# Winning on the Stock Market

## Second Edition

# Other titles in the *Millard on . . .* Series

# Winning on the Stock Market

## Second Edition

### Brian J. Millard

JOHN WILEY & SONS

Chichester • New York • Weinheim • Brisbane • Singapore • Toronto

First edition published by John Wiley & Sons, 1993
This edition copyright © 1998 by John Wiley & Sons Ltd,
                            Baffins Lane, Chichester,
                            West Sussex PO19 1UD, England

                            National       01243 779777
                            International   (+44) 1243 779777
                            e-mail (for orders and customer service enquiries):
                            cs-books@wiley.co.uk
                            Visit our Home Page on http://www.wiley.co.uk
                            or http://www.wiley.com

*Other Wiley Editorial Offices*

John Wiley & Sons, Inc., 605 Third Avenue,
New York, NY 10158–0012, USA

WILEY–VCH Verlag GmbH, Pappelallee 3,
D-69469 Weinheim, Germany

Jacaranda Wiley Ltd, 33 Park Road, Milton,
Queensland 4064, Australia

John Wiley & Sons (Asia) Pte Ltd, 2 Clementi Loop #02-01,
Jin Xing Distripark, Singapore 129809

John Wiley & Sons (Canada) Ltd, 22 Worcester Road,
Rexdale, Ontario M9W 1L1, Canada

***Library of Congress Cataloging-in-Publication Data***

Millard, Brian J.
   Winning on the stock market / Brian J. Millard — 2nd ed.
      p.   cm. — (The Millard on — series)
   Includes index.
   ISBN 0-471-97053-0 (pbk.)
   1. Stocks.   2. Investments.   3. Speculation.   I. Title.
II. Series: Millard, Brian J. Millard on — series.
HG4661.M54   1998
332.63'22—dc21                             97–41438
                                               CIP

***British Library Cataloguing in Publication Data***

A catalogue record for this book is available from the British Library

ISBN 0-471-97053-0

Typeset in 10.5/12pt Times by Dorwyn Ltd, Rowlands Castle, Hampshire
Printed and bound in Great Britain by Redwood Books, Trowbridge, Wiltshire
This book is printed on acid-fee paper responsibly manufactured from sustainable forestation, for which at least two trees are planted for each one used for paper production.

# Contents

# Preface

It is now five years since the first edition of *Winning on the Stock Market* was published. At that time a large number of private investors held shares which they had acquired from the various privatisations during the 1980s. Now these numbers have been swelled as a result of the building society conversions which have taken place in the last few years.

The vast majority of these investors are "static" investors, i.e. once they have acquired the shares, they will continue to hold them until such time as they might need some capital, in which case they then sell. The behaviour of the stock market over the past ten years or so, with the market outperforming almost all other forms of investment has tended to reinforce the view that holding for the long term is the correct strategy. However, this long term rise in share prices tends to obscure the fact that within the long term share prices rise and fall. They can fall at the beginning of a year and recover by the end of that year. They can also fall constantly throughout the year and then regain this loss and add even more value the next year. This book will show that investors who take advantage of these rises and falls can achieve much better gains than the investor who buys for the long term. It is also shown that better profits can be made from those shares whose historical rises and falls have been above average than those shares which are less volatile.

In this book you will find four major concepts. The first is the overriding importance of the overall investment climate. The odds against making a profit are greatly increased when the investment climate is running adversely. A simple method is presented by which the investor can determine when the general investment climate is favourable. The second concept is that of the dominant trend. In a sense this can be looked at as the investment climate for a particular share. Again, this is readily determined, and it is shown how easy it is to find those shares whose dominant trends have just begun to move up. The third concept is that of the investment trends. These are the short term trends, and a knowledge of when they start and end is vital in enabling the investor to buy at the time of maximum potential for gain. While these first three concepts are concerned with making sure that the investor buys shares at the best time, the fourth, but equally important aspect is to insure against losing the gain that has been made, and the investor is shown how to use a percentage stop-loss to do this.

The reader is also given an introduction to the technique of channel analysis, a topic which is the subject of another book in this series. It will be seen that channel analysis combines all of the four major concepts in one simple method, a method which can be used equally by the pencil and paper investor and the investor with the very latest in computer technology.

Unlike many others, the methods in this book have withstood the test of time. They have worked well for many years, and should continue to do so in the future. They do demand patience from the investor in waiting for the correct time to invest. Never forget that an impatient investor is a losing investor!

Brian J. Millard<br>
Bramhall

# 1

# Introduction

It is a sad fact that for every investor who makes money out of the stock market by buying and selling shares, there are another two who do not. There are many reasons for failure, but foremost among these is inconsistency of approach, with impulse buying featuring at the top of the list. Naturally, a consistent approach is useless if it lacks the wherewithal to make profits, but investors will find that the methods discussed in this book have stood the test of time, and have led over the long term to very useful profits for those who have followed them carefully.

The prime objective of an investment in the stock market is to make money. It might be thought that this is so obvious that it needs no stating in this introduction, but this is not the case. Many investors have subconsciously changed their focus so that their objective is simply to hold shares. This is particularly true of new investors who have become involved in the stock market through the many privatisation issues or who have been lucky enough to have received free shares from the many building society flotations. They have no clear idea of what to do once they have received the share certificates. This is partly due to ignorance, not so much ignorance of the mechanics of selling shares, since the High Street banks are full of notices about how they can do this for you, but ignorance of how share prices rise and fall and the timescale over which they do this. The recent building society flotations have also drawn attention to another category of investor—the investor who is frightened of holding shares and elects to receive the money instead. Such investors have made far less money from the auction of these unwanted shares than those who stayed in even for just the first day of trading.

## MISPLACED LOYALTY

There is constant talk in the press of the advantages of investor loyalty and of holding shares for the long term. This is total poppycock on two counts. Firstly, as we will see later, the penalty for going for the long term can be to see the real value of a holding greatly reduced, not only owing to the ravages of inflation but because of a fall in the share price.

Secondly, loyalty should be a two-way process, but UK companies consider it to be nothing of the sort. If shareholders stay with their holdings for extended periods of time, then the costs of maintaining the share register are reduced, and the share price could stay firmer. While talking about difficult trading conditions, the directors often award themselves large and totally unjustifiable increases in salary or directors' fees. The last thing such directors want is a stampede by investors to shed themselves of their shareholdings. **The only loyalty required by an investor is to the value of his or her shareholdings.**

A share certificate has no emotional standing, and except for nostalgic certificates of long-gone Victorian railway companies and the like, no intrinsic value as a work of art. The certificate is simply a means to an end, the end being to increase the value of an investor's shareholdings. If a particular share ceases to contribute to the upward momentum then it must be sold.

## THE OBSTACLES TO PROFIT

Private investors have a major cross to bear in the form of dealing costs and the spread between quoted buying and selling prices of shares. In the absence of these costs, an investor who just buys and sells on a purely random basis should hope to break even over a long time period, although the aim of breaking even is not a very ambitious one! With these costs added in, the same investor must lose over the long run, since all profitable transactions must have these costs deducted from the profit, while all losing transactions have these costs added to the loss.

An investor who just buys and sells at any time he or she feels inclined to do so is therefore almost certain to lose. Buying opportunities have to be chosen carefully so as to maximise the potential gain while reducing the potential loss, and the aim of this book is to discuss ways in which this can be done.

Besides the fine detail of the timing decisions of share buying and selling, there is one simple requirement for investment success: *There should be more profitable transactions than unprofitable ones.* The question which arises from this is "How many more?".

An investor who is correct 50% of the time cannot make a profit because of the effect of dealing costs. How much more of the time he should be correct in order to move into profit depends upon the level of these dealing costs and the average profit or loss per transaction. While we know the dealing costs, the average profit and loss depends upon the individual investor's decision making and the state of the market. In the absence of any other information, we could hazard a guess that the investor needs to be correct 75% of the time, i.e. three transactions out of every four should be in profit.

This is a very demanding requirement, unlikely to be met by more than a handful of investors, and even then they would not be able to maintain this level of success for any extended period of time.

Besides the negative influence of dealing costs on the overall profitability of stock market investment, there is also the unavoidable mathematics of profit and loss in a world where we look at everything in percentage terms. *The percentage gain necessary to retrieve a loss is greater than the percentage which was lost.* A simple example, which ignores dealing costs, serves to clarify this.

Supposing an investor starts with £1000 and loses 20% of this on his first investment. He is then left with £800. Now to claw back the lost £200 and restore the capital back to £1000 a gain of 25% is required on the £800.

The situation gets rapidly worse as the percentage loss increases. Suppose our investor loses 50% of the starting £1000. He is now down to £500, and requires a 100% gain to restore the original £1000.

Figure 1.1 shows how rapidly the gain required to offset a loss rises as we move from modest to large losses. The gains are achievable when we are talking about small losses of, say, less than 25–30%, but by the time we reach large losses we require impossible gains to compensate.

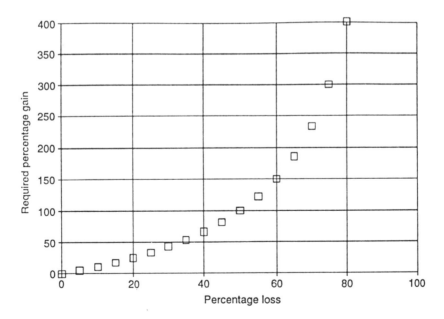

**Figure 1.1**   How the percentage gain required to offset a particular percentage loss rapidly reaches levels which are impossible to achieve

Thus it is vital to develop a method which will keep our losses down to the level of those at the left-hand corner of the graph in Figure 1.1. As a spin-off, the method will also improve the situation so that the investor need not be correct such a high proportion of the time. The method is to place a restriction on the maximum loss which can be made from the losing positions, while having no such restriction on the profitable positions. This is done via what is called a "stop-loss", and the mechanics of determining the stop-loss level and applying it to share price movements are discussed fully later in this book.

## THE FUNDAMENTAL AND TECHNICAL VIEWPOINTS

There are two basic schools of thought in choosing shares to buy.

The fundamentalists take the view that a thorough study of the fundamentals of a company will show whether its share price is too low, too high, or just about correct. They arrive at this decision by doing a large amount of work on the published accounts of the company, analysis of the markets in which it operates, the current and future competition, the quality of the top management, the quality of the products, the export potential of the product, and so on. It doesn't take much imagination to see that a vast amount of effort has to be expended in order to arrive at a conclusion that a share should be bought, sold or held. Just suppose that a private investor had the energy to put into such an effort, and came to the conclusion that the share was undervalued, and should be bought. His reasoning is that eventually the market will come to realise that the share is out of line, and the price will rise until it either correctly reflects the worth of the company, or has gone to the other extreme and overvalues the worth of the company. The major flaw in this reasoning is the belief that the market will come to realise that the share is undervalued. It may not do so, or may take such a long time to do so that the investor spends a long time in the situation where he has not even covered his dealing costs in buying the share.

In practice, the situation is rather better than this. The professional fundamentalists publish their findings in the press and in brokers' circulars. Thus a large number of investors simultaneously read that the share of company ABC are worth buying. We then have a self-fulfilling prophecy, since this excess of demand will make certain that the share price rises in the short term. The trouble is, the short term may be too short for a sensible profit to emerge once dealing costs are taken into account, and it lies in the lap of the gods as to whether a longer term upward trend has been established.

From the foregoing, the reader will perceive that I am not impressed by what we might call the result to effort ratio. An awful lot of effort has been put in by somebody, be it the investor or a professional analyst, for a result that may still be of questionable value as far as realised profit is concerned.

The technical analysts take a rather different view of share price evaluation. They believe that the whole story is told by the price itself, and rather than go through the extensive analysis of the fundamentalists, it is only necessary to observe the movement of the share price. An increasing interest in a share, for whatever reason, will be reflected in a rise in the share price, and part of the job of the technical analyst is to determine whether the rise will be an extensive and therefore profitable one.

Since this book is not about fundamental analysis, then on the broad definitions used above it falls into the technical analysis category. That being said, it should be pointed out that technical analysts form a very broad church indeed. The methods shown in the following chapters, while owing much to the subject at large, are also very much the author's own view of how decisions can be arrived at from analysis of share price data.

Although the effort involved in developing the skills to analyse share price movements in this way can be considerable, the resulting expertise can be applied to any one share in a fraction of the time needed for a fundamental analysis of the same company. The advent of software packages to run on personal computers (see Appendix) takes a great deal of the drudgery out of technical analysis, and can even take the decision making right out of the hands of the investor. The power of computers to store data, present charts and perform extensive calculations in a few seconds is to be welcomed, and indeed this book would have taken twice as long to write and ten times as long for the research to have been carried out without a computer. Having said that, the black-box approach of entering the share prices and then obeying the instructions to buy or sell which the computer prints out is not one that I favour. A good analogy is that of driving a car. The driver who never cares what is under the bonnet but simply uses the vehicle to get from A to B is the driver who is more likely to suffer a breakdown on the road. The driver who is in sympathy with his car knows every noise and rattle, and will often begin to sense when something is starting to go wrong, taking appropriate action in plenty of time. The investor who understands the process behind the investment decision making will also be able to take appropriate action to limit the risk to his or her investments.

## THE SCIENCE OF INVESTMENT

Investment has always been seen as an art rather than a science, and indeed a very famous investment book of yesteryear had the title *The Art of Investment*. Art is almost totally subjective—a pile of bricks arranged in a neat cube in the Tate Gallery is one person's thing of beauty and another's pile of bricks. Artistic people can also be very suggestible, and many can be persuaded to see eventually that the pile of bricks is not just a pile of bricks but something of wonderment. Art is also subject to fashions, and new fashions rise while old ones decline. Investors also suffer from the same shortcomings, many of them being very suggestible to the shadier type of investment operator. Sectors of the stock market also become fashionable, such as the banking sector over 1996–97, but as in the world of art, they will suffer the inevitable decline. On the other hand, science is, or should be, highly objective. It is based on facts and on the development of theories from those facts. Until I became interested in the stock market, I spent some 15 years as a university scientist in a branch of chemistry known as mass spectrometry. Although such a background may seem to be totally irrelevant to my later calling as an investment writer, nothing could be further from the truth. The scientific method imposes a discipline that is essential for success in the stock market. There is nothing magic about it; the scientific method is actually just an attitude of mind. Fortunately, this attitude can be developed by investors without having to take A-levels in physics or chemistry, and reading and following the methods discussed in this book should suffice.

Put simply, the stepwise scientific approach is as follows:

1. Make some observations and gather some facts.
2. Propose a theory to explain all the facts.
3. Make further observations.
4. If they are in line with theory, the theory is strengthened. If they are not, discard the old theory and go back to 2.

There have been many scientific scandals in the past, and there will continue to be more in the future, where a worldwide reputation has been made by scientists who have stopped at step 3 above. The scientist is so excited by his new theory that he is totally convinced that it is correct. He gets on a bandwagon which carries him along, and new facts that are not in line with this theory are ignored. It is not until later that it turns out that other scientists are unable to repeat the original work. A prime example is the question of the availability of virtually unlimited energy from cold fusion.

Investors are extremely prone to this failing. They come to some conclusion and then become blind to facts which subsequently negate the conclusion. While not damaging a world reputation, this will certainly damage their investments!

## DEALING WITH RANDOMNESS

The methods used in this book are based on the manipulation of numbers, the numbers being share prices. As will be shown later, the movements of share prices are partly random, and the degree of randomness in the movement changes from one period of time to another. Thus there will be no such thing as a cast iron, 100% certain prediction of price movement, even if the prediction is limited to the simple question of whether the price will rise, fall or remain the same. The only way forward in such situations is to think in terms of the probability of a particular outcome. Thus we could determine the probability of the price of ICI shares rising on any particular day, or we could determine the probability of the price of ICI shares rising by exactly 10p on any given day. These two probabilities will be different, since quite obviously the probability of a specific rise of 10p is much less than the probability of a rise of any magnitude.

It is quite simple to determine the probability of such outcomes in the stock market from past data. Taking a simple example, we could determine that over the last 100 days of ICI prices, there have been 20 occasions when the price has remained unchanged from that of the previous day, 43 days when it rose, and 37 days when it fell. This is irrespective of the actual amount by which the price rose or fell.

With the proviso that the share price will continue in the same way into the future, we can say that there are 20 chances in 100 that it will remain unchanged tomorrow, 43 chances in 100 that it will rise and 37 chances that it will fall.

These can be converted to percentages such that:

Chance of unchanged price = 20%
Chance of price rise = 43%
Chance of price fall = 37%

Thus there is a slightly better chance that the price will rise tomorrow than that it will fall, and a poor chance that it will remain unchanged.

It should be pointed out that the probabilities shown above are not exact values, but estimates provided by the data from which they have been calculated. The estimates get better the more data we use to perform the calculations on, and get worse the fewer data we use. Thus the estimates obtained if we could be bothered to use, say, 10 years' worth of ICI data (over 2500 daily values) would be better than those above. They are also likely to be slightly different in actual value.

Here we hit a theme which is constant throughout this book: a balance has to be struck between the amount of effort which should be employed and the results which can be achieved from that effort. It is a waste of time doing calculations on, say 2500 share prices if there is only a small improvement over the results obtained from 500 share prices. We will see this particularly with the question of using daily prices as opposed to weekly prices. It will become obvious later in this book that we do not improve our gains by a factor of five if we use daily prices (five per business week) as opposed to weekly prices. The choice is entirely up to the investor as to how much effort he is prepared to put into the analysis of share prices. That being said, there is certainly a minimum level below which the results will be disappointing, to say the least.

It is only if the chance of a rise is 100% that we can be absolutely certain that that is what will happen. If the chance is only 99.9%, then there is still a finite possibility that the price will not rise.

Looked at in this way, probabilities are extremely simple, but extremely necessary since, unless they are totally ignored, they prevent the investor from investing in a situation where the odds are totally against him.

Looking at the three probabilities above, an investor is bound to lose over the long run if he continues to bet on any one of the three outcomes. Such are the vagaries of chance that he may well be correct 10 times in a row, but over a large number, say 100 times, he will inevitably lose out.

Thus, just as probabilities become more meaningful as we use more data in their calculation, so do future results get closer to the ones predicted by such probabilities as we amass more of them. This fact is so fundamental to the methods shown in this book that it must be clearly understood by the investor. *It is only by consistent application of the techniques over an extended period of time that we can be more and more certain that the expected results will be achieved.*

A humorous example will serve to highlight both the workings of probability and the way in which individuals can fool themselves that probabilities always act in a certain way for them which may be quite different from normal expectation.

We have all had the experience of a buttered slice of bread skidding off the plate and on to the carpet. It is a common belief that more often than not, it lands so as to cause the maximum inconvenience, i.e. buttered side downwards. Most people would imagine that the explanation has something to do with aerodynamics or the centre of gravity, causing the buttered side to end up underneath during the flight from the table to the floor.

There is an excellent distinction here between what people think and what actually happens. Two experiments serve to clarify both of these:

1. Carry out a poll of people.
2. Carry out an experiment with buttered bread.

When asked "Do you think if you accidentally drop a buttered slice of bread it will land face down on the carpet?", 18 people out of 20 said "yes".

In an experiment in which 1000 slices of buttered bread were flipped into the air from a machine specially designed to eliminate bias, the bread landed face down 505 times and face up 495 times. These results are so close that there is virtually an equal chance of the bread landing either way up.

There are two vital messages here for the investor: fist, that all preconceptions must be emptied from the mind, and secondly, that probability wins over the long term. **Thus investors, having read this book and begun to implement the methods here, should not become disheartened if the first few investments go wrong.** Their continued application will sooner bring the investor into profit. Conversely, the investor who finds that he makes a large profit from each of his first few investments should not think that he has found the Holy Grail. He is bound to make a few counter-balancing losses before long.

## THE DARTBOARD INVESTOR

Wherever possible in this book, the probabilities of certain outcomes, or a rough estimate of them, are given. This enables the investor to take a much more informed view of the investment possibilities in certain situations. These probabilities are best expressed through the use of a mythical "dartboard investor".

The dartboard investor is the rival of every investment author who puts forward any theory, method or system for making money out of the stock market. The dartboard investor operates by using a very simple technique. On one wall of his garage is fixed a large sheet of chipboard. On the chipboard he has pasted the lists of UK shares which are found in the back pages of the *Financial Times*. Alongside these two pages he has an enlarged version of the FT Actuaries Table of market sectors. He has a dartboard in which all of the odd numbers have been marked by small red stickers bearing the word "sell", while all of the even numbers are accompanied by small green stickers bearing the word "buy". Finally, he has also pasted on the chipboard a total one-year calendar.

The dartboard investor now has all of the tools available to enable him to take decisions. He can select a market sector by throwing a dart at the FT Actuaries Table, he can select shares by throwing a dart at the share pages of the FT, he can decide about buying or selling by throwing a dart at the dartboard itself, while finally he can decide on which day to do something by throwing a dart at the calendar.

In order to allow the laws of chance to operate freely, he should do this with his eyes shut. By this means we arrive at an investor whose decisions are made purely by chance.

*It is incumbent on every investment author to show that, over the long term, the dartboard investor will not outperform him*. If this turns out not to be the case, then the thousands of hours spent writing the book and the many more thousands accumulated by its readers will have all been totally wasted.

## CHARTS

Producing a chart of a share price or index is the most logical way in which the movements can be shown over a period of time. The alternative is to show columns of figures, but very few individuals other than those with accountancy training are able to gain very much from this method of presentation. There are three types of chart in use today: linear, logarithmic, and point and figure charts. The last have no place in this book and are not discussed further. Suffice it to say that they are based on price movements in a particular direction, and can only be used in the sense of drawing trendlines, support lines and the like on them as an aid to decision making.

Both linear and logarithmic charts have two meaningful axes. The horizontal one is always taken to be the time axis, and is linearly divided according to the timescale being used. Short term price movements may be shown with daily divisions, longer ones with weekly or monthly divisions, while extended time periods will require yearly divisions.

It is in the vertical (price) scale that linear charts differ from logarithmic ones. The logarithmic scale is one of constant ratios, so the distance between the divisions representing 10p and 20p is exactly the same as the distance between the divisions representing 100p and 200p. An example of such a chart is shown in Figure 1.2.

The advantage of such charts lies in the fact that a specific percentage change in a price gives the same apparent movement whatever the price. Thus the change from 800p to 1200p represents a 50% change, as does the change from 1000p to 1500p, and as pointed out above, the distance on the chart is the same.

The disadvantage of such logarithmic charts is the loss of sensitivity to price movements in the upper part of the chart, i.e. at those points representing the higher prices. The chart appears to be flattened out. This also makes it difficult to determine the amplitude of cyclic movements.

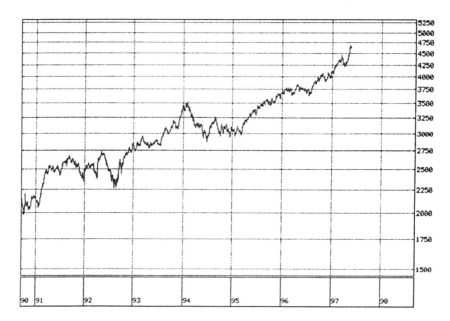

**Figure 1.2**   A logarithmic chart of the FTSE100 Index. The vertical distance between say 2000p and 3000p is the same as that between 3000p and 4500p. Thus the chart is based on constant ratios

Perfect cyclic movements are symmetrical in terms of peak to peak distance, and are also symmetrical in terms of trough to peak distance (amplitude). A logarithmic scale distorts this vertical distance.

Since an analysis of price movements is the central theme of this book, all subsequent charts will be of the linear type, as shown in the example in Figure 1.3. Here a specific price difference rather than a ratio gives the same apparent movement. Thus the distance from 10p to 20p will be the same as the distance from 100p to 110p. For those who wish to construct price charts manually by plotting daily or weekly prices, a linear chart is far easier to maintain.

## TOOLS OF THE TRADE

For the operations described in this book, the only requirements are graph paper for those who wish to construct their own charts, paper ruled with columns for maintaining price histories and simple calculations, and a calculator. Chart paper in the form of pads of A4 linear charts can be obtained from any good stationers, as can pads of paper ruled with squares. Better still would be an accounts book or accountant's ruled pad with columns already in place for calculations.

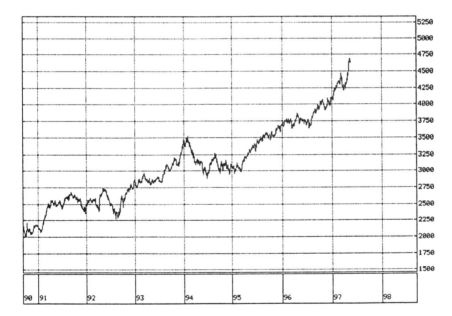

**Figure 1.3**  A linear chart of the FTSE100 Index. The vertical distance between 2000p and 3000p is the same as that between 3000p and 4000p. Thus the chart is based on constant differences

The calculations are trivial and require only simple addition and division.

As a short cut, printed values of many years of share price histories and linear share charts of the same shares can be obtained at modest cost (see Appendix).

## MICROCOMPUTERS

The availability of relatively inexpensive microcomputers has taken much of the drudgery out of the manipulation of share price data. Now that such data can be acquired throughout the day via several commercial data feeds down a telephone line, it is feasible to maintain a database of all UK share data. The ability to store all these share price data and plot a chart of a selected share is invaluable, but allied to this is the fact that micro-computers can perform calculations and display results in a fraction of the time it would take by hand.

Unless the investor has the ability to program the computer, it is of little use without a program to do the required tasks. There are numerous software packages currently available for the investor. However, not all of them can carry out some of the apparently simple but nevertheless essen-tial calculations and plotting shown in this book, such as presenting cen-tred moving averages. The charts of share prices and indices displayed in this book have been produced using MICROVEST 5.0 (see Appendix).

Since the plotting of a chart requires historical price data, the avail-ability of extensive price histories on a large number of shares on diskette in a variety of program formats, or even as printed values, at modest cost simplifies the task of compiling a database (see Appendix). The data can be updated manually or by means of the data feeds mentioned above.

# 2

# Brokers and Financial Information

Prior to the "Big Bang", whenever there was a change in interest rates, or the balance of payments figures were horrendous, it was always the practice of the TV companies to send a camera crew to view the trading floor of the Stock Exchange. Viewers would see a scene of frantic activity with members rushing to and fro, usually waving bits of paper at each other. The floor was the place where jobbers, who dealt in shares, quoted prices to members of stockbroking firms who were acting to buy or sell shares on behalf of clients.

Since the Big Bang, the floor is deserted, because dealings are done through computer screens using the SEAQ system. In place of the jobber is the market maker, who decides on the buying and selling prices of the various shares in which they make a market. The shares of any one company may be handled by more than one market maker, and in fact for a share to be classed as an alpha share it is a Stock Exchange requirement that there must be at least two market makers for that share. The broker now stays back in his office, since all he has to do to quote a price to his client is to look at his SEAQ screen. The market maker updates the prices frequently, but has to deal at the price he is showing at any one time.

In the old days, if you requested a price from your broker, he would have to ask his representative on the trading floor to get a quotation. He would then call you back with this price. You then decided that you would buy or sell at this price, and by the time the request was sent back to the representative, the price may well have changed. To overcome this, it was necessary to give your broker some flexibility, using a phrase such as "buy at the market", meaning buy whatever price was being quoted. The advantage of having today's instant response is obvious. You know as soon as you place your phone call what price you will be having to pay, or what price you are getting for your shares. You know your commitment instantly.

There are very few newcomers to the stock market who did not participate in one of the privatisation issues, but the way in which these were sold to the public is quite different from the way in which the secondary, or after, market operates. The investor filled in his application form, either cut out of a newspaper or obtained through a registration system, specified the appropriate number of shares requested, and enclosed a cheque for the correct amount. At some time in the future he then received an allocation of all, part, or even none of the shares requested. Although stockbrokers were involved in this process, they were acting behind the scenes and were not obvious to the investor.

When the time came to sell the privatisation shares, investors found that they needed the services of either an intermediary or a stockbroker. As far as buying shares is concerned, unlike the privatisation issues where the investor put the money up front, the secondary market in shares (the market in shares which have already been issued) is built on trust.

Shares now have to be paid for within five working days of the deal being made. Unless you are maintaining an account with your broker in which he is investing on your behalf in the money market, the broker is trusting you to pay virtually by return of post for the shares you have bought. If you are selling, you expect to be paid, and you will receive the proceeds once you have returned the share certificate.

Note that for dealing in gilts, the settlement is slightly different. These have to be paid for on the day following the transaction. You may buy gilts through the Post Office, paying for them at the time.

For dealing in traded options, the settlement is again due the day after the transaction.

The most obvious intermediary for an investor to use will be his High Street bank, presuming he has a satisfactory relationship with it. There are no worries about the financial standing of the bank, and other than the fact that they occasionally make mistakes, your bank account will be credited without further intervention by you with the proceeds of any shares sold, or debited with the costs of any shares bought.

Another route which may look attractive is through one of the telephone dealing firms which usually advertise on Teletext. They appear to offer lower minimum commissions than banks or brokers, but this may be offset by a wider spread between the quoted buying and selling prices. There are also a few "share shops" which may be viewed in the same light.

If an investor wishes eventually to deal in traded options, then it is better if he finds a broker rather than uses a bank. Since trust is involved, a broker will not take on a client totally unknown to him unless the client provides bank details for a reference or is recommended by a well-known existing client of the broker. As mentioned above, this is no problem if you have a normal relationship with your bank. If not, change banks before testing the water with a broker!

In order to find a broker in your area, you can either look in Yellow Pages, ask a friend, ask your bank, or write to the Stock Exchange in London (see Appendix). Obviously telephone calls are cheaper if your broker is in your local telephone area, but be prepared to go beyond this if you find a broker with a better rate of commission which will more than offset the extra telephone charges.

# BROKER SERVICES

Brokers offer a number of services, for which they, like any other business, have to charge. The minimum possible, which except for special circumstances is all that readers of this book require, is a "dealing only" service. Other levels of service include an advisory service and a full discretionary service.

## *Dealing Only Service*

All you want from the broker is that he executes the buying or selling orders that you give him. You will receive confirmation of the order the next day in the form of a contract note, specifying exactly what you have bought or sold, the price you paid or received, the amount of commission, etc.

## *Advisory Service*

Here you may wish to ask advice about a particular share, and your broker will also send you recommendations and printed material from time to time.

## *Discretionary Service*

This is for the investor who wishes to do nothing but place his cash or portfolio in the hands of the broker. Hopefully any investor reading this book would not fall into this category. The broker buys and sells as he sees fit, sending you a monthly or perhaps quarterly report on the performance of your portfolio, or perhaps we should say his performance of your portfolio.

## *Traded Options*

As mentioned earlier, unlike the position with shares, traded options deals have to be paid for the next morning. An investor who wishes to deal in traded options must complete a set of forms which his broker will send him. These acknowledge that the investor recognises the risks inherent in traded options.

The broker will not deal in traded options for you under credit. You have to deposit sufficient funds to cover any deals. In the case of cheques or drafts, these funds will have to be cleared before dealings commence.

## HOW MUCH MONEY IS NEEDED TO DEAL WITH A BROKER?

Many investors have an inflated idea of how much money you should be investing before you can expect a broker to act for you, but by today's standards, not very much is needed. You may carry out a transaction in which only £500 worth of shares is bought or sold, but the dealing costs will be quite high as a percentage of this amount. For this reason, deals of less than that are not advised. There may be occasions with privatisation issues in which you have been allocated only a paltry number of shares. Many banks or building societies offer a good deal if these shares are used as the basis for a new account, and it is much better to liquidate such small holdings in this way. Dealing costs fall in percentage terms as the value of the transaction rises, and it is best to view a deal of £1000 as about the minimum you would normally contemplate.

For a discretionary account, a sum of the order of £25 000 is probably the minimum that would interest most brokers.

## COMMISSION

Commission is worked out as a percentage of the value of the deal. The value of the deal is termed the "consideration", and is simply the price obtained or paid for the shares multiplied by the number of shares sold or bought. Thus 2000 shares sold at 132p will give a consideration of £2640.

The commission structure is complicated in two ways. Firstly, there is a minimum commission, which varies from about £15 for a country broker to £25–£30 for a big-city, and especially London, broker. Secondly, there are often commission bands, so that the percentage falls once the consideration rises above a certain amount, say £5000 or £10 000.

Most commission charges for deals of below a few thousand pounds are in the range 1.5–2.25%. The investor must shop around in order to obtain the best deal, comparing the quotes from several brokers. For an active investor, the difference may amount to several hundred pounds a year— well worth the cost of a few telephone calls at the outset.

It is the minimum commission that is the killer for small deals. Thus if the minimum is £25 and the percentage rate is 1.5%, the percentage of the consideration taken up by the commission rises rapidly as the value of the consideration falls, as can be seen in the third column of Table 2.1.

In addition, there is a contract charge of £5 per deal. This leads to the final column of Table 2.1 where total dealing costs are expressed as a percentage of the consideration.

An investment must be considered as a two-way transaction, since in order to realise the profit the security has to be sold again. The above percentages naturally apply to both sides of the transaction. In

**Table 2.1** The increasing importance of dealing costs as the size of deal decreases

| Consideration (£) | Commission (£) | % of consideration | % including charge of £5 |
|---|---|---|---|
| 5000 | 75 | 1.5 | 1.6 |
| 2000 | 30 | 1.5 | 1.75 |
| 1000 | 25 | 2.5 | 3.0 |
| 750 | 25 | 3.3 | 4.0 |

approximate terms, if you buy £1000 of shares and sell them later at £1000, you will be paying £30 twice, i.e. a total of £60. This represents 6% on the round trip, as it is called.

From this discussion of dealing costs, etc., the advantage of keeping deals comfortably above £1000 is obvious.

## SPREADS

There is another source of costs which represent a considerable percentage operating to the disadvantage of the investor: the "spread" of prices. The closing prices quoted in newspapers are so-called "middle" prices. If a middle price is quoted as 250p, you will be disappointed to find that you will have to pay say 252p for the shares. Conversely, you will also be disappointed to find that when you sell them, you will only receive say 248p for them. The difference between these buying and selling prices at any one time is called the spread. The above spread, of about 4p for a share around the 350p mark, is typical of a share in the top 350. This spread is therefore building in an additional cost to the investor of about 1.5% on the round trip.

Taking into account the dealing costs discussed above, for a round trip in £1000 in the shares of a FTSE100 Index constituent, the investor could pay as much as 6% + 1.5%, i.e. 7.5%.

There is a great advantage in dealing with the top 350 shares because of the effect of spreads on dealing costs. Once you move outside these shares the spread can become extremely large in percentage terms. For those investors who have succumbed to the blandishments of telephone share pushers, it may be extremely difficult to sell such shares at other than knockdown prices.

At the 7.5% level for top 350 shares, the investor has a substantial deficit to overcome by a share price before moving into profit. It is very easy to get carried away when the share price rises by say 5% within a few days of buying the shares, but such a rise is only just getting to the point at which a profit will be produced. For the medium term investor, dealing costs will be offset to a great extent by dividends received. As will be seen shortly, these are normally a small percentage of the money invested in the share.

## CONTRACT NOTES AND SHARE CERTIFICATES

Within a very few days of doing a deal with your stockbroker, you should receive a contract note with the date and time of the bargain, the settlement date, a contract reference and the details of the bargain, i.e. the quantity of shares and their price. The consideration is calculated, and then in the case of a buying operation, the commission and contract charge will be added to the consideration, giving the total payable to the broker. In the case of a selling operation, the commission and contract charges are deducted from the consideration to give the total payable to you.

You should return any tear-off part of this with your payment, and in any case never send a cheque without a note attached to it listing the contract reference or references. The accounts staff of brokers, like the rest of us, can and do make mistakes from time to time, and having the correct number helps to reduce the chances of an error.

If you are expecting payment and do not receive a cheque within a day or so of the settlement date, call up the accounts department of the broker to find out why. Besides the obvious mistake of a cheque lost in the mail or overlooked, it sometimes happens that there is a delay in clearing a bargain.

## FINANCIAL INFORMATION

The most accessible place for financial information is the newspaper. The quality dailies carry listings of share prices, as do many provincial evening papers. None carry as complete a range of information as the *Financial Times* (the FT). For the serious investor, especially one who deals in traded options, access to price movements during the day is essential. The Teletext pages of BBC2 and Channel 4 carry listings of many hundreds of share prices, updated frequently throughout the day, as well as announcements about changes in bank rate, company results and the like.

Unfortunately, it has to be said that the small private investor appears to be somewhat of a nuisance to the Stock Exchange. Rather than provide a service in the form of a real-time display of the FTSE100 Index, which would act as an encouragement to small investors to become more active, the Stock Exchange became involved in a dispute with the broadcasting authorities over payment by the latter for the provision of the data. As always the investor is the loser, since the FTSE100 Index as displayed on Teletext is running some 20 minutes behind real time. Institutions, of course, have access to their own real-time displays.

A useful mine of financial information is the *Investors Chronicle*, published weekly, which presents an abundance of company information.

Shares used to be marked in the FT with their category (alpha, beta, etc.). Now they are not separated in this way, but listed together. There is now an indication of shares which are actively traded by means of the bullet symbol (●). The only separation is into "sectors" of the market, reflecting the markets in which the company operates. Thus there are banking, engineering, insurance, industrial and many other categories. New shares such as the recent electricity power generator shares are often kept for some time under a separate heading of "New Issues".

In the FT the data are presented in columns. The first three entries under "Chemicals" at the time of writing are shown in Table 2.2. The meaning of the various annotations in the lists of data is as follows.

**Notes:** Small letters with an explanation at the end of the list. For example:

| | |
|---|---|
| g | assumed dividend yield after rights issue |
| xd | ex-dividend |
| xc | ex-scrip issue |
| φ | figures or report awaited |

**Price:** Yesterday's middle closing price, sometimes with "xd" or "xc" or some other symbol whose meaning is clarified in the Notes section. "xd" means that buyers of the share do not get the dividend; this goes instead to the previous owner of the shares. "xc" means that the buyers of the share do not get the scrip issue.

**+ or – :** Whether the price rose or fell from the previous day's close.

**1997 high and low columns:** These are the highest and lowest prices reached during the year so far.

**Mkt Cp£M:** This is the market capitalisation, the product of the share price and the number of shares in issue. It is given in units of £million.

**Yield Gr's:** This is the gross yield, derived from the dividend expressed relative to the share price before applying Advanced Corporation Tax at the appropriate rate (25% at the time of writing).

**P/E:** This is the price to earnings ratio, given by the current share price divided by the earnings per share, where earnings are the after-tax profits.

## PRICE TO EARNINGS (P/E) RATIOS

These are worth a section of explanation since they are widely used by the investment community to attempt to value the shares of a company. If an

**Table 2.2**  A typical newspaper presentation of share price information

| Notes | Price | + or – | 1997 | | Mkt | Yield | P/E |
|---|---|---|---|---|---|---|---|
| | | | High | Low | Cp£M | Gr's | |
| Akzo Fl ................ | **£82⅝** | ................ | £95⅝ | £79⅜ | **5,864** | 2.6 | 13.8 |
| Allied Colloids .. | **128.5** | +1 | 137 | 118.5 | **885.15** | 2.7 | φ |

investor knows the profits and the number of shares in that company issued, he can calculate the P/E figure, although the FT carries this out for you.

The number of shares in issue and the earnings of the company are obtained from the latest report of the company to its shareholders. By writing to the company secretary, you should be able to get hold of a copy of this even if you are not a shareholder. You could certainly telephone to find out these latest figures.

In the figures given for the two shares in the Chemicals sector, only one had a P/E figure. That was Akzo with a value of 13.8. By itself, this is a meaningless figure, because the investor needs to be able to compare Akzo with other shares, and even better to compare it with other shares within the same sector. Without this comparison, all that one can say is that a high P/E ratio means that other investors think the prospects for the company are good, while a low P/E ratio means that investors do not think very much of the prospects for that company. The trouble with high P/E values is that unrealistic expectations may be built into the share price. A smart investor may be able to find a company with a low P/E ratio which has been overlooked by the market in general, where the prospects have the potential to become transformed. He can then expect that the share price will take off rapidly.

Fortunately, the FT does provide us with a way of ranking one company against other companies in terms of their P/Es. This lies in the table of FT Actuaries Share Indices to be found on the inside pages. The great value of this table is that details are kept for each sector—not only estimated P/Es for each sector, but special indices for each sector. By plotting the histories of these just as though they were shares, investors can spot sectors which are out of fashion and which may provide an opportunity to invest in before they become fashionable.

From the P/E point of view, at the time of writing the P/E values ran from 9.30 for the water companies up to 35.5 for oil exploration companies. The number of companies in that sector is also stated, e.g. 12 for water companies and 12 also for oil exploration. Taking specific companies in these sectors, Yorkshire Water had a P/E of 7.7, below the sector average, while Lasmo in the oil exploration sector had a P/E of 76.2, above the sector average.

The market therefore judges that there is an excellent earnings potential for Lasmo, but has much lower expectations for Yorkshire Water.

Investment analysts spend a great deal of time analysing the P/E ratios for companies and analysing closely the companies within a sector that interests them. They pay visits to these companies and talk to higher management. The management goes along with this in the hope of a favourable recommendation from the analysis, which usually comes out as a broker's circular. A favourable report will elevate the share price, allowing the management to glow with satisfaction. Sometimes, to the fury of the management, analysts come away with a "sell" recommendation for that company's shares.

Although the background information given in the financial press is useful as an aid towards understanding the overall investment climate, the methods discussed in this book focus simply on the price of the share, and the way in which this price has moved over the course of time. Thus the investor needs to do no more than update his share price histories from whatever source he uses—newspaper, Teletext, direct feed of prices from a databank via the telephone line, or prices on diskette. He should avoid shares which are not labelled as being active stocks, and stay mainly with the shares with the highest market capitalisations. By this means he will reduce the unfavourable spread of prices to the minimum.

# 3

# Market Influences

There is an important question to be asked about the stock market that will influence totally the way in which we approach investment. The question is this: does the market act more like an indivisible whole, or more like a set of completely individual shares all doing their own thing?

The focus of newspapers and TV on the FTSE100 Index as the barometer of share price movement may lead investors to the conclusion that it is the market itself which is of overriding importance, and individual shares simply mirror the movement of the market. A moment's thought dispels this idea, since obviously an individual share must also reflect the view that investors have of that particular company. This may lead to the opposite view of the market, that it is simply a collection of unique shares, each behaving in complete isolation from every other share. As is frequently the case, the truth lies somewhere between these two extremes, since several influences act on an individual share price. The important influences are summarised in Figure 3.1. There are four of these: world markets, the UK market, the sector influence and the feeling about the company itself.

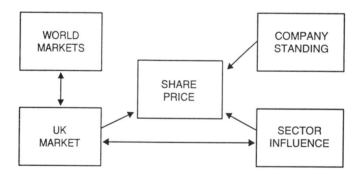

**Figure 3.1**   The share price of an individual company is affected directly or indirectly by world markets, the UK market, UK sectors and the perceived standing of the company itself

Anyone who held shares at the time of the 1987 crash will appreciate the effect of world markets, since the crash started in Wall Street before reverberating around the world. The term "world markets" is something of a misnomer, since there are just three markets of any importance: Wall Street, which is measured by the Dow–Jones Index; Tokyo, measured by the Nikkei–Dow Index; and London, measured primarily by the FTSE100 Index. Of these "Big Three", Wall Street is by far the most influential. There are a host of minor markets, such as Hong Kong and Sydney, but these exert very little influence in global terms.

The UK market is conveniently divided into sectors, which are listed in Table 3.1. The share pages of the *Financial Times* have now been radically altered so as to allocate shares more rationally into appropriate sectors. Just as the market as a whole is measured by the FTSE100 Index, then so are the sectors also measured by their respective sector indices. These are to be found on the inside pages of the *Financial Times* in the FT Actuaries Table, a very valuable compact source of information.

We can take the view, therefore, that the various market influences result in a general "feel good" factor, upon which will be grafted the investor's feeling about the individual share. The question is whether we can determine the importance of this general "feel good" factor as opposed to the specific feeling about a share. If it turns out that the "feel good" factor is vitally important, then we should focus most of our attention on the market and sector indices themselves, whereas if the factor is of very little importance, we should give the market and sector indices only a passing glance.

In order to determine the importance of the "feel good" factor we need to analyse, simply but carefully, the relationships shown in Figure 3.1.

**Table 3.1**   The major sectors in the UK stock market

| | |
|---|---|
| Banks (Merchant) | Leisure and Hotels |
| Banks (Retail) | Life Assurance |
| Breweries | Media |
| Building/Construction | Oil Exploration/Production |
| Building/Materials | Oil/Integrated |
| Chemicals | Other Financial |
| Distributors | Paper/Packaging/Printing |
| Diversified Industrial | Pharmaceuticals |
| Electricity | Property |
| Electronics/Electrical | Retailers (Food) |
| Engineering (Vehicles) | Retailers (General) |
| Engineering | Spirits/Wines |
| Extractive Industries | Support Services |
| Food Producers | Telecommunications |
| Gas Distributors | Textiles |
| Health Care | Tobacco |
| Household Goods | Transport |
| Insurance | Water |

## WORLD MARKET INFLUENCES

Wall Street, the US market, is the major world market, so we can simplify the analysis by comparing movements in Wall Street, measured by the Dow–Jones Index, with movements in London, measured by the FTSE100 Index. Charts of the two indices from April 1987 to May 1997 are shown in Figures 3.2a and 3.2b. The general impression is given that the two markets move more or less in sympathy with each other, since major peaks and troughs occur at the same points in time. It is also seen that the markets have risen substantially over the time period shown.

It is possible to calculate the relative performances of one index against the other by calculating the ratio of the two indices. This is done by taking, one week at a time, the Friday closing value of the FTSE100 Index and dividing it by the corresponding value of the Dow–Jones Index. The result is shown in Figure 3.2c.

If the markets were performing similarly then the ratio would be more or less constant. It can be seen that this was the case over the first half of the chart, but since then the ratio has dropped steadily. This shows that Wall Street has outperformed the FTSE100 Index consistently since about 1993.

It requires a study of the actual price changes to look at the shorter term relationship between the two markets. In order to allow for the widely

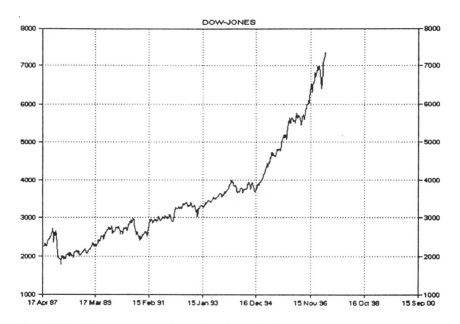

**Figure 3.2a**   The movement of the Dow–Jones Index from April 1987

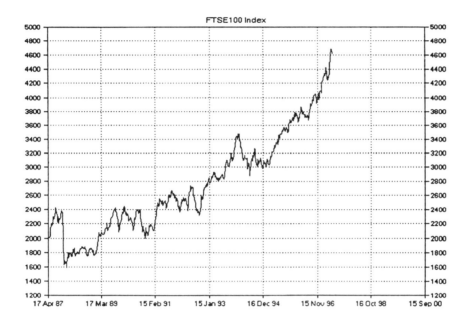

**Figure 3.2b**   The movement of the FTSE100 Index from April 1987

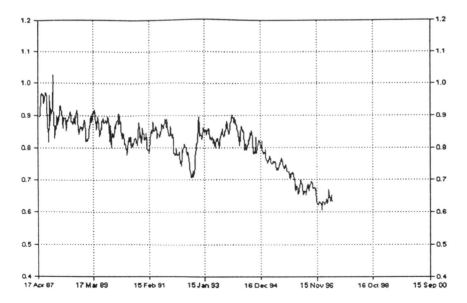

**Figure 3.2c**   The ratio of the FTSE100 Index to the Dow–Jones Index on a weekly basis. Over the last few years the Dow–Jones has outperformed the UK market

differing time zones between the two markets, the change in each market over a week, i.e. from Friday to the next Friday, would seem to be a more appropriate measure of sympathetic movement. Such a weekly span allows investors to take full cognisance of normal trends and unusual occurrences in each market.

Over the last five years, from April 1992, there were 250 weekly price changes for each market. None of the changes were zero, i.e. in no case did a Friday closing price stay the same for the following Friday. Of the 250 changes, 157, i.e. 63% or about two-thirds, were in the same direction in both markets. This was also true of the five years from April 1987. In that case 165, i.e. 66% (again two-thirds) of the weekly changes were in the same direction. Thus there is a consistency over the whole ten-year time period that for two-thirds of the time the two markets move in unison.

Only the following four possibilities can occur for price movements in New York and London:

- Rise in New York, fall in London
- Rise in New York, rise in London
- Fall in New York, fall in London
- Fall in New York, rise in London

It may seem to the average investor that we are being excessively trivial in writing down these obvious possibilities, but in any determination of probabilities, some of which may be much more complex than this present example, it is always necessary to specify the different combinations which can occur.

In this present case, two of the possibilities out of four are for a movement in the same direction in both markets, either a rise or a fall. Thus, if there were no connection whatsoever between the two markets over the time period being studied, we would have expected only 50% of the movements to be in the same direction.

Thus it is obvious that New York and London are not totally isolated markets, but do move partly (not completely) in sympathy with each other.

## THE IMPORTANCE OF EXTREMES

It is the normal in stock market behaviour that tends to be unexciting, whereas the abnormal gets investors sitting up and taking notice. We will see that this is an important generalisation for the investor. The more extreme a movement in a market, sector or price, the greater is its effect on the other markets, sectors or prices.

This can easily be demonstrated for the New York–London situation. The greater the weekly change, the more likely is the change to be reflected in the other market. Taking, over the last five years, weekly changes of 1% or greater (either rises or falls), then out of 55 such changes, 45, i.e. 82%, were in the same direction in both markets. Taking the first five years, there were 122 such changes, of which 103, i.e. 84%, were in the same direction.

As far as the UK investor is concerned, it is not necessary to do any more than keep a weather eye on New York, since a study of the London market will provide basically the same information. It is when more extreme movements occur in New York which are yet to be reflected in London that the investor should pay even closer attention to the FTSE100 Index than normal.

## INFLUENCE OF THE UK MARKET ON SECTORS

Most investors would think that when the market, as measured by the FTSE100 Index, is falling, then all sectors would do the same. Similarly, when the market rises, they would expect all sectors to rise. If there are any differences between sectors, these would be seen by some sectors rising more than others in a rising market, and falling more than others in a falling market.

A simple test of this view is easily carried out by taking three separate periods of one year, chosen so as to show respectively no change in the market, a fall in the market, and a rise in the market as measured by the difference between the Index at the start and end of the yearly periods.

During period 1, from 1st October 1993 to 30th September 1994, the Index virtually stood still, moving from 3039.3 to 3026.3, a fall of only 0.4%. For period 2, from 28th January 1994 to 27th January 1995, the Index fell from 3447.4 to 3022.2, a fall of 12%. For period 3, from 5th September 1995 to 4th September 1996, the Index rose from 3532.4 to 3872.7, i.e. gained 9.6%.

In each period, the gains or losses in the 36 sectors (those listed in Table 3.1) have been determined. These gains or losses have been sorted into ascending order for each period, and plotted as bar charts in Figures 3.3a, 3.3b and 3.3c.

Where the market started and ended at similar levels over a one-year period, it would be expected that the behaviour would be mixed, with a few sectors staying at similar levels and the rest apportioned about equally between risers and fallers. This is seen to be the case in Figure 3.3a for the period 1st October 1993 to 30th September 1994. Six of the sectors changed by less than 2% over the period, and of the other 30, 16 fell and 14 rose. What is perhaps not expected is the large discrepancy in gains and losses between the two extremes. Thus the largest fall was 19% and the largest rise was 26%. Investors with shares in the largest falling sectors would be rather disgruntled to rack up losses when the market had hardly changed over the year, especially if they had friends with shares in the winning sectors.

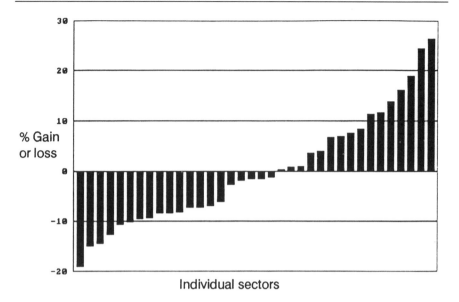

**Figure 3.3a**   The behaviour of the sectors from Table 3.1 during the year from 1st October 1993 to 30th September 1994

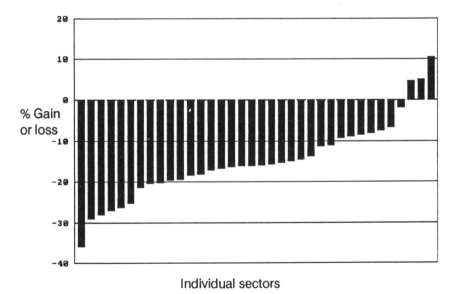

**Figure 3.3b**   The behaviour of the sectors during the year from 28th January 1994 to 27th January 1995

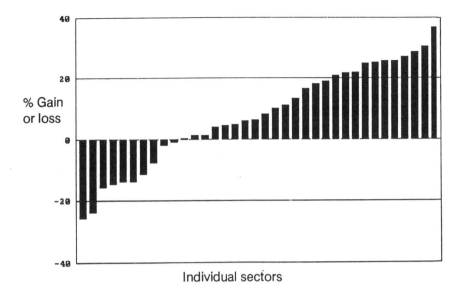

**Figure 3.3c** The behaviour of the sectors during the year from 5th September 1995 to 4th September 1996

In the case of a falling market, the prediction of course would be for a much higher proportion of losers. It would also be expected that the losing sectors would see far greater losses than the 19% seen above for a market standstill. One might also expect that the highest gains would be less than the 26% seen during a market standstill. All three of these predictions are seen to be true from Figure 3.3b for the period 28th January 1994 to 27th January 1995 when the FTSE100 Index fell by 12%. Only three sectors showed a gain during this period, with the overwhelming proportion of 33 showing a loss. The largest loss was 36% and the highest gain 10%.

The reverse situation would be expected for the behaviour of sectors during a rising market. This is shown to be true in Figure 3.3c for the period from 5th September 1995 to 4th September 1996 when the FTSE100 Index rose by 9.6%. This time 10 sectors showed a fall and the other 26 rose. The largest gain was 36.7% and the largest fall 25.6%. It is slightly surprising that the largest fall was greater during this rising market than the largest fall during the standstill.

The overall influence of the market can best be illustrated by looking at our old friend the dartboard investor. Where the Index subsequently fell by 12%, this investor had only three chances in 36, i.e. an 8% chance, of selecting a winning sector by throwing his dart at the FT Actuaries Table. On the other hand, when the market rose by 9.6%, the dartboard investor would have had 26 chances out of 36, i.e. a 72% chance of being correct.

As the rise or fall in the FTSE100 Index increases, then the proportion of sectors following the market also increases. Having said that, it would take a very large rise or fall in the Index, of greater than say 30%, before all sectors follow suit. With larger falls in the Index, the falls in the worst-performing sectors increase in magnitude. Conversely, with higher rises in the Index, the rises in the best-performing sectors increase in magnitude.

**These figures put into perspective the great importance of the market direction itself. The chance of beating an adverse market trend is minuscule, while with a favourable market trend, the chance of coming to grief is small.**

## INFLUENCE OF THE MARKET ON INDIVIDUAL SHARES

Naturally, within a sector which contains a large number of shares of what may still be a relatively diverse set of companies, there will still be a wide variation in share performance. Even in a sector which declines over a yearly period, there may still be shares which make a profit, while within a losing sector, winners may still be found. Thus it is possible to cast more light on the importance of the market by examining the behaviour of a set of individual shares. To do this, a pool of 123 top shares (mainly the FTSE100 constituents plus shares from the Traded Options list) was examined for their performance over the same time periods as were used for the sector evaluation.

Figure 3.4a shows the gains and losses, sorted into ascending order, of these 123 shares during the year from 1st October 1993 to 30th September 1994 when the Index was almost unchanged. It can be seen clearly that, as with sectors, the shares are split fairly evenly between winners and losers. As far as extremes go, the largest loser saw a fall of 42% and the largest gainer a rise of 37%. The gainers averaged a gain of 12.6%, while the losers averaged a loss of 12.2%. The overall performance was for a gain of 1.3%.

For the period from 28th January 1994 to 27th January 1995 when the Index fell by 12%, the overwhelming majority of shares made a loss, as shown in Figure 3.4b. Out of 123, no fewer than 105 shares (about 85% of the total) made a loss or no change, and only 18 made a gain. The worst loss was 48% and the best gain was about 23%. The average loss of the 105 losing shares was over 17%, while the average gain of the 18 gaining shares was 7.7%. The overall performance of the 123 shares was for a loss of more than 13%.

Finally, Figure 3.4c shows the case for the year from 5th September 1995 to 4th September 1996, the Index rising by 9.6% over the year. This time, 81 shares (66% of the total) made a gain while 42 lost. The gainers averaged a gain of 17.9%, while the losers averaged a loss of 16.3%. The overall performance of the 123 shares was for a gain of more than 6.2%.

Thus a study of the behaviour of shares during falling, sideways and rising markets reinforces the message of the behaviour of market sectors. When the market is falling, the chance of finding a profitable share at random is very small. The dartboard investor would have about a 15% chance of success for the period shown in Figure 3.4b. On the other hand, the chance of finding a profitable share at random during a rising market is high, the dartboard investor being correct 66% of the time during the period shown in Figure 3.4c.

As with sectors, the greater the rise in the overall market during the period, the greater is the chance of picking a winner. Conversely, the greater the fall in the market during the period, the smaller is the chance of picking a winner.

**As a cardinal rule, investors must take a view as to the probable direction of the market over the period of time for which it is envisaged that the shares will be held.** Ways of arriving at such a view are discussed later in this book.

## THE "80:20 RULE"

There is wide applicability, in many spheres of activity, of what might be called the "80:20 Rule". Thus, in warehousing stock control, it is found that 20% of the stocked items move rapidly, while the other 80% are much slower to move, tending to gather dust. In a variety of businesses, 80% of the profit is made from 20% of the variety of goods being sold. For simplicity, we can take the stock market as being another area in which this rule can be applied. The figures of 85% and 87% discussed above can be considered to be small aberrations from this rule. It is then much easier to remember that as long as the market is rising or falling, then most of the time 80% of the shares will follow the direction of the market itself, while 20% will do the opposite.

The rule will not apply during periods of prolonged sideways movement of the market.

## BEHAVIOUR OF SHARES DURING MARKET TOPS AND BOTTOMS

The preceding discussion was based on a rather inflexible view of the actions of investors in the market. It simply took large blocks of time, such as one year, and compared the position at the start of the block with that at the end. Even within this limitation, we did arrive at the 80:20 rule, which gives a valuable indication of the probability of success for an investor who follows the market trend, and of failure for the investor who bucks the market trend. However, the whole thrust of this book is that an investor

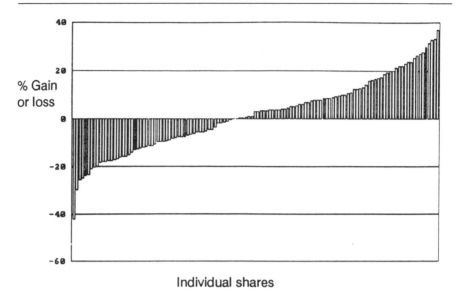

**Figure 3.4a**   The behaviour of the individual shares during the year from 1st October 1993 to 30th September 1994

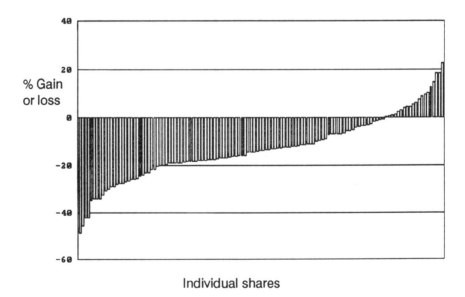

**Figure 3.4b**   The behaviour of the individual shares during the year from 28th January 1994 to 27th January 1995

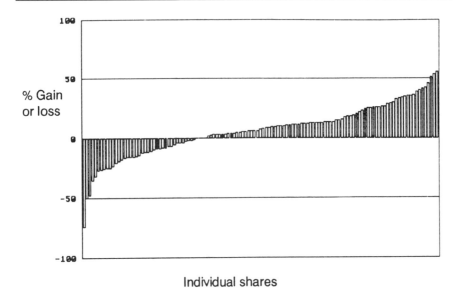

**Figure 3.4c**   The behaviour of the individual shares during the year from 5th September 1995 to 4th September 1996

brings to bear rather more analytical expertise to the timing of an investment than simply buying at a random point in time and selling exactly one year later.

Since the FTSE100 Index has seen such a sustained rise over recent years, we have to go back to January 1994 in order to find an isolated peak in the Index, i.e. one which stayed as the high point for nearly a year afterwards. The chart of the Index about this peak (21st January when weekly data are used) is shown in Figure 3.5.

The question now arises as to how the individual shares themselves behave at a market top such as this. Does the 80:20 rule hold good in the sense that 80% of the shares also top when the Index tops and 80% bottom out when the Index bottoms out?

The comparison that has to be made is between the behaviour of the FTSE100 Index over this period, up to say four months either side of the peak point on 21st January 1994, and the number of shares topping or bottoming each week during the period. This is done in Figure 3.6, where the number of shares topping out each week is plotted against the number of weeks for which that point leads or lags the week in which the Index topped out.

A number of interesting observations can be made from Figure 3.6. One might expect that the majority of shares would top out at the same week as the Index, but this is not the case. Rather more topped out five weeks after the peak in the Index. The most important point that comes through from

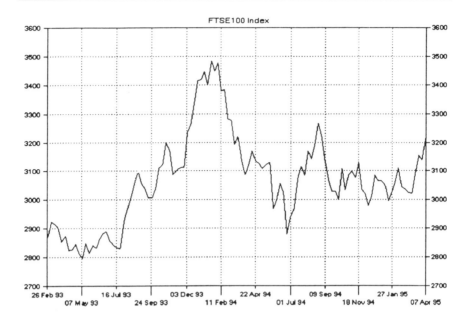

**Figure 3.5**  A market top in the FTSE100 Index. The Index peaked on 21st January 1994

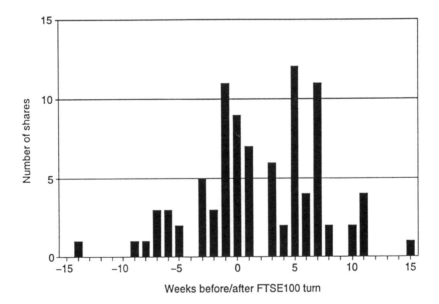

**Figure 3.6**  The numbers of shares topping out each week either side of the peak in the FTSE100 Index which occurred at week 0. The left-hand side of the chart represents early topping shares and the right-hand side late topping shares

the figure is that individual shares top out over a time period that is centred around the time of the market peak. The time period extends for about 10 weeks either side of this central point. Thus the 80:20 rule does not apply to the actual point at which shares top out. Only a small proportion of shares will top out at the same time as the Index.

Since, at the time of writing, there has not been a market bottom of any significance over the last five years, it is not possible to analyse the recent behaviour of shares during a market bottom. Suffice it to say that in the past we have seen exactly the same behaviour as with the market tops, where shares bottom out over a time window stretching over many weeks either side of the low point in the FTSE100 Index.

It should be pointed out that there is an unavoidable delay of one week for weekly data or of one day for daily data in defining a peak or trough. This is because a peak is not a peak until the price falls back from it, and similarly a trough is not a trough until the price rises from it. Even with the most perfect system of calling the market high or low point, it will not be possible to sell at the exact high or buy at the exact low, but only at the prices prevailing on the next daily or weekly close.

Many investment authors do themselves a disservice by measuring the buying and selling points achieved by their particular method against the market or share price low and high, points which it is theoretically impossible to determine by any logical method (other than the totally illogical blind chance), whereas they should measure these points against the price prevailing the day after the low or high.

As we will see later, much effort has been expended by many authors in the search for the most consistent method of determining peaks and troughs in share prices with the shortest delay after the actual event. The analysis of a pool of shares, such as the 123 used in this present example, gives a valuable insight into the formation of peaks and troughs in the FTSE100 Index itself, and thus gives a great deal of help in determining the direction of the market. This is for two reasons:

1. For sharp peaks and troughs in the market, the 80:20 rule holds, since 80% of the top shares will be seen to have peaked or troughed at the same time. Once we have established that such a sharp peak or trough has occurred (subject to the unavoidable delay in this determination as mentioned above), then there is a high probability that any share which has not yet followed suit will do so very shortly. This is particularly important for market peaks, since warning is being given to pay particular attention to any shares which have not given their individual selling signals according to the various methods discussed later in this book.
2. The rounded peaks or troughs are the most useful because they give much more of that precious commodity, time. It is with these types of peaks and troughs that we can see the great value in studying the individual behaviour of a pool of shares, such as the alpha shares, rather

than just a measure of the whole market such as the FTSE100 Index. We will see more and more of the pool of shares begin to follow the crowd headed either north or south. The crowd movement never becomes the lemming-like rush of the sharp peaks and troughs.

A closer look at Figure 3.6 from the point 15 weeks before the peak in the FTSE100 Index shows how the information gradually builds up. The trigger point can be considered to be when at least 10% of the shares in the pool (of 123 shares in this example) peak out at the same time. In this case the trigger point is the week before the FTSE100 peaks. This triggering would normally take place within about three weeks either side of the FTSE100 peak. However, in the case of a very sharp market top or bottom, it is to be expected that most shares would top out at the same time, probably putting the trigger point in the same week as the FTSE100 peak or trough.

## BACK THE MARKET, DON'T BUCK THE MARKET!

This chapter has aimed to bring home to the investor the great importance of the market itself. It is vital that the investor attempts to determine the direction of the market by methods discussed later. The chance of making a profit when the market is moving adversely is so greatly reduced that the risk is unacceptable.

Finally, this chapter has also attempted to show how much valuable information is lost by looking at the market simply as one homogeneous entity whose sole measurement is the FTSE100 Index. At the cost of some extra work in tracking peaks and troughs in a pool of shares such as the 100-constituents of the FTSE100 Index itself, or the slightly larger pool which includes the Traded Options shares, the increasing probability of an individual share changing direction to join the general market direction can be determined quite clearly.

# 4

# Trends in Share Prices

The prime objective of any investor is, or should be, to buy when a share price is low, and sell when it is high. While this appears to be stating the obvious, it is a fact that a high proportion of investors do not achieve this objective. This is primarily because of the lack of a clear understanding of what constitutes low and high share prices.

The vehicle for producing a profit in the stock market is a price trend. A trend takes the price from a low point to a high point, while a different trend will take the price back down again to another low point, which may be higher or lower than the previous low. Since trends connect low points to high points and vice versa, we can distinguish between a rising trend (uptrend) and a falling trend (downtrend). There are occasions when the trend is sideways, and from some points of view such situations can be considered to be periods of zero trend.

The problem of deciding what is a low point and what is a high point in a share price is typified by the chart of Allied Domecq shown in Figure 4.1. The timescale of this chart covers the period from October 1986 to June 1997. The lowest price reached in the period was on 11th December 1987 at 329p, while the highest point reached was 680p on 31st December 1993. An investor who bought at 329p and sold at 680p would be reasonably happy in making such a profit of 106% over six years.

What about an investor who only became interested in stocks and shares in the middle of 1988? He would have missed the low point of Figure 4.1. If, though, he was in ignorance of the previous low of 1987, then he would consider the low of 27th April 1990 to be a prime investment opportunity. He could then have bought for 412p and still have sold at the same time as the 1987 investor, in December 1993 at 680p, for a final profit of 65%.

What about an investor who only began to take an interest in the market in 1995? He would have missed the high point in late 1993. However, suppose he was operating in ignorance of the early lows and highs. He would have noticed a low point on 10th November 1995 at 480.5p, and having bought at that point, could have sold on 5th January 1996 at 550p

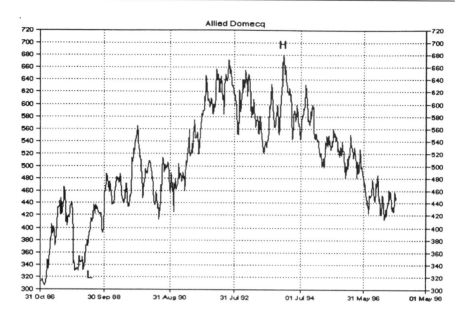

**Figure 4.1**   The Allied Domecq share price from October 1986 to June 1997. The major low and high points are marked L and H

for a useful profit of 14%. What these three examples tells us is that the concept of low and high prices depends upon the timescale of investment, and whether or not we have knowledge of previous lows and highs. In Figure 4.1 it is easy to see at a glance the major low point and major high point. These are marked L and H respectively. They are about six years apart. The 1988 investor would see the picture shown in Figure 4.2. Again, the low and high points are marked L and H, and this time are about three and a half years apart. Our 1995 investor would see an even shorter timeframe, shown in Figure 4.3, with the low and high again marked L and H. These two points are about two months apart. Taking an even more restricted view, an investor active only over the month of May 1997 would see the portion shown in Figure 4.4, with the low and high points marked as before. He could have bought on 2nd May at 425p and sold two weeks later on the 16th at 458p, giving a gain of 7.75% in just two weeks.

Figures 4.1 to 4.4 should bring home to the investor the important fact that trends have to be qualified by having a timescale associated with them. Since uptrends join low to high points, we saw the existence of a six-year uptrend in Figure 4.1, a 3.5-year uptrend in Figure 4.2, a two-month uptrend in Figure 4.3 and a two-week uptrend in Figure 4.4. These are but a small selection of the dozens of uptrends that can be distinguished in Figure 4.1. A similar situation holds for downtrends.

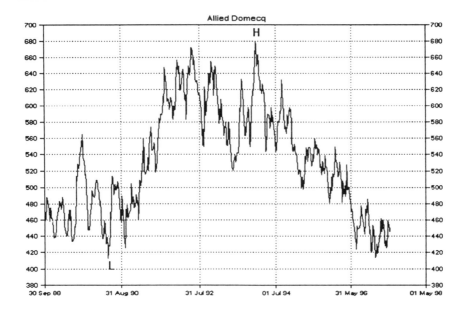

**Figure 4.2** An investor entering the market in Allied Domecq in 1988 would have a different perspective of high and low points from that in Figure 4.1

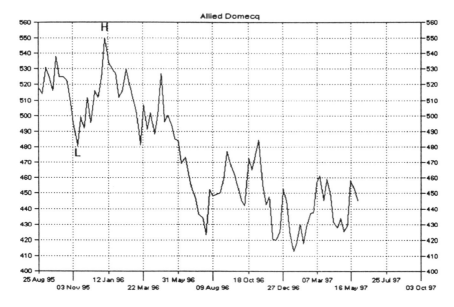

**Figure 4.3** An investor entering the market in Allied Domecq in 1995 would have a different perspective of high and low points from that of the 1988 investor

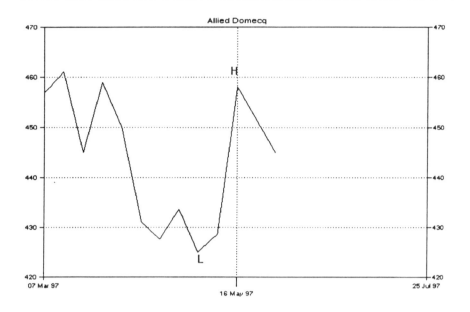

**Figure 4.4**  An investor entering the market in Allied Domecq in May 1997 would have a different perspective of high and low points from that of the 1995 investor

It is useful at this point to tabulate the length of time for which these particular trends lasted, and the percentage gain that the price made during the lifetime of the trend. This is done in Table 4.1.

We can see that the percentage gain goes down as we decrease the length of the trend. Thus it would appear that an investor would make large profits if he could take advantage of long term trends by investing right at the start of such a trend. As we will see later, this seductive argument has to be qualified quite heavily, and it is the *quality* of the gain made, expressed as a rate of gain per week, that is the most important factor. **Riding on the back of a long term rise may not be as profitable as taking advantage of two successive shorter term trends.**

The relationship between the length of a trend and the percentage rise which the trend yields is not an exact one. This can be shown by an analysis of the Allied Domecq share price in Figure 4.1 for the more

**Table 4.1**  The lengths of four different trends in the Allied Domecq share price. The percentage gain in the share price caused by the trends is also shown

| Length of trend (weeks) | Percentage gain |
| --- | --- |
| 316 | 106.0 |
| 192 | 65.0 |
| 8 | 14.0 |
| 2 | 7.75 |

obvious uptrends. The results, expressed as the length of the trends in weeks and the percentage gains made for each trend, are shown in Table 4.2.

Some trends cause larger percentage rises than some others of longer duration. This is especially true of very short term trends. Thus a four-week trend caused a rise of 6.2% while a five-week trend caused a rise of 3.5%. It is possible, however, to come to the conclusion that the gains to be made from trends increase as the duration of the trends increases.

## THE ADDITIVE NATURE OF TRENDS

Much of the anomaly in the relationship between the lengths of trends and the percentage rise made by the trend is caused by the fact that the method of measuring them was to mark off the low and high points of the trend on a chart similar to that shown in Figure 4.1. No provision was then made for the additive nature of trends. The short term trends in Table 4.2 occurred while one or more longer term trends were in progress. Because of this, what we were actually measuring when measuring a short term trend was the rise due to the short term trend plus the rise made by that portion of the longer term trends over the timespan of the short term trend. In other words, we have not been looking at the effect of the various trends in isolation.

The additive nature of trends can be illustrated by a simple example. Suppose we have a short term uptrend which lasts for four weeks and would cause the share price to rise by say 20p. Assume this is followed by a similar downtrend which also lasts for four weeks and which would cause the share price to fall back by 20p. This sequence of two short term trends is shown in the upper left part of Figure 4.5.

Now suppose at the same time we have a long term trend of say 40 weeks' duration which causes the share price to rise by say 80p. This trend is shown (not to scale) in the lower left part of Figure 4.5. If the two trends start at the same point in time, then the resulting trend which we actually see would have the form shown on the right of Figure 4.5. Over the first four weeks, the long term trend of 80p in 40 weeks would by itself cause the price to rise by 8p. Since the short term trend causes a price rise of 20p, what we actually see is the sum of these two, i.e. a rise of 28p over the four

**Table 4.2** The length of various uptrends in Allied Domecq shares and the percentage gains made for each trend. Note that over the period of measurement there are two instances of each of the trends of length 2–7 weeks

| Weeks | 2 | 3 | 4 | 5 | 6 | 7 |
|---|---|---|---|---|---|---|
| % Gain | 7.75 | 1.1 | 3.2 | 3.5 | 4.0 | 6.2 |
| | 2.2 | 3.5 | 6.2 | 6.1 | 3.5 | 5.5 |

| Weeks | 8 | 16 | 64 | 192 | 316 |
|---|---|---|---|---|---|
| % Gain | 7.5 | 17.0 | 30.1 | 65.0 | 106.0 |

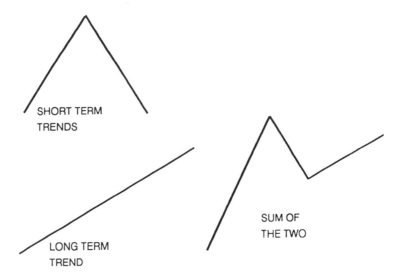

**Figure 4.5**   The co-existence of the short term and long term trends on the left gives
the result on the right. The short term uptrend appears to rise faster because of the
additive effect of the rising long term trend. The short term downtrend appears to fall
less for the same reason

weeks. This is what we would measure on the chart, and what we would
report the short term trend as doing if we ignored totally the fact that there
is a coincident long term trend. What we have done is to exaggerate the
rise which we attribute to the short term trend. Note that the effect on the
short term downtrend over the next four-week period is to add a contribution of 8p to a fall of 20p, giving a net effect of a fall of 12p. Thus the fall
due to the short term downtrend has become understated because of the
existence of the underlying long term uptrend.

The effect of adding a long term downtrend to the short term trend of
Figure 4.5 is shown in Figure 4.6. We assume a long term downtrend of the
same absolute value as the previous long term uptrend but in the opposite
direction, i.e. a fall of 80p in 40 weeks. Now the short term uptrend giving a
rise of 20p should have an amount of 8p subtracted since this is the amount of
fall due to the long term trend. Thus the apparent rise over the first four
weeks is 12p. Over the second four weeks, the fall of 20p due to the short term
trend has this additional fall of 8p added to it, giving an overall fall of 28p.

Thus with a rising long term trend, the rise over the first four weeks of
the short term uptrend is 28p, whereas with a falling long term trend, the
rise over the first four weeks is less than half of this, 12p. The fall over the
second four weeks is only 12p with a rising long term trend, but very much
larger at 28p with a falling long term trend.

The additive effect is easily demonstrated by a real example such as the
chart of Reed International, shown in Figure 4.7. This share is one of the

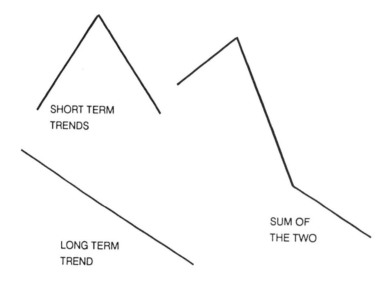

**Figure 4.6**  The effect of a falling long term trend added to the short term trends. The short term uptrend appears to rise more slowly because of the subtractive effect of the falling long term trend. The short term downtrend appears to fall more quickly for the same reason

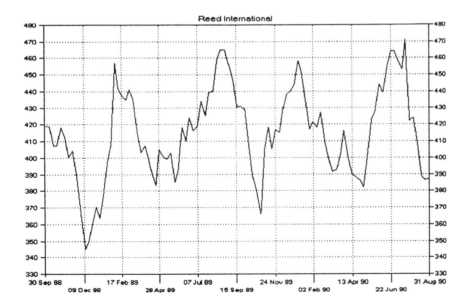

**Figure 4.7**  The share price of Reed International provides a good example for isolating the contribution made by short term trends since the long term trend in this portion of the chart is horizontal and makes a zero contribution

few which has shown a horizontal long term trend, and as such was used as
an example in the previous edition of this book. Since no better example
can be found it is presented here again.

Taking the time period from 1989 to the middle of 1990, we have a
number of short term uptrends and downtrends occurring at a time when
the long term trend is sideways, i.e. zero. We can thus establish the rises
and falls due entirely to short term trends (we can ignore the very short
term trends superimposed on the short term trends). The short term
trends rise from a floor of about 375p to a ceiling of about 475p and then
fall back to the floor. Thus the short term uptrends give a rise of about
100p and the short term downtrends a fall of about 100p.

To show the additive effect of a long term trend, it is only necessary to
move back in time to early 1987 (Figure 4.8), where we can see a short
term trend that started at 300p and took the price up to 450p over the same
short timescale as the short term trends discussed above. This rise of 150p
is therefore half as large again as that which would be caused by a short
term uptrend in isolation. Because the price history of Reed does not
contain an equivalent downtrend, it is not possible to demonstrate the
reverse position, but we can deduce what it would be by analogy. Since the
long term uptrend was responsible for adding 50p to the overall rise, an
equal and opposite long term downtrend would be expected to subtract
50p from the normal 100p rise to give a resulting rise of 50p.

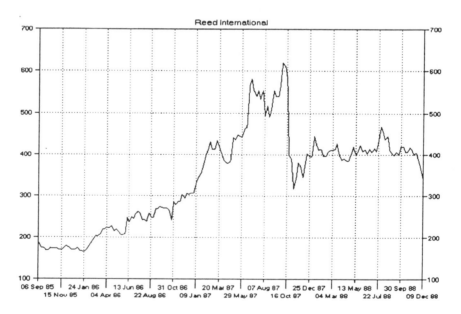

**Figure 4.8**  Early in 1987 the share price of Reed International shows the effect of a
short term and long term uptrend co-existing. The combined effect took the price from
about 300p to about 450p in a few months

These results can be displayed in a 2 × 2 matrix:

|  | | LONG TERM | |
|---|---|---|---|
|  | | Down | Up |
| SHORT TERM | Down | −150p | −50p |
| | Up | 50p | 150p |

The various combinations of short term and long term uptrends and downtrends give four results, from a loss of 150p if both trends are down to a gain of 150p if both trends are up. The rises and falls can be expressed as percentages if we assume that the action is taking place at a price level of 400p. These are shown in the same matrix.

|  | | LONG TERM | |
|---|---|---|---|
|  | | Down | Up |
| SHORT TERM | Down | −37.5% | −12.5% |
| | Up | 12.5% | 37.5% |

These figures have to be adjusted downwards for two reasons. Firstly, dealing costs of say 5% have to be taken into account. Secondly, as we will see later, because of the time lag involved in deciding when long term trends have started and ended, we are forced into using short term trends to decide on our buying and selling points. Adjusted for dealing costs, the percentages would be:

|  | | LONG TERM | |
|---|---|---|---|
|  | | Down | Up |
| SHORT TERM | Down | −42.5% | −17.5% |
| | Up | 7.5% | 32.5% |

Thus, the combination which gives a good profit is when, using the beginning of a short term uptrend as the buying trigger, we have correctly determined that the underlying long term trend is also upwards. A wrong decision on the status of the long term trend will probably lead to a loss. We will assume the investor does not get both trends wrong, since the losses in that case would be horrendous!

Thus it is imperative that the long term trend—known as the dominant trend—is running favourably before any investment is made on the basis of short term investment trends.

## THE INVESTMENT TIMESCALE

The trends discussed above, although conveniently characterised as short term (investment trends) or long term (dominant trends), cover, as we have seen, virtually all timespans from a few days up to many years' duration. We have suggested that we should use short term trends as our prime investment target, as long as those are riding upwards on the back of a long term dominant trend.

Although it is obvious that we should seek to invest as close to the start of such a short term uptrend as possible, what is not so obvious is whether we should get out of the investment at the end of the short term uptrend, or stay invested to take advantage of the underlying dominant trend. If we stay invested, we have to soldier on through the downward legs of the short term trends, but we also have the possibility of further impetus being given to the investment by subsequent short term uptrends. Thus the picture is not completely clear about the advantage of staying invested.

One point upon which it is possible to be clear is that the optimum buying point for a share is where the start of a long term uptrend and a short term uptrend coincide, or where there is the minimum delay between the start of the long term uptrend and the start of the short term uptrend. We have the great advantage of the initial surge of the short term trend allied to the gentler rise of the dominant trend. Such a point may be called a primary investment point. This is shown in Figure 4.9 in the chart of GEC.

Although such a point is the optimum as far as the potential for profit is concerned, there will normally be at least one and sometimes more points where useful profits will be made by correct timing to take advantage of a subsequent short term trend riding on the dominant trend. These may be called secondary investment points. Four such points are also shown in Figure 4.9. The last one is at a point where the dominant trend is about to top out, and therefore would be the last buying opportunity for some time. The profit potential from this last point is obviously less than that from the previous three for this reason.

By analogy with the prime investment point, we would expect that the optimum selling point would be one where the end of the long term

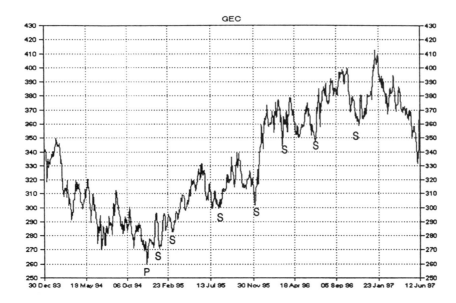

**Figure 4.9** A primary investment point, marked P, is a point at which a long term and a short term uptrend both start at approximately the same time. Secondary investment points, marked S, are those points where a short term trend begins against the background of an already rising long term trend. The latest secondary point occurs just before the long term trend peters out

uptrend coincided with the end of a short term uptrend, or where there is the minimum delay between the two. However, in practice this is not as clear cut as it would appear to be. The reason for this is that it is not the absolute gain that matters so much as the rate of gain, although the period over which the particular gain is made is also important.

The way in which the rate of gain can decrease even though the absolute gain has increased is easily shown by a simple example such as that shown in Figure 4.10. Suppose the time period between the prime investment point P and the point T at which both the long term and a subsequent short term trend terminate is one year. If the absolute gain is say 30%, then the rate of gain is 30% per annum, or 15% in six months. Now suppose there is a short term trend which terminates at exactly six months. It is perfectly possible that the gain at this point, while less than the 30% obtained by staying invested until the end, could be say 20%. Thus the rate of gain is 20% in six months, which is higher than the rate of gain obtained by staying invested until the termination of the long term trend. There would be a great advantage in selling at this six-month point provided we could find another share which was at a primary or secondary investment point in order to continue to benefit from similar rates of gain. As we shall see shortly, it is not sufficient to go for the time period which produces the

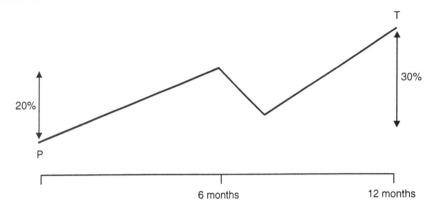

**Figure 4.10**   An investor buying at point P and selling at the end of the long term uptrend at T may make 30% over the year, equivalent to 15% over six months. If he sells at the end of the short term uptrend at six months he makes 20%, which is a better rate of return

highest rate of gain if such a period is very short, since dealing costs of say 5%, for example, will mop up a considerable proportion of the absolute gain. This proportion obviously gets larger the smaller the absolute gain, so that 5% in dealing costs out of an absolute gain of 10% is half of the absolute gain, whereas 5% out of an absolute 50% gain is only 10% of the absolute gain.

This apparently complex situation is best approached by means of a real life example, based on the FTSE100 Index. In Figure 4.11 we have drawn a long term trend which started in December 1987. At the time of writing (June 1997) the trend is still in existence. The last obvious short term peak was on 14th March 1997. The final few months of the chart are cut off so as to improve the vertical scaling of the points of interest.

The primary investment point (marked X here) can be considered to have occurred on 4th December 1987, when the Index was at 1582.8. The final selling point at which both a short term uptrend and the long term trend terminated was on 19th April 1996.

Between these two extremes, we have a number of points at which short term uptrends terminated, which therefore represent possible selling points prior to the final one in January 1990. Both the primary buying point and these various selling points are also shown in Table 4.3. The primary point is labelled X, while the selling points are labelled from A to U.

Not every obvious peak has been labelled. This is because the points have been selected with the important proviso that each selling point should be at a higher level than the previous one, so that there is no penalty to the investor in terms of giving up some of the absolute gain if he remains invested. Since each successive selling point is higher than the previous one, it follows that the percentage gains increase as we move down the table. The gains range from 13.2% to 179.4%.

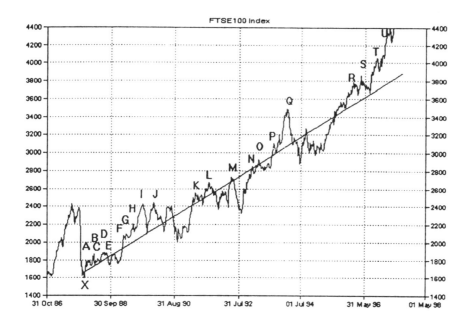

**Figure 4.11** A chart of the FTSE100 Index, showing the prime investment point (X) on 4th December 1987. A number of obvious selling points are labelled from A to U. The straight line represents the direction of the long term trend

Table 4.3 is important in helping us to settle the argument about either staying with the long term trend or switching the investment at some point prior to this. We should state at this point that the prices of any share could have been used, since the general picture remains the same. It is convenient to use the FTSE100 Index as being representative of all shares.

The first impression is that the longer we stay invested, the higher is the return, as we would expect. However, it is the quality of the return that is important. Taking the simplest illustration of this, by selling at point J, a gain of 54.5% is obtained, whereas by staying invested to point K, well over a year later, only an additional 6.3% is squeezed out of the investment. Clearly, therefore, there is an advantage to be obtained by not staying invested in the FTSE100 Index until the end of the long term trend. At market conditions of the time, a return better than this 6.3% could have been obtained by putting the proceeds from point J into the money market for a year.

This is the simpler of the two questions to be answered. What is much more complex is to determine the optimum length of time for which an investor should stay invested now we have determined that the optimum time is obviously not at the end of the long term trend. The answer depends upon several imponderables.

**Table 4.3**  The various selling points which could have been used following an investment in the FTSE100 Index on 4th December 1987. Also shown is the number of weeks from 4th December 1987 to each selling point, and the corresponding absolute percentage gain over that period

| Point | Date | FTSE100 | Weeks expired | % gain |
|---|---|---|---|---|
| X | 04/12/87 | 1582.8 | — | — |
| A | 27/12/87 | 1791.3 | 3 | 13.2 |
| B | 04/03/88 | 1834.5 | 13 | 15.9 |
| C | 18/03/88 | 1855.5 | 15 | 17.2 |
| D | 24/06/88 | 1871.3 | 29 | 18.2 |
| E | 08/07/88 | 1877.2 | 31 | 18.6 |
| F | 03/02/89 | 2069.9 | 61 | 30.8 |
| G | 10/03/89 | 2085.2 | 66 | 31.7 |
| H | 19/05/89 | 2204.7 | 76 | 39.3 |
| I | 08/09/89 | 2423.9 | 92 | 53.1 |
| J | 05/01/90 | 2445.5 | 109 | 54.5 |
| K | 05/04/91 | 2545.5 | 174 | 60.8 |
| L | 06/09/91 | 2667.4 | 196 | 68.5 |
| M | 08/05/92 | 2725.7 | 231 | 72.2 |
| N | 05/03/93 | 2922.1 | 274 | 84.6 |
| O | 27/08/93 | 3100.6 | 299 | 95.9 |
| P | 22/10/93 | 3199.0 | 307 | 102.1 |
| Q | 21/01/94 | 3484.2 | 320 | 120.1 |
| R | 02/02/96 | 3781.2 | 426 | 138.9 |
| S | 19/04/96 | 3857.1 | 437 | 143.7 |
| T | 18/10/96 | 4053.1 | 463 | 156.1 |
| U | 14/03/97 | 4423.3 | 484 | 179.4 |

If we sell at some intermediate point, where are we going to put the proceeds? Can we find another share immediately which is at its own individual primary or secondary investment point so that we can continue to make a high rate of return?

If not, and we put the money into the money market at a rate of $x\%$ per annum, will this give us a higher return over the period for which we could have remained invested in the FTSE100 Index or share than if we had stayed where we were?

We also have to bear in mind that if we switch to another share, we will have another set of dealing costs of say 5% to contend with. There will be no such additional penalty either for staying with the original share or for switching into the money market.

At the time of writing, the return to be obtained from the money market is about 5%, but this could rise or fall in the future, and hence the arithmetic of a situation could change. Even so, the general principles remain the same. Since the gains shown in Table 4.3 are all higher per annum than that from the money market, a switch to another share will obviously be the preferred route to take for the future investment. Having said that, at times when the long term trend is running upwards, we can tolerate small periods of time invested in the money market while waiting for the next primary or secondary investment point in another share (or even the same share—see later). Note that we will continue throughout this book to put forward the message that investments should not be made unless the long term trend is upwards. If it is running adversely, then we will have to remain in the money market for long periods or else adopt various traded options strategies (see *Traded Options Simplified*, details in Appendix).

One way of approaching the problem which we have already touched on is to look at the rate of return rather than the absolute gains. The rate expressed as a percentage per week is simply the overall gain divided by the number of weeks invested. There is one important adjustment to be made before we do this. We should deduct from each gain the 5% taken up by dealing costs if we are to arrive at a real life representation of the situation. This is done in Table 4.4.

The weekly rates of return are high for the very short term investments, and then fall very gradually, dropping to the 0.3% level for the long term investments of more than 109 weeks.

Clearly, then, it is not an advantage to stay invested for more than two years, since the rate of return will have flattened out. This is illustrated graphically in Figure 4.12. A strong case can be made from both Table 4.4 and Figure 4.12 that the most advantageous length of time to remain invested is somewhere around 20 weeks, since the return per week falls rapidly after that.

**Table 4.4**  The rates of gain calculated from the data in Table 4.3. An adjustment is made for dealing costs of 5% before the calculation is carried out

| Point | Date | FTSE100 | Weeks | % gain | Adjusted | % gain/week |
|---|---|---|---|---|---|---|
| X | 04/12/87 | 1582.8 | — | — | — | — |
| A | 27/12/87 | 1791.3 | 3 | 13.2 | 8.2 | 2.7 |
| B | 04/03/88 | 1834.5 | 13 | 15.9 | 10.9 | 0.84 |
| C | 18/03/88 | 1855.5 | 15 | 17.2 | 12.2 | 0.81 |
| D | 24/06/88 | 1871.3 | 29 | 18.2 | 13.2 | 0.46 |
| E | 08/07/88 | 1877.2 | 31 | 18.6 | 13.6 | 0.44 |
| F | 03/02/89 | 2069.9 | 61 | 30.8 | 25.8 | 0.42 |
| G | 10/03/89 | 2085.2 | 66 | 31.7 | 26.7 | 0.40 |
| H | 19/05/89 | 2204.7 | 76 | 39.3 | 34.3 | 0.45 |
| I | 08/09/89 | 2423.9 | 92 | 53.1 | 48.1 | 0.52 |
| J | 05/01/90 | 2445.5 | 109 | 54.5 | 49.5 | 0.45 |
| K | 05/04/91 | 2545.5 | 174 | 60.8 | 55.8 | 0.32 |
| L | 06/09/91 | 2667.4 | 196 | 68.5 | 63.5 | 0.32 |
| M | 08/05/92 | 2725.7 | 231 | 72.2 | 67.2 | 0.29 |
| N | 05/03/93 | 2922.1 | 274 | 84.6 | 79.6 | 0.29 |
| O | 27/08/93 | 3100.6 | 299 | 95.9 | 90.9 | 0.30 |
| P | 22/10/93 | 3199.0 | 307 | 102.1 | 97.1 | 0.32 |
| Q | 21/01/94 | 3484.2 | 320 | 120.1 | 115.1 | 0.36 |
| R | 02/02/96 | 3781.2 | 426 | 138.9 | 133.9 | 0.31 |
| S | 19/04/96 | 3857.1 | 437 | 143.7 | 138.7 | 0.32 |
| T | 18/10/96 | 4053.1 | 463 | 156.1 | 151.1 | 0.33 |
| U | 14/03/97 | 4423.3 | 484 | 179.4 | 174.4 | 0.36 |

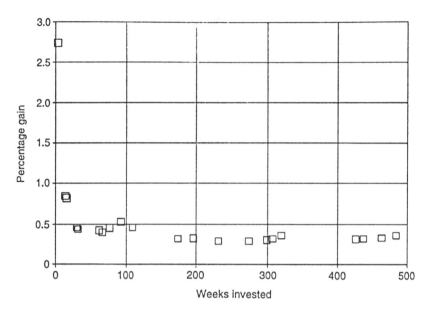

**Figure 4.12**  The rate of return per week, adjusted for dealing costs, plotted against the number of weeks invested. The initial high rates of return fall quite rapidly once the length of time invested exceeds about 20 weeks

Another way of casting some light on the problem of selecting the best time period is to see what the rate of gain would be for the period between one selling point and the next. This gives us a very good idea of the advantage, if any, that would be obtained by staying on until the next selling point. These rates of gain are shown in Table 4.5.

Columns four and seven in the table should be compared, since these show the rate of gain up to the particular selling point, and the rate of gain over the subsequent period to the next selling point. It is only if the latter is larger than the former that we can say that there is an advantage in remaining invested. We can see from the entries in these columns that out of the 20 entries, nine gave a better overall return per week from remaining invested. However, in the first 10 selling points, on only two occasions, at points G and H, is there an advantage in staying on until the next selling point. Since we have already decided that to hold for a long term investment is bad practice, these points at the end of many years are irrelevant.

Although such a positive conclusion cannot and should not be made from such a small number of results, it is a fact that similar exercises carried out on a much larger number of shares give much the same values. Thus we cannot improve our rate of return by staying invested. The rule tells us to sell as soon as we are at a peak in the short term trend.

In the absence of any other qualification, it therefore appears that we should sell as soon as the first selling point is reached, since we should not,

**Table 4.5** The rates of gain obtained for the period until the next selling point, assuming that the investor holds on until this next point

| Point | Weeks | Adjusted % | % gain per week | Weeks to next sell point | Additional % gain | % gain per week over this period |
|---|---|---|---|---|---|---|
| A | 3 | 8.2 | 2.7 | 10 | 2.7 | 0.27 |
| B | 13 | 10.9 | 0.84 | 2 | 1.3 | 0.65 |
| C | 15 | 12.2 | 0.81 | 14 | 1.0 | 0.07 |
| D | 29 | 13.2 | 0.46 | 2 | 0.4 | 0.20 |
| E | 31 | 13.6 | 0.44 | 30 | 12.2 | 0.41 |
| F | 61 | 25.8 | 0.42 | 5 | 0.9 | 0.18 |
| G | 66 | 26.7 | 0.40 | 10 | 7.6 | 0.76 |
| H | 76 | 34.3 | 0.45 | 16 | 13.8 | 0.86 |
| I | 92 | 48.1 | 0.52 | 17 | 1.4 | 0.08 |
| J | 109 | 49.5 | 0.45 | 65 | 6.3 | 0.10 |
| K | 174 | 55.8 | 0.32 | 22 | 7.7 | 0.35 |
| L | 196 | 63.5 | 0.32 | 35 | 3.7 | 0.11 |
| M | 231 | 67.2 | 0.29 | 43 | 12.4 | 0.29 |
| N | 274 | 79.6 | 0.29 | 25 | 11.3 | 0.45 |
| O | 299 | 90.9 | 0.30 | 8 | 6.2 | 0.78 |
| P | 307 | 97.1 | 0.32 | 13 | 18.0 | 1.38 |
| Q | 320 | 115.1 | 0.36 | 106 | 18.8 | 0.18 |
| R | 426 | 133.9 | 0.31 | 11 | 4.8 | 0.44 |
| S | 437 | 138.7 | 0.32 | 26 | 12.4 | 0.48 |
| T | 463 | 151.1 | 0.33 | 21 | 23.3 | 1.11 |
| U | 484 | 174.4 | — | — | — | — |

under the laws of probability, expect to achieve a better rate of return by waiting for the second or subsequent selling points. Fortunately, there are other qualifications that show that it is better to stay invested for rather more than just the few weeks that a blind application of the rule would suggest.

Firstly, there is the fact that the present discussion is concerned with the exact length of the various trends. In practice, when investing in any of the trends, we will find that it is impossible to get in at the exact troughs and peaks. As a result, we will probably lose something of the order of 8–10% of the available gain. Thus we have to use a selling point that yields considerably more than 8–10% gain after dealing costs are taken into account. This would certainly rule out a very short period of investment such as the three weeks at selling point A. This leaves acceptable selling points from B down to F, or time periods of 13 weeks down to 61 weeks.

Secondly, we must take into account the availability of another home for the investment once it has been sold. Money market rates at present are about 5%, which in simple terms can be viewed as a rate of 0.1% per week. This is much inferior to any of the rates of gain obtained at any of the selling points in Table 4.5. Thus, quite clearly, if we sell at any point, we have to try very hard to find an alternative share which is at the correct phase of its long term and short term trends. Since long term uptrends do not last for much longer than one to two years, then once the time for which we have been invested in any one share extends much beyond one year, we are going to find it more and more difficult to find a new share whose long term uptrend has any length of time left in it. On the other hand, the shorter the time for which we have been invested in one share, the more likely it is that we can find another share with plenty of head of steam left.

These considerations lead to the conclusion that the optimum period of investment in any one share lies between about 13 weeks and just over one year.

## REINVESTING IN THE SAME SHARE

We mentioned earlier that there are sometimes occasions when having sold out of a share, there is no other share available at that time in which to reinvest. There is then a delay, hopefully short, before the next investment opportunity arises. It is perfectly possible that this opportunity will arise in the very share that we had previously sold out of. We may still be in a position to make similar profit levels in this same share as those made in the earlier investment.

This can be demonstrated easily by reference to the FTSE100 Index as before. The chart is shown again in Figure 4.13. There are many buying

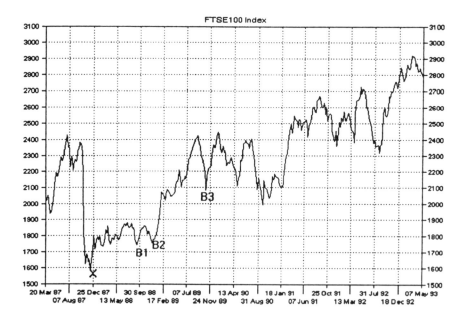

**Figure 4.13**  As well as the buying point X, previously shown in Figure 4.11, many other buying points will give useful profits, for example the three labelled B1, B2 and B3

points over the period since 1983, but in order to illustrate the profits to be obtained from other buying opportunities it is simply necessary to examine just a few of those which occur in the period immediately following the prime buying point. In Figure 4.13 we have labelled, as well as the original buying point X, three further points at which it would appear at the time that profitable investments could be made. These are labelled B1, B2 and B3. B1 occurred on 2nd September 1988 with the FTSE100 Index at 1746.9, B2 on 9th December 1988 at 1750.7 and B3 on 27th October 1989 at 2082.1.

Taking the first of these as the buying point, we can use the selling points F to J, which gives the unadjusted gains shown in Table 4.6. With B2 as the buying point, the gains shown in Table 4.7 are obtained, while using B3 we are left with the one selling point in January 1990 (Table 4.8).

It is easy to see that the levels of gains obtained from these subsequent buying points are only slightly inferior to those obtained from the original

**Table 4.6** The various selling points which could have been used following an investment in the FTSE100 Index on 2nd September 1988. Also shown is the number of weeks from this date to each selling point, and the corresponding absolute percentage gain over the period

| Point | Date | FTSE100 | Weeks | % gain | Adjusted | % gain/week |
|---|---|---|---|---|---|---|
| B1 | 02/09/88 | 1746.9 | | | | |
| F | 03/02/89 | 2069.9 | 22 | 18.5 | 13.5 | 0.61 |
| G | 10/03/89 | 2085.2 | 27 | 19.4 | 14.4 | 0.53 |
| H | 19/05/89 | 2204.7 | 37 | 26.2 | 21.2 | 0.57 |
| I | 08/09/89 | 2423.9 | 53 | 38.8 | 33.8 | 0.64 |
| J | 05/01/90 | 2445.5 | 70 | 40.0 | 35.0 | 0.50 |

**Table 4.7** The various selling points which could have been used following an investment in the FTSE100 Index on 9th December 1988. Also shown is the number of weeks from this date to each selling point, and the corresponding absolute percentage gain over the period

| Point | Date | FTSE100 | Weeks | % gain | Adjusted | % gain/week |
|---|---|---|---|---|---|---|
| B2 | 09/12/88 | 1750.7 | | | | |
| F | 03/02/89 | 2069.9 | 8 | 18.2 | 13.2 | 1.65 |
| G | 10/03/89 | 2085.2 | 13 | 19.1 | 14.1 | 1.08 |
| H | 19/05/89 | 2204.7 | 23 | 25.9 | 20.9 | 0.91 |
| I | 08/09/89 | 2423.9 | 39 | 38.5 | 33.5 | 0.86 |
| J | 05/01/90 | 2445.5 | 56 | 39.7 | 34.7 | 0.62 |

**Table 4.8** The selling point which could have been used following an investment in the FTSE100 Index on 27th October 1989. Also shown is the number of weeks invested and the absolute percentage gain over the period

| Point | Date | FTSE100 | Weeks | % gain | Adjusted | % gain/week |
|---|---|---|---|---|---|---|
| B3 | 27/10/89 | 2082.1 | | | | |
| J | 05/01/90 | 2445.5 | 10 | 17.5 | 12.5 | 1.25 |

buying point. This justifies our assertion that it is perfectly possible to make respectable profits when it is necessary to dip into and out of the same share.

We have 10 points from Table 4.4, five points from Table 4.6, five points from Table 4.7 and one point from Table 4.8, making 21 points in all. This is certainly enough now to draw a firm and final conclusion about the optimum time period to stay invested. We can see that, as was deduced from the original 10 selling points, the best rates of return are obtained with investment periods of less than about 15 months. Coupled with the requirement to make a sufficient absolute percentage gain to offset the fact that we will not get our investment timing 100% perfect, we can conclude that a period of between four months and just over one year is the optimum.

# 5

# Insuring against Loss

By and large, falls in the market occur at a faster rate than rises. Because of this we need slightly different approaches to the way in which we make buying and selling decisions.

As we have discussed earlier, our decision to buy depends not only upon the price movement of the share which we are considering buying, but also upon the long term status of the market being favourable. Although we buy when the market is favourable, the corollary is not true. There is no necessity to sell once the market becomes unfavourable. We should wait for the share itself to give a selling signal. If this is done we have the prospect of squeezing out extra profit if our share still continues upwards after the general turnaround in the market. Naturally, the ultra-safe option is to sell the share once the market peaks out, since the 80:20 rule tells us that there is only a small chance that our particular share will continue in a contrary fashion to the market itself. However, as long as we recognise that we are in a situation of much higher risk than usual because of the contrary behaviour of the share, then we can take out an appropriate insurance against this risk.

Once a share is in this situation of following the 20% rather than the 80% of the 80:20 rule, then the most frequent occurrence is a very sharp correction to the share price so as to catch up with the rest of the pack in the shape of the declining market. This correction will occur with very little or no warning, so that the more normal methods we have of deciding that a share price has run its course may not apply. It is in this situation that we need some kind of insurance to protect as large a proportion as possible of our hard-won gains in that share. Failure to do this will see what was a profitable situation change dramatically into a losing one.

## THE PERCENTAGE STOP-LOSS

As is often the case, the simplest system is also the best, and this is a method which uses a percentage stop-loss. It is called a stop-loss for obvious reasons—its function is to stop us losing our money. In return for this, we have to pay, just as with any other insurance, a premium. This premium is a percentage of the share price which has been reached, and hence the full term "percentage stop-loss".

There are two outcomes to a fall of a share from its peak price. Either the price will continue to fall, perhaps with feeble and unsuccessful attempts to rise, or it will recover from its fall, hopefully to move into higher ground than its previous peak. Both of these possibilities are shown in Figure 5.1.

The question now comes down to a consideration of how long the downward leg of Figure 5.1(a) continues before we give up hope of a recovery and sell the share, i.e. how long is it before we stop waiting for the situation in Figure 5.1(b) to occur? The biggest problem we are up against here is investor psychology. By and large, the private investor will continue to watch while the situation in Figure 5.1(a) continues to eat away at the accumulated profit, because he or she is convinced that the price will bounce back tomorrow, the day after or the day after that. The private investor is always too reluctant to sell, and therefore the only protection we can give the private investor is to put forward an entirely mechanical system that must be followed objectively.

Such a mechanical system must take into account the rate at which the probability of recovery diminishes as the latest peak price recedes into the past. Since such a system is based on probabilities, over the long run we will always come out ahead over any other method based on intuition or the whim of the investor.

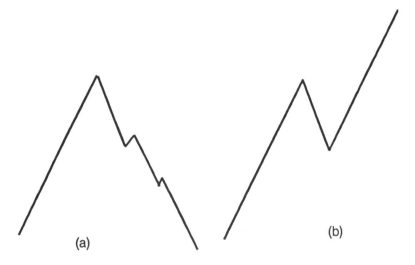

**Figure 5.1**  The two outcomes of a fall from a share price peak. In (a) the price continues to fall back with perhaps small attempts at a recovery. In (b) the price recovers from a limited fall and moves into higher ground

With a percentage stop-loss, the value of this percentage down from the share price is known as the floor. As the share price rises this floor value is raised. The floor value is never lowered when the share price falls, since the selling trigger is when the share price falls below this floor. As the share price rises, therefore, the profit so far is consolidated by this constant raising of the floor. The system must be used totally automatically, the share being sold the instant it falls below this floor. There must be no question of an investor convincing himself that the price will recover if he waits just that little longer. Although occasionally the investor may be correct, this approach will inevitably cause higher losses in the long run.

The operation of the floor is shown in Figure 5.2. The floor can tolerate small falls in the share price, but is triggered at the point shown.

The only variable which can be changed by the investor is the percentage value being used. This percentage value is a compromise. If it is too low, so that the floor is not very far below the rising price, then a small fall in the share price will trigger it off, even though the price then recovers to move higher. A large percentage will prevent such premature selling signals but will build in a large loss which may reach unacceptable proportions.

The relationship between the percentage stop-loss and the percentage of the accumulated gain is not as simple as a straightforward trade-off.

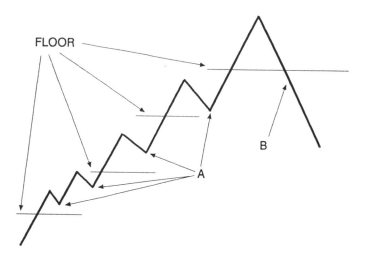

**Figure 5.2** The operation of a stop-loss. As the price moves upwards, the floor moves up so as to remain a constant percentage below the rising price. If the price falls the floor is left at its previous position. Only if the price fall takes the price below the floor is a sale triggered such as at point B. The system is able to tolerate small falls in price of less than the floor percentage such as those points labelled A

This is for two reasons. Firstly, the price fall is usually not obliging enough to stop just half a penny or one penny below the floor. The fall may often be a vertical one that takes us several pence below the floor. It is the price we receive for the share when selling that determines the profit, not the absolute value of the stop-loss floor. Secondly, a loss of 5% off the peak price is not the same as 5% off the overall gain. This latter point can be illustrated by taking an actual example. Suppose we buy at 100p and the peak price reached is 150p. This would give a potential gain of 50%. If we set a stop-loss of 5%, then at the peak of 150p, the floor is at 142.5p.

Since the price must fall below the floor, the best price that we can achieve is 142p. This gives us a gain of 42% instead of the maximum 50%. We have thus lost a sixth of the potential gain.

It is important to understand the real cost of applying a stop-loss, which is relatively high for small gains and lower for large gains. The effect of various stop-losses on a series of gains from 10% to 100% is shown in Table 5.1. These were calculated by assuming that the original gains were made on a base price of 100p. Thus a gain of 10% would take the price to 110p, but the application of a 1% stop-loss would trigger a sale when the price fell back from 110p to 108.9p, giving an eventual gain of 8.9%. The effect of a 7% stop-loss on a small gain of 10–20% is particularly high, whereas a 5% stop-loss operating on a 100% gain still leaves the investor with a 90% gain.

Because of the effect of Table 5.1, we can see that it is in our interest to use as small a value as possible. On the other hand, small values for the stop-loss will take us out of the share for even the most minor corrections in price, leaving us with a smaller profit than could have been made by staying invested in the share for longer. Quite obviously, we are faced with a compromise. We have to choose a stop-loss which maximises our potential for gain by taking advantage of trends of longer duration in the share price, while leaving us with as large a proportion of this gain as possible.

Many investors pluck a figure out of the air and hope for the best. Thus I have seen values of 2%, 3%, 4%, 5% and even 10% put forward as

**Table 5.1**  The final gains made when stop/losses of 1–8% are applied to the peak gains of 10–100% shown in the left-hand column

| %   | 1%   | 2%   | 3%   | 4%   | 5%   | 6%   | 7%   | 8%   |
|-----|------|------|------|------|------|------|------|------|
| 10  | 8.9  | 7.8  | 6.7  | 5.6  | 4.5  | 3.4  | 2.3  | 1.2  |
| 20  | 18.8 | 17.6 | 16.4 | 15.2 | 14.0 | 12.8 | 11.6 | 10.4 |
| 30  | 28.7 | 27.4 | 26.1 | 24.8 | 23.5 | 22.2 | 20.9 | 19.6 |
| 40  | 38.6 | 37.2 | 35.8 | 34.4 | 33.0 | 31.6 | 30.2 | 28.8 |
| 50  | 48.5 | 47.0 | 45.5 | 44.0 | 42.5 | 41.0 | 39.5 | 38.0 |
| 60  | 58.4 | 56.8 | 55.2 | 53.6 | 52.0 | 50.4 | 48.8 | 47.2 |
| 70  | 68.3 | 66.6 | 64.9 | 63.2 | 61.5 | 59.8 | 58.1 | 56.4 |
| 80  | 78.2 | 76.4 | 74.6 | 72.8 | 71.0 | 69.2 | 67.4 | 65.6 |
| 90  | 88.1 | 86.2 | 84.3 | 82.4 | 80.5 | 78.6 | 76.7 | 74.8 |
| 100 | 98.0 | 96.0 | 94.0 | 92.0 | 90.0 | 88.0 | 86.0 | 84.0 |

sensible stop-loss levels. It is important to apply at least a small amount of logic to the situation. This can only be done by experimenting with different values on a number of shares to see what the effect is of changing the stop-loss level.

A good starting point is the data we have already presented in Chapter 4 on the various selling points in the FTSE100 Index following a buying signal on 4th December 1987. For the purposes of the stop-loss evaluation, it is necessary to have details of how far back the Index falls after each peak, i.e. the value of the intermediate trough. These are shown in Table 5.2.

The lowest percentage fall-back from a peak is 0.7%, found at two points—after peak B and after peak D. The largest is the fall after the final peak J, 18.6%.

Since the stop-loss floor has to be above the level to which the price falls back from the peak if the stop-loss has to trigger, then any stop-loss of less than 4.4% will be triggered at point A, leaving us invested for only three weeks. Increasing the stop-loss to slightly more than 6.1% would prevent us being triggered at point A, and would also take us past point C. Such a stop-loss would be triggered at the trough following point E. In order to stay invested past this point, the stop-loss would have to be at a level of say

**Table 5.2**  The fall-back in prices from the selling peaks following the buying point in the FTSE100 Index on 4th December 1987. The various points labelled X and A to J are those shown previously in Figure 4.11

| Point | Weeks | Value | Date of trough | Value | % fall-back |
|-------|-------|-------|----------------|-------|-------------|
| X | 0 | 1582.8 | | | |
| A | 3 | 1791.3 | 01/01/88 | 1712.7 | 4.4 |
| B | 13 | 1834.5 | 11/03/88 | 1811.6 | 1.2 |
| C | 15 | 1855.5 | 01/04/88 | 1742.5 | 6.1 |
| D | 29 | 1871.3 | 01/07/88 | 1858.2 | 0.7 |
| E | 31 | 1877.2 | 09/09/88 | 1738.4 | 7.4 |
| F | 61 | 2069.9 | 24/02/89 | 2019.5 | 2.4 |
| G | 66 | 2085.2 | 31/03/89 | 2045.7 | 1.9 |
| H | 76 | 2204.7 | 02/06/89 | 2102.6 | 4.6 |
| I | 92 | 2423.9 | 07/10/89 | 2082.1 | 14.1 |
| J | 109 | 2445.5 | 28/09/90 | 1990.2 | 18.6 |
| K | 174 | 2545.3 | 28/06/91 | 2414.8 | 5.1 |
| L | 196 | 2667.4 | 20/12/91 | 2358.1 | 11.6 |
| M | 231 | 2725.7 | 28/08/92 | 2312.6 | 15.2 |
| N | 274 | 2922.1 | 07/05/93 | 2793.7 | 4.4 |
| O | 299 | 3100.6 | 24/09/93 | 3005.2 | 3.1 |
| P | 307 | 3199.0 | 12/11/93 | 3099.1 | 3.1 |
| Q | 320 | 3484.2 | 24/06/94 | 2876.6 | 17.4 |
| R | 426 | 3781.3 | 15/03/96 | 3644.5 | 3.6 |
| S | 437 | 3857.1 | 27/07/96 | 3673.3 | 4.8 |
| T | 463 | 4053.1 | 08/11/96 | 3910.8 | 3.5 |
| U | 484 | 4423.3 | 11/04/97 | 4270.7 | 3.4 |

7.5%. With such a level, we would not be triggered until we reached the fall-back after point I.

Rounding these values off, we can see that stop-losses of 4.5%, 6.5% and 7.5% would take us out after peaks C, E and I respectively. This would allow us to stay invested for at least 15, 31 or 92 weeks respectively, although the exact period would depend upon how quickly the Index falls to a point below the stop-loss level after each peak.

The points at which the Index would be sold, and the gain made for each, are shown in Table 5.3.

Compared with the price at the exact peak, using stop-losses we lose 7.5% for peak C, 3.2% for peak E and 8% for peak I. We can see that there has been no advantage in moving from a 4.5% stop-loss to a 6.5% stop-loss, since the return from the latter of 5.4% is only marginally better than the 5% return of the former, and has taken twice as long to achieve. Thus the rate of return is more than halved. There appears to be an advantage in moving to a 7.5% stop-loss, since it enables us to stay invested for 97 weeks for an adjusted gain of 36.1%. However, the rate of return of 0.37% per week is only slightly higher than the 0.31% per week from the investment which was terminated just after peak C by the 4.5% stop-loss. In view of comments in the last chapter about the disadvantage of staying invested for these long periods of time, we can see that the 4.5% stop-loss was slightly superior.

This extremely limited set of data is not sufficient to give us more than an indication of the thought processes that need to be applied to the problem of stop-losses. We need to use a stop-loss that will keep us invested for the optimum duration, which as we saw in Chapter 4 was from about three months to just over a year.

We have used only the one buying point that was discussed in Chapter 4. A section of the long term chart of the FTSE100 Index, as shown in Figure 5.3, shows that there are seven obvious buying points in this period to May 1993, following the primary buying point, which we can use for an evaluation of stop-loss effectiveness.

Percentage stop-losses of from 1 to 10 have been applied, and the average number of weeks from the buying point to the trigger points determined for the same buying points, as have the average percentage gains for that stop-loss. The results are shown in Table 5.4. Thus the table is a

**Table 5.3**  Selling points and gain at each point made by various values of the stop-loss. The adjusted gain is the gain after subtracting dealing costs of 5%

| Point | Value | Stop-loss % | Date | Value | Weeks | % gain | Adjusted % gain | % gain/week |
|-------|-------|-------------|------|-------|-------|--------|-----------------|-------------|
| X | 1582.8 | | | | | | | |
| C | 1855.5 | 4.5 | 25/03/88 | 1767.9 | 16 | 10.0 | 5.0 | 0.31 |
| E | 1877.2 | 6.5 | 02/09/88 | 1746.9 | 39 | 10.4 | 5.4 | 0.14 |
| I | 2423.9 | 7.5 | 13/10/89 | 2233.9 | 97 | 41.1 | 36.1 | 0.37 |

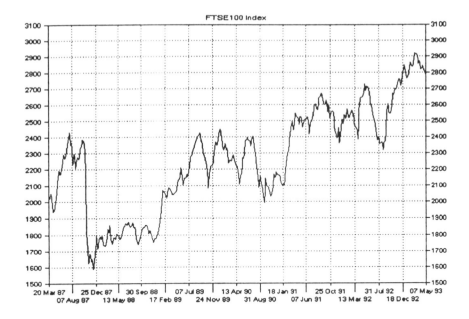

FTSE100 Index

**Figure 5.3** This chart of the FTSE100 Index from 1987 shows that there are seven good buying points over the period

compression of 70 trigger points—sufficient data now to draw a firm conclusion.

This conclusion can only be arrived at by taking the gains, adjusting them for dealing costs, and then calculating the rate of gain per week as in Chapter 4. The final column of Table 5.4 shows this rate of gain for each of the 10 stop-loss percentages. The interesting point is that this rate of gain passes through a maximum at 0.52% per week, thus pointing quite clearly

**Table 5.4** The average number of weeks invested, average gains, and average gains per week by employing various stop-losses to seven buying points in the FTSE100 Index

| Percentage stop-loss | Weeks to trigger | Average % gain | Average % gain per week | Adjusted for dealing costs |
|---|---|---|---|---|
| 1 | 4.0 | 5.64 | 1.410 | 0.160 |
| 2 | 8.0 | 7.41 | 0.926 | 0.301 |
| 3 | 11.4 | 9.03 | 0.792 | 0.354 |
| 4 | 14.4 | 11.21 | 0.778 | 0.432 |
| 5 | 20.9 | 15.84 | 0.758 | 0.519 |
| 6 | 33.7 | 18.96 | 0.563 | 0.414 |
| 7 | 55.3 | 28.56 | 0.516 | 0.426 |
| 8 | 63.5 | 34.45 | 0.543 | 0.464 |
| 9 | 67.3 | 33.53 | 0.498 | 0.424 |
| 10 | 91.0 | 35.78 | 0.393 | 0.338 |

to the best stop-loss being the level of 5%. The average length of time for which this stop-loss keeps us invested is 21 weeks, while the average absolute gain given by this stop-loss after adjusting for dealing costs is 10.8%.

The increase in absolute gain achieved, and the fact that the rates of gain show a clear maximum, are shown in Table 5.4. This optimum value of 5% for a stop-loss gives similar results to those shown in the table when applied to shares. There are occasions when a stop-loss of 4% can give slightly better results, but whether or not an investor uses this smaller value for a particular share depends upon whether he is prepared to carry out a similar study to that above for several buying points in the past history of that share.

## USING HIGHER STOP-LOSS PERCENTAGES

The stop-loss levels suggested here are arrived at by a balance between the most sensible levels of risk and reward, and also were based on perfect timing of the buying point. In practice such perfect timing will not be possible, so that the gains made from real buying situations will be somewhat less. However, we will see in other chapters that we will only buy at times when there is a high probability of a long term trend continuing its upward path. Because of this fact, the buying points will be at times of low risk, i.e. the probability is for a good gain to be accumulated provided we can ride the long term trend. Since we will develop techniques to monitor constantly the status of the long term trend in order to decide when it has reversed direction, we can be more relaxed about the stop-loss level since its function will be as a backup to the other methods of deciding upon the correct time to sell. It will be found that a stop-loss of the order of 7.5% will give good overall performance, preventing us being thrown out of an investment when we can determine that the long term trend has not yet changed direction. We will find that there will be many occasions when the price falls by 5% from a peak when we know that the underlying dominant trend is still rising. Since we will wish to continue to reap the benefit of such dominant trends while they continue at a good rate of gain, it would be inappropriate to be taken out of the investment by a 5% stop-loss.

## EARTHQUAKES

Nine times out of ten, or even 99 times out of 100, the share price will fall below the stop-loss floor by only a small margin. The course of action is then obvious—the share must be sold. There is a situation, however, in which a rather more subjective approach can be taken. This is when the share price falls by a considerable amount, e.g. 10%, 20%, 30% or even 50% in a day. I call such catastrophic falls "earthquakes". Selling at such a time when the stop-loss floor has been penetrated by such a huge margin will crystallise a large loss for the investor. The question arises therefore as to whether it is better to stay invested in such a share in the expectation that some recovery may take place, thereby reducing the scale of the loss, even though it is not envisaged that the whole of the loss will be recouped.

Statistically, the answer is "yes". About two-thirds of such situations result in the share price making a recovery, and often it will regain all of the lost ground over a period of several weeks or months. The share price then continues in the same direction as it did before the sharp fall. This is the reason for the description "earthquake", because a chart of the price movement looks as if an earthquake has struck, with a section of the price movement displaced vertically downwards. Such a formation can be seen in the chart of P&O shown in Figure 5.4, the price falling by 10% extremely quickly.

These rapid falls also offer good opportunities for the investor who is not holding that share, since very large percentage gains can be made from such situations. For both types of investor, one who is deciding whether to ignore the stop-loss trigger, or one looking at the possibility of buying the share, it is essential that a number of requirements are satisfied:

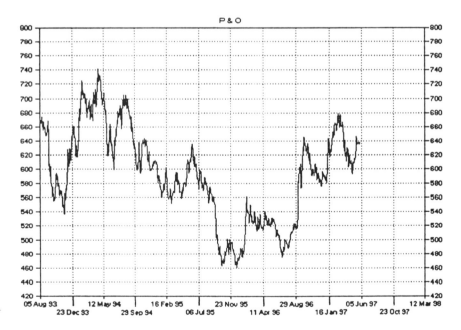

**Figure 5.4** This chart of P & O shows an earthquake formation in the middle of the chart. The price fell from 550p on 11th September 1995 to 501p within a week

1. The dominant trend (see Chapter 9) of the market as measured by the FTSE100 Index is upwards.
2. The dominant trend of the share itself had changed for the better within the last few months.
3. No sinister reason for the fall has been mentioned in the press, such as a Fraud Squad investigation, the calling in of Customs and Excise, potentially disastrous litigation in a US court, etc. A gloomy forecast by a City analyst for sharply reduced profits does not fit into this category! Such forecasts normally have only a very short term effect on the share price, as can be proved by any investor making notes on share price charts of adverse comments as they occur.
4. There is no better opportunity in another share.

Provided the share passes these tests, it is acceptable to ignore the stop-loss and continue to hold the share. If not, the share must be sold, or avoided as an investment.

# 6

# Investment Tools

The tools which we will use to help us with our investment decisions are few in number and simple to apply. Before discussing these, it is necessary to discuss in rather more detail the job which has to be done. Since success in the stock market depends upon the identification of the beginning and end of trends which cause a large enough rise in the share price to give us a profit, we need rather more information about trends than has been given so far in earlier chapters.

## CYCLES IN THE STOCK MARKET

So far we have discussed the way in which trends are additive, the optimum length of trends as far as profit is concerned, and the way in which they influence the choice of stop-loss. Although we did not emphasise the point, it was obvious that for every uptrend there was a corresponding downtrend. The problem was that the additive nature of trends meant that in a complex mixture of such trends, the trend in the opposite direction would not have appeared to be of equal duration or percentage change.

The reason that we have uptrends and downtrends is the existence of cyclical behaviour in share prices. The complex mixture of trends is simply the manifestation of a complex mixture of cycles or waves. An example of a waveform is shown in Figure 6.1. Waveforms are characterised by two properties—the wavelength or peak to peak (and trough to trough) distance, and the amplitude, which is the height from trough to peak.

Now we can see that since the wave rises from trough to peak, this corresponds to an uptrend of the type discussed in the last chapter, while the fall from peak to trough is a downtrend.

In stock market terms, the wavelength is a time in days, weeks or years, while the amplitude is a value in pence, pounds, dollars or, in the case of an Index, points. Since an uptrend is just one half of a wave, i.e. the portion of the cycle from trough to peak, an uptrend of say 20 weeks' duration is the uprising part of a cycle of 40 weeks' wavelength.

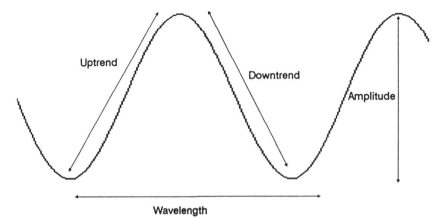

**Figure 6.1** A waveform has two properties of interest to investors, the wavelength, i.e. the trough to trough distance, and the amplitude, i.e. the trough to peak distance. A portion of the waveform from one trough to the next is one complete cycle. Thus we can see that an uptrend is the rising half of a cycle while a downtrend is the falling half

A share price movement is a complex mixture of waves of various wavelengths from a few days right up to many years. Just like ripples on water, the ripples of a few days' duration have very little height, i.e. they move the price by only a few pence. On the other hand the stock market equivalent of the huge Atlantic rollers can have wavelengths of a year or more, and may move the price by many pounds. This is why in the last chapter we emphasised the importance of the long term trends—they cause much larger rises in price than short term trends.

As we will see shortly, the most important of the simple tools which we have available to us, the moving average, has a particular effect when applied to stock market waves, so that it is important to grasp that share price movement is based on cyclical waveforms.

## THE PROBLEM

From the point of view of making a profit out of investment in a share, we have seen that it is important to buy as close to the beginning of an uptrend as possible and sell as soon after the end of this trend as possible. Thus, ignoring the question of the type of trend being analysed—whether short or long term—the most important piece of information we can obtain is that the trend has reversed direction. This fact will encompass buying points, where the trend changes from a downtrend to an uptrend, and selling points, where the trend changes from an uptrend to a downtrend. From this determination we can also arrive at the current status of a trend—if it is not at the point of reversal then it is still continuing to move in the same direction.

It is appropriate at this point to emphasise that there is no cast iron, 100% method of determining that a trend is changing direction at the time it is doing so. As time passes after the turning point of the trend, we will become more and more certain that that point was the end of the trend, finally reaching a point in time at which we are 100% certain that that particular trend has reversed direction. Thus in the examples in the last chapter, we are 100% certain that the trends changed direction because we have the benefit of the historical perspective.

The change from uncertainty to certainty is best illustrated by means of an example. A portion of the price movement of Blue Circle Cement shares is shown in Figure 6.2. What we can see from our historical perspective is that we had an uptrend that started in September 1993 and lasted until late January 1994. It then reversed direction and the downtrend continued until the end of June. Superimposed upon these two medium term trends are a number of short term trends, occurring at odd times over the whole timescale of the chart. As we shall see, it is these short term trends that cause our difficulty in deciding at the time that the direction of the medium term trends has reversed. Since all trends have other shorter term trends superimposed on them, with durations often as short as one day, we can see that the problem is a universal one.

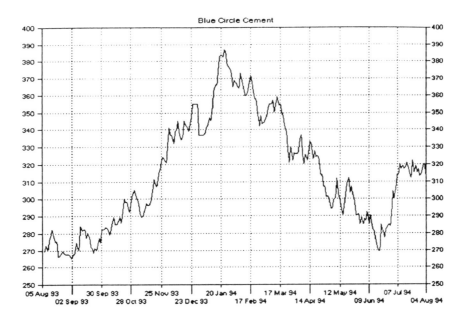

**Figure 6.2** A portion of the Blue Circle share price showing an uptrend that lasted from early September 1993 to January 1994 and a downtrend that lasted from January to June 1994

At the exact peak of the three-month uptrend, which occurred on 24th January 1993, the share price was 387p. The position at this time is shown in Figure 6.3.

We cannot predict whether the price will rise, fall or remain the same the next day. If we ignore the possibility of the price remaining the same, in order to simplify the argument, we can say that there is a 50% chance of a rise and a 50% chance of a fall on 24th January. Since by definition an uptrend can only come to an end if the price falls, on 24th January we have a 50% chance of the trend coming to an end.

By 1st February (Figure 6.4), the price has fallen to 365p, i.e. 22p below the price on 24th January. Now we begin to think that the trend may have ended. Thus the probability of it having ended on 24th January is greater than 50%, although we cannot at this stage determine an exact probability. We still think there is a chance that the price may recover and move higher than the 387p of a few days earlier, and therefore we do not believe that there is a 100% probability that the trend ended on the 24th. The reason for thinking this is that we saw many occasions from September 1993 onwards of the price falling back from the rising trend due to the interference of shorter term trends, only to recover within a few days once the shorter term trends petered out. Thus we feel that this present fall may be due to a similar short term trend of limited duration. This is an important

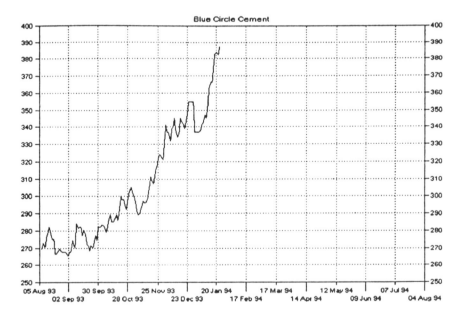

**Figure 6.3** At this point in the Blue Circle share price (24th January 1994), it is impossible to know whether the upward price trend will continue. Later it was seen that this was the peak price (387p)

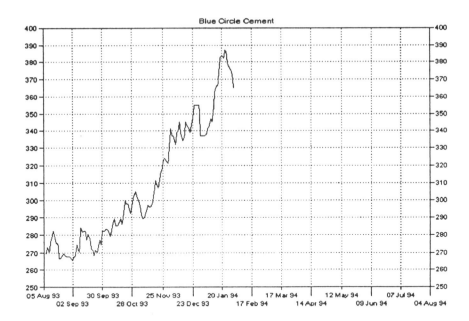

**Figure 6.4** By 1st February 1994, the price has fallen by 22p from the peak of 387p on 24th January. The probability is increasing that the uptrend has come to an end

fact. Our perception that the trend may not have ended is coloured by our past experience of the limited duration of these shorter term trends.

If there had been no such short term trends, then the position might well appear like that in Figure 6.5. Since we had not previously seen such a fall of 22p during the upward phase of the trend, we would certainly come to the conclusion that the trend had reversed direction, and we would put the probability of this being correct at somewhere not far short of 100%.

At what point in this real example, short term trends and all, do we become satisfied that the trend has reversed? This must occur when the price has fallen for longer without recovering than our previous experience of such falls. In Table 6.1 we show the duration of the short term trends that had occurred since the beginning of June. The duration is taken as the time from one of the short term peaks to the point at which the price has recovered back to this value before proceeding higher.

We can see that the longest such duration was 5 days. Thus, by the time we have gone six days after this peak, a recovery is overdue on historical grounds. By the next day, 2nd February, the price moved up a penny, then fell back the following day to 364p. It then moved up to 373p on 8th February before falling back again to 370p on the 9th. We are at the position shown in Figure 6.6, and have now stayed below the peak value for longer than at any time since the start of the uptrend in September 1993. We are thus moving into the territory at which we are becoming

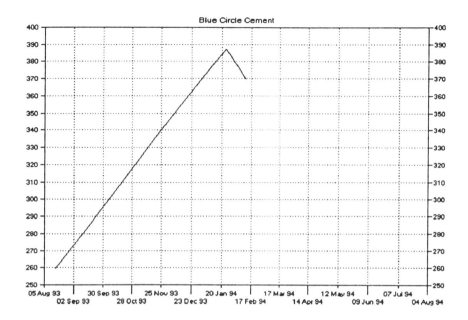

**Figure 6.5**   The shorter term trends in Figure 6.4 are responsible for our uncertainty that the longer term uptrend has ended. If there were no such short term trends, the prediction of the end of the trend would simply depend upon a change in direction as in this figure

more and more convinced that the uptrend terminated on 24th January. Note that even at this point, there is still some chance that the short term trend is one that has a duration of 11 or 12 days or longer, but the probability that the fall from the peak is due to a trend of such a slightly longer term diminishes rapidly as the days go by. It would be necessary to analyse a much longer history of Blue Circle in order to determine the distribution of short term trends with better accuracy. In spite of this, these numbers do enable us to give a reasonably quantitative answer to this question of how long must elapse before we are confident that the uptrend has reversed direction. We can say that after 12 days we are about 95% confident of this. As far as our 80:20 rule is concerned we would be 80% confident of the reversal of the trend about seven days after the peak price.

**Table 6.1**   The duration of short term trends in the Blue Circle share price from September 1993 to January 1994. The duration is measured from a peak value to the point at which the price recovers back to the peak

| Duration in days | 2 | 3 | 4 | 5 |
|---|---|---|---|---|
| No. of occurrences | 6 | 2 | 3 | 1 |

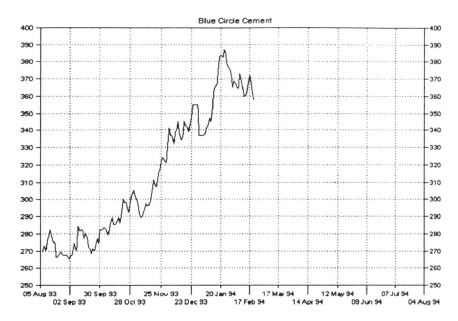

**Figure 6.6** By 9th February, we have spent longer below the recent high peak than below previous high peaks on other occasions in the price history. Thus the probability is high that the uptrend terminated at the peak on 24th January

# MOVING AVERAGES

We have seen that one way of deciding that a trend has ended is by analysing the short term trends in order to confirm that at a certain point past the peak value, the chance of a short term uptrend is extremely small. There is an alternative way of arriving at a conclusion, and that is by some means of removing the contribution made by the short term trends. The application of a moving average to share price data can achieve just this effect.

## Calculation of Moving Averages

A moving average is simply the average of a number of successive prices. All moving averages are characterised by a "span", which is simply the number of prices being averaged. Thus we can have a five-day average in which five consecutive daily prices are added together and the total divided by 5, or we can have, for example, a 40-week average in which 40 successive Friday closing prices can be added together and this total divided by 40. The adjective "moving" simply arises from the fact that we keep the average process going, moving down the series of prices and carrying out the averaging process until there are no more prices left. Thus if we have say seven daily prices, we can calculate the first value of a five-day average from the first five prices. We calculate the second value from the prices from day 2 up to day 6 and the final value from the data for days 3 up to day 7. At that point we have run out of data. The way in which a five-day average can be calculated for Blue Circle over 14 days of daily prices is shown in Table 6.2.

Adding up the first five entries in Table 6.2 gives a total of 1853, which is put in the column alongside the last of these five entries. This is divided by 5 to give the five-day average of 370.6.

Although the next average could be calculated by starting with the value of 366 on 14th January and adding the next four values to this to achieve a total of 1874, there is a short cut which is particularly valuable if averages of large span are being calculated. The method is to add in the next value in the series, i.e. 384 on 20th January, and subtract the first value of the previous calculation, i.e. the value of 363 on 13th January. This also yields 1874, but requires only one addition and subtraction instead of five additions. With, say, a 200-day average we would have just one addition and one subtraction instead of 200 additions! The column marked "Subtract" is to remind you which value should be subtracted the next time you come to continue the calculation. Thus we would have put our X opposite the first entry when we have calculated the very first total of 1853. When we come to calculate the next, the X tells us to subtract the 363, and naturally the value to be added in is the next value that we have not yet used, the 384. Having calculated the second value of 1874, we put our X in the line for 14th January.

The method is extremely simple and fast, and you may check for yourself that you get the same results as shown in the last two columns.

**Table 6.2**  Calculation of a five-day moving average of the Blue Circle share price

| Date | Price | Subtract | Five-day total | Five-day average |
|------|-------|----------|----------------|------------------|
| 13/01/94 | 363 | x | | |
| 14/01/94 | 366 | x | | |
| 17/01/94 | 366 | x | | |
| 18/01/94 | 375 | x | | |
| 19/01/94 | 383 | x | 1853.0 | 370.6 |
| 20/01/94 | 384 | x | 1874.0 | 374.8 |
| 21/01/94 | 382.5 | x | 1890.5 | 378.1 |
| 24/01/94 | 387 | x | 1911.5 | 382.3 |
| 25/01/94 | 386 | x | 1922.5 | 384.5 |
| 26/01/94 | 379 | | 1918.5 | 383.7 |
| 27/01/94 | 377 | | 1911.5 | 382.3 |
| 28/01/94 | 375 | | 1904.0 | 380.8 |
| 31/01/94 | 372 | | 1889.0 | 377.8 |
| 01/02/94 | 365 | | 1868.0 | 373.6 |

Note this important point which we will be discussing later. Once we have calculated the first average point, the subsequent value depends upon two quantities—the next point which we are adding in, and the point which we have subtracted. The latter will be referred to as the "drop-point" for obvious reasons. Thus an average will change direction from rising to falling because the next point is of a lower value than the drop-point. In the opposite sense, an average will change direction from falling to rising because the next point is of a higher value than the drop-point.

Looking at the average values in Table 6.2, we can see that the highest value occurred on 25th January, one day after the peak price. This would not become apparent until the next business day, 26th January, when the average, at 383.7, was lower than the previous value of 384.5. We are not particularly interested in the actual values of the average, but only in the fact that it has reversed direction.

When the five-day average is calculated for all of the points since September 1993 and plotted, we get the situation shown in Figure 6.7. When we compare the plot of the average with the plot of the actual prices themselves, we can see that most of the short term fluctuations have been removed. This is because a moving average acts as a smoothing device for the data. When a moving average of a specified span is applied to data which contain cyclical movement, cycles with wavelengths equal to the span of the average are completely removed. Those with wavelengths less

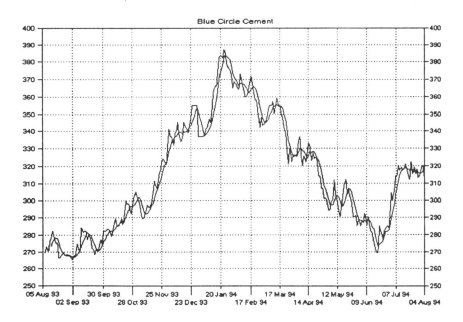

**Figure 6.7** By using a five-day average of share prices, most of the short term fluctuations are removed

than the span of the average are partially removed, i.e. their importance, reflected as their amplitude, is greatly reduced. Wavelengths greater than the span of the average are unaffected.

As far as the plot of the five-day average is concerned, we know from Table 6.1 that in the rising half of the share price the times between each peak and the following trough fell in the range 2–5 days, while after the peak there was a gap of six days to the next trough. Since from Figure 6.1 we can see that the wavelength is the time from one peak to the next or from one trough to the next, the wavelengths of these short term fluctuations are twice these values of 2–6 days, i.e. fall into the range 4–12 days.

On the basis of what we have just said, therefore, we would not expect to have removed all of these by the averaging process, but only those of wavelength less than five days, leaving those of eight, 10 and 12 days to come through. These should still appear as kinks in the average, and it can be seen that this is indeed the case by a closer inspection of Figure 6.7.

Thus it is obvious that to smooth out the short term fluctuations in this particular example, we should employ an average span of at least 12 days, if not longer. A 21-day average is plotted in Figure 6.8. We can see that we are correct in that the average line is much smoother than that of Figure 6.7. We have now approached the ideal situation that we put forward in Figure 6.5, i.e. of a trend that has no interference from the short term trends, so that we can take a down turn in this trend as being significant the

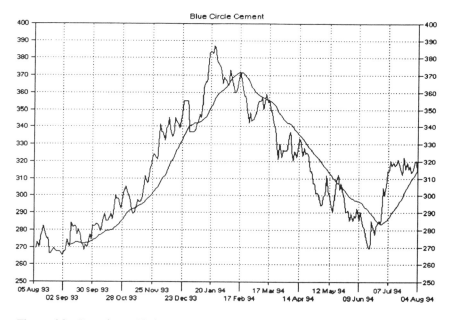

**Figure 6.8** By using a 21-day average, many more of the short term fluctuations are removed

moment it occurs. Here we come to another important fact. The moment the 21-day average peaked out is not the same day as when the price peaked out. The price peak was on 24th January, whereas the peak in the 21-day average occurred on 11th February. Thus 14 business days elapsed before the fall in the moving average told us that the trend had peaked out. This is the unavoidable penalty we have to pay for the increased certainty that the uptrend has reversed direction. In the case of the five-day average we had to wait three business days for the average to fall. In general, the larger the span of the average, the longer the delay from the actual reversal point of the trend to the time at which the average reverses.

## Selecting the Correct Span

For investors with a computer program, the selection of the correct span for a set of circumstances is straightforward. It is a matter of trial and error, selecting the average of shortest span which gives a smooth result. We should always use the shortest span we can get away with for the reasons stated above—the delay in generating a reversal signal increases as we increase the span of the average.

For investors doing this work by hand, it is out of the question to calculate and plot large numbers of different averages. The only way forward is by the method shown above. Look at the short term cycles which are interfering with the trend in which you are interested and jot down how long it takes the price to recover to a higher level than the previous peak. The span of the average should be chosen to be at the longer end of this set of times.

Having calculated the average, it should be plotted in the case of analysis of short term investment trends at the day or week alongside which it occurs in the table of calculation, similarly to the way in which the values in Table 6.2 were plotted. Where dominant trends are concerned, there is another way of plotting averages which will be addressed later.

The above comments apply to those investors who wish to carry out some research on the effect of various moving averages in order to understand them more completely. The alternative approach is to use the result of other people's research, such as mine. In this way the investor can use a value or values for the span which have been shown to yield good results across a wide variety of shares. Although each share exhibits subtle differences so that the optimum span for one share is not the same as the optimum for another share, these spans are sufficiently close together that a universal value can give good results.

Slightly better results will obviously be obtained by using the correctly determined value for a share, but investors always have to balance the amount of work needed to do this against the extra performance that can be obtained.

# Daily or Weekly Data

In the last chapter, we discussed the various trends that were present in prices that were obtained weekly, i.e. the Friday closing prices. Hence such trends were characterised by their duration in weeks. On the other hand, the discussion of Blue Circle in this chapter concentrated on the daily closing values. It is necessary, before proceeding to apply moving averages to share price data, to point out the difference to the investor between using daily or weekly data.

If daily data are readily available to the investor via a computer system in which the data can be downloaded automatically, then it makes sense to use this as the basis for analysis. If the data have to be laboriously typed in, or if the calculations are carried out by hand, then quite obviously the investor is faced with five times as much work if analysing daily compared with weekly data. The question must then be asked as to whether using daily data under such circumstances is an efficient use of time. The answer is no, since, although a better overall performance will be obtained, the difference does not warrant the considerable amount of work entailed.

As far as moving averages are concerned, a popular span used for determining buying and selling points due to short term trends is one of 25 days, whereas longer trends are investigated by 200-day averages. The weekly equivalents to these are the five-week average and the 40-week average. For reasons discussed later the five-week and 41-week averages are the ones used extensively in this book. There is virtually no difference between the results obtained for the analysis of long term trends either from using a 200-day average on daily data or from using a 40-week average on weekly data, since such averages are not used to fine tune a buying or selling point but to determine the background climate to the investment. Thus the only point at issue is the question of the 25-day average of daily data as opposed to the five-week average of weekly data. The performance of these two averages will be compared in a later chapter, but one aspect needs to be emphasised now. A portion of the Boots daily price is shown in Figure 6.9. The Friday closing prices, i.e. the points which would be obtained by using weekly data, are shown superimposed as stars on the daily line plot. If we joined together these stars, we would see that this line is much smoother than that for the daily data. The reason is that sampling every fifth point imposes its own smoothing of the data, since after a Friday value there are four more daily values to come before the next Friday value, giving four chances for the data to be higher or lower than the Friday close. Thus the extremes of the daily data are reduced, which will lead to a smoother average. Thus we would expect a five-week average of weekly data to be somewhat smoother than a 25-day average of daily data. This is confirmed by Figures 6.10 and 6.11 where these two types of average are compared.

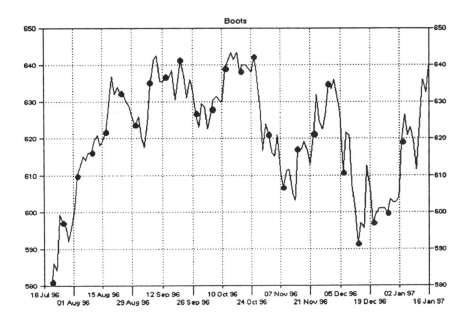

**Figure 6.9** The Friday closing points in this daily chart of a section of the Boots share price shows that weekly data remove some of the extremes of the daily data, giving a smoother plot

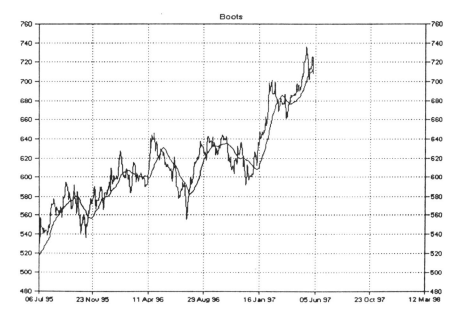

**Figure 6.10** A close inspection of this 25-day average of the Boots share price will reveal that there are many small kinks in its apparent smoothness

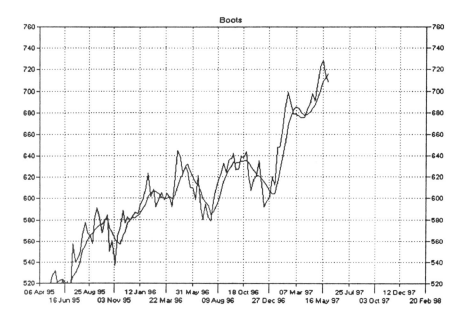

**Figure 6.11** When the five-week average of the weekly closing prices are used, the average is much smoother than that in Figure 6.10, with only a few kinks

We will see later that this extra smoothness is of great value in reducing the number of false buying signals which can be generated by short span averages.

## Delays in Average Turning Points

We pointed out earlier that there was a one-day delay between the peak in the Blue Circle share price and the peak in the five-day average. In the case of a 10-day average there was a delay of four days before the average peaked out. In general, this gap increases as we increase the span of the average, although the relationship cannot be expressed exactly. It is important to understand the reasons for this delay, since the estimation of the current status of a long term average such as one of 41 weeks is crucial to the reduction of risk in investment.

The reason for the delay becomes clear if we look more closely at the relationship between the price values and the way in which the average is calculated. A simple case is the five-day average, and we have already presented the set of data for this calculation in Table 6.2.

Of the 14 prices given between 13th January and 1st February, the highest peak was 387p on 24th January. We noted previously that the current value of the running total is calculated from the previous value of the running total by adding in the current price and subtracting the first price in the set of five used for the previous calculation, i.e. the price five days ago. It is useful to use the notation "NOW" to represent the current, i.e. latest, price, and "NOW – 5" to represent the price which is subtracted, i.e. the price we call the "drop-point" to avoid confusion over which points are added and which are subtracted in producing the running total.

The five-day average will continue to rise if the price at NOW is higher than the price at NOW – 5. In general, an *n*-day average will continue to rise if the price at NOW is higher than the price at NOW – *n*. Taking the data in Table 6.2, although the price fell back from its peak at 387p on 24th January to a value of 386p on the next day (the 25th), the average did not fall. This is because the price on the 25th, i.e. NOW, being 386p, was higher than the price at NOW – 5, i.e. 375p on 18th January. It is only on the next business day, the 26th, that the price of 379p is less than the price at the new NOW – 5, i.e. 383p on 19th January. The position is shown in Figure 6.12.

## Minimum and Maximum Delay

In later chapters in this book we shall use the turning points in moving averages. Since the delay in the change of direction of the five-day average following the change in direction of the share price average depends only upon the difference between the price at NOW and the price at NOW – 5,

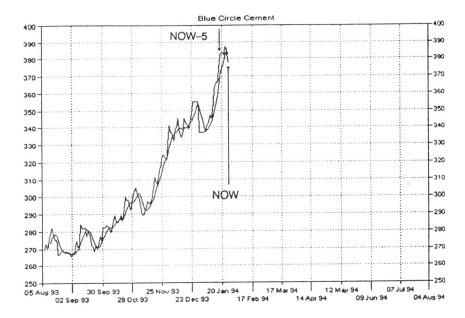

**Figure 6.12** The position in Blue Circle on 26th January. The five-day average has reversed direction because the price of 379p on 26th January (NOW) is lower than the price of 383p on 19th January (NOW – 5)

then the timing of the reversal of the average simply depends upon when this difference changes from being positive to negative in the case of a peak, or from negative to positive in the case of a trough. The minimum delay can therefore be zero, i.e. the average changes direction when the price changes direction. Such an example is shown in Figure 6.13.

While delays of zero are not uncommon in five-day averages, they get less common the larger the gap becomes between NOW and NOW – $n$, where $n$ is the span of the average, and $n$ is notionally in days. Thus for a 25-day average a zero delay is virtually unknown. Since the delay in a five-week average is 25 business days, zero delays in a five-week average are also virtually unknown. The reason for this is quite simple. The further back in time we go from the peak point, the greater is the price gap between this point and the peak price. Thus the required fall in price from the peak to reverse the rising average must get larger. With larger spans of averages, the probability of such a large one-day fall for daily averages or of a one-week fall for weekly averages rapidly diminishes until it is vanishingly small. This is shown in Figure 6.14, where the required price fall in one day is much larger than any fall experienced during the history of the share.

While the minimum delay is zero, the maximum possible delay is one day (or one week for weekly data) less than the span of the average. This

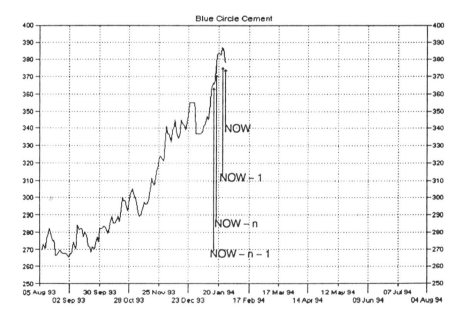

**Figure 6.13** The minimum delay possible between a reversal in a rising price and a reversal in the rising moving average is zero. This will happen only when the price at NOW is lower than the price at NOW – $n$, where $n$ is the span of the average, while the price at NOW – 1 is higher than the price at NOW –1 – $n$

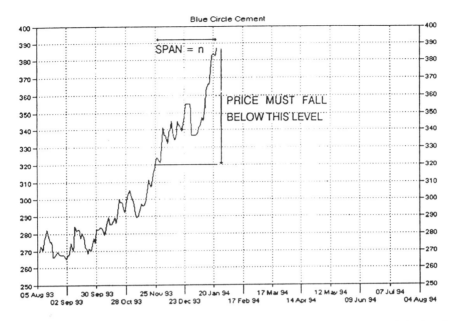

**Figure 6.14** The larger the span of the average, and hence the further back in time is NOW − *n*, the larger the next price fall must be to reverse the average with zero delay

can occur when the price falls back in such small steps that the price level which prevailed at the point immediately before the peak price is not reached within another *n* − 1 days, where *n* is the span of the average. Such an example is given for a five-day average in Table 6.3. The price peaked out at 575p on 5th June, and the average peaked out at 565p on 11th June, four business days later.

Since the maximum delay is *n* − 1 and the minimum is zero, the delays in the averages of a variety of shares are spread around a mean value of a delay of about half a span. The spread is such that only a few are at the extremities of the minimum and maximum possible, most being around half a span.

**Table 6.3** A set of prices that would delay the reversal of the five-day moving average for five days, i.e. the peak in the average occurs five days after the peak in the prices

| Date | Price | Subtract | Five-day total | Five-day average |
|---|---|---|---|---|
| 04/06/97 | 545 | x | | |
| 05/01/94 | 575 | x | | |
| 06/06/97 | 570 | | | |
| 09/06/97 | 565 | | | |
| 10/06/97 | 560 | | 2815 | 563 |
| 11/06/97 | 555 | | 2825 | 565 |
| 12/06/97 | 550 | | 2800 | 560 |

# 7

# The Investment Climate

We have seen earlier that the most beneficial trends are those which last from about 20 weeks to just over a year. These were called dominant trends because they caused larger price movements than shorter term trends. The latter, the investment trends, are used primarily to generate buying signals in order to get on board a dominant trend at an opportune time.

In Chapter 3, we also saw that the 80:20 rule applied to share price movements over periods such as a year, i.e. periods which encompass the timescale of dominant trends. There is only about a 20% chance that any one share will continue to move in a fashion contrary to the market. Thus it is obvious that it is vital to keep track of dominant trends in the market itself in order to select the most profitable periods for investment. However good the prospects look for a particular share, with the dominant trend having begun to move up, and the investment trend giving a buy signal, we are betting against the market, i.e. putting our money on a 20% chance instead of an 80% chance if the dominant trend in the market itself is moving unfavourably. On the other hand, if the dominant trend in the market is moving in the right direction, then it gives us quite a bit of leeway with the timing of an investment in a particular share. We can still make a mistake as regards the timing of a buying operation through an analysis of the investment trend, but the upward sweep of the dominant trend in the market itself will more often than not put things right for us.

Thus it is apparent that we must not make any investment decision until we have established the direction in which the current dominant trend in the market is moving. In fact, monitoring the current dominant trend in the market should be a constant task.

The prime measurement of the investment is the FTSE100 Index. Since the dominant trend in the FTSE100 Index is by definition an uptrend or downtrend of at least 20 weeks' duration, then we need to filter out as far as possible cyclical movements which give rise to trends of shorter duration than this. Since a 20-week uptrend or downtrend is just half of a complete cyclical waveform, then we need an average which will remove fluctuations of wavelength 40 weeks or less. For a reason which will shortly become obvious, we should concentrate on moving averages of an odd rather than an even span, so an average with a span of 41 weeks is appropriate for the examination of trends of duration of 20 weeks upwards.

One of the greatest causes of failure in investment in shares when such an investment is based on a moving average is the confusion between a moving average and a trend. Many investment methods are based on rules such as "buy when the price rises above the 25-day average as long as the 200-day average is rising". The second part of this rule really means ". . . when an uptrend of at least 200 days' duration is at an early point in its existence". Because the 200-day average is not the same as such a trend, such rules frequently fail. What the average does is filter out trends of at least 100 days' duration, i.e. either the rising or falling leg of a 200-day cycle, thereby giving a clearer picture of what is going on.

Since we have come to the conclusion that a 41-week average is a good tool for studying dominant trends in the market, we can use the application of such a moving average to the FTSE100 Index in order to illustrate the difference between the moving average and the trend or trends which the average allows through.

Figure 7.1(a) shows a curved uptrend of more than two years' duration between its start at point A and its end at point B. During the lifetime of this uptrend a number of short term uptrends and downtrends occur. As long as these are of lesser periodicity than 41 weeks from peak to peak, then we would expect them to be removed by the application of the 41-week average to these data. We would expect the two-year uptrend to be unaffected by the averaging process. Using the calculation methods of the last chapter, we end up with a sequence of average values, the last of which is in the same line of the calculation table as the last value of the FTSE100 Index itself. If these values are plotted on the chart at the same dates at which they have been calculated, we arrive at Figure 7.1(b).

When we compare the actual trend in Figure 7.1(a) with the plotted 41-week average in Figure 7.1(b), two conclusions are immediately obvious:

1. The shape of the average plot is very similar to that of the original trend.
2. The position in time of the average bears no resemblance to the position in time of the original trend.

Thus the moving average has allowed through a trend which looks similar to the one which we drew in the first place, but which is offset in time. Quite clearly, therefore, the average itself is not the trend, and this is where methods which confuse the two come to grief.

The reason for the offset position of the trend which the average has allowed through is a very simple one: investors and many investment writers misunderstand the averaging process itself. They add up the values just as we did in Table 6.2, and put the values in the same line as we did in Table 6.2. This was done for clarity and to avoid confusion over which

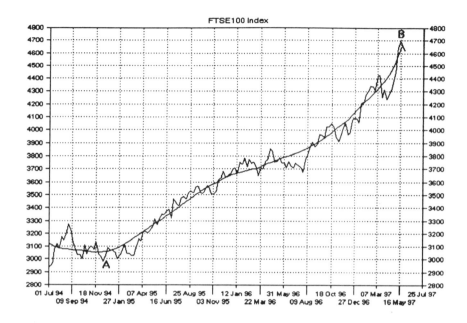

(a)

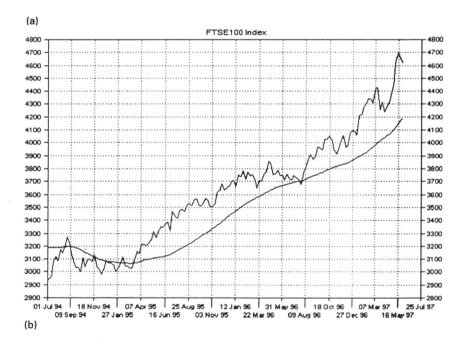

(b)

**Figure 7.1**   (a) A trend of more than two years' duration in the FTSE100 Index. The trend started at point A and is still in being at point B. (b) A plot of the 41-week average of the data

points have already been used, which have to be added in, etc. What is missing from Table 6.2 is a statement that shows the actual relationship between a calculated average point and the timescale.

The averaging process needs to be complete in both the price domain and the time domain. If we have five successive days of prices, such as 100p, 120p, 95p, 115p and 110p, then:

average price is $(100 + 120 + 95 + 115 + 110)/5 = 108p$
average time is $(1 + 2 + 3 + 4 + 5)/5 = 3$

i.e. the central point of the five days.

Thus the important point is that the value of a calculated average should be associated with the central point of those points being averaged. If we are only interested in whether the latest value that we have calculated for an average is continuing to rise or fall, or has changed direction, then it is perfectly in order to calculate and present the averages in exactly the same way as in Table 6.2. However, if we are interested in the use of averages to isolate trends that we wish to visualise by plotting, then we should construct another column in Table 6.2 in which the average values are moved back up the table so that each calculated value is alongside the central point of the span. The data from Table 6.2 with this extra column are shown in Table 7.1. Now we can see why it is useful to use averages with an odd span. The central point of an even-spanned average would occur at a point *between* two days or two weeks, thereby losing its meaning. The value by which an average needs to be offset back in time is given by (span – 1)/2. Thus the offset for the five-day average shown in Table 7.1 is 2 days, as can be seen if we compare the values in the final column with those in the previous one. The offset for a 41-week average is 20 weeks.

**Table 7.1** Calculation of a five-day moving average for Blue Circle as in Table 6.2. The final column shows how averages can be set back half a span (two days) in time, to produce a centred average

| Date | Price | Subtract | Five-day total | Five-day average | Centred average |
|------|-------|----------|----------------|------------------|-----------------|
| 13/01/94 | 363 | x | | | |
| 14/01/94 | 366 | x | | | |
| 17/01/94 | 366 | x | | | |
| 18/01/94 | 375 | x | | | |
| 19/01/94 | 383 | x | 1853.0 | 370.6 | 378.1 |
| 20/01/94 | 384 | x | 1874.0 | 374.8 | 382.3 |
| 21/01/94 | 382.5 | x | 1890.5 | 378.1 | 384.5 |
| 24/01/94 | 387 | x | 1911.5 | 382.3 | 383.7 |
| 25/01/94 | 386 | x | 1922.5 | 384.5 | 382.3 |
| 26/01/94 | 379 | | 1918.5 | 383.7 | 380.8 |
| 27/01/94 | 377 | | 1911.5 | 382.3 | 377.8 |
| 28/01/94 | 375 | | 1904.0 | 380.8 | 373.6 |
| 31/01/94 | 372 | | 1889.0 | 377.8 | |
| 01/02/94 | 365 | | 1868.0 | 373.6 | |

If we now plot the 41-week average of the data from Figure 7.1(a) in this fashion, 20 weeks back in time, then we see the plot shown in Figure 7.2. Averages plotted in this way are known for obvious reasons as "centred averages". Clearly, the centred 41-week moving average has allowed through a version of the trend which is very similar to the original trend as shown in Figure 7.1(a). Under these circumstances, it is not bending the truth too much to use the average as a very good (but not perfect) representation of the trend itself, and to use the term "trend" and "centred average" interchangeably.

Plotted as a centred average, we can see and understand more readily the prime dilemma of moving averages. The latest point for which we have a value can be described as "NOW". Since we have offset the average back in time by 20 weeks, the last calculated plot appears at a point also 20 weeks back in time, i.e. at NOW – 20. This is the reason we were careful to describe the centred average as not a perfect representation of the trend itself. We know from Figure 7.1(a) that the actual trend continued right up until point B, whereas the averaged version of it is missing 20 points. The missing 20 points are the mathematical penalty we have to pay for being able to get as close as we have done to the shape and position in time of the actual trend. The way we have to interpret this is that we know the true position of the trend only as it was 20 weeks back in time, and not as it is at present at the time of the last calculation.

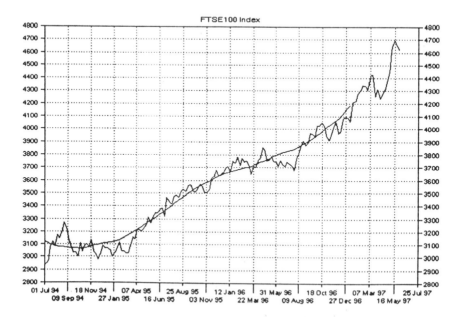

**Figure 7.2**   By using a 41-week centred average, the trend which is allowed through is now similar in shape and position in time to the original trend

We can now understand why methods depending upon moving average direction are frequently wrong. Such methods are looking at what a trend was doing in the past, and not what it is doing at the present. If the trend has changed direction between the last true point of the average and the present time, then any system which depends upon the trend at NOW still moving in the direction as the average was moving at NOW – 20 will come to grief. We can describe such systems or methods as "NOW = NOW – X", where X represents half the span of the average. In the present case of the 41-week average, the system can be described as "NOW = NOW – 20", abbreviated to NN20.

## PERFORMANCE OF "NOW = NOW – 20" SYSTEMS

It is necessary to use some real data from the FTSE100 Index in order to show the pitfall of using an NN20 system, i.e. one in which we assume that the latest calculation of the 41-week average represents the actual trend at the time of calculation, and takes no notice of the fact that the trend may have changed direction in the meantime.

Since NOW = NOW – X systems and methods have been in use for half a century or longer, it would be reasonable to think that their underlying philosophy must be correct, otherwise surely somebody would have started complaining about the performance of such methods. In fact, such systems are a good variation on the theme of "fooling some of the people some of the time", in that they fool all of the people some of the time. By this I mean that there are periods in stock market history when such systems work very well, and other periods when they are nothing less than catastrophic. Markets go through periods of ordered behaviour, periods of disordered behaviour, and periods of chaotic behaviour. The term "chaos" is not the same as "disorder" but has a rather special meaning. There are several books on this subject for those readers interested in this type of behaviour. Stock market systems will perform quite differently under these different sets of conditions.

Graphically it is very easy to show the periods at which the NN20 method is good and periods when it is bad. This can be done by plotting the 41-week average twice, in its centred form and in its plotted up-to-date form. This is done for the FTSE100 Index in Figure 7.3 from 1986 to the time of writing (June 1997). The offset version, i.e. the plot with the left-hand of the two peaks in 1987, gives the most correct representation of the actual trends. The up-to-date version, i.e. the plot with the right-hand of the two peaks in 1987, is the one in which it is assumed that the latest calculation of the average represents the position of the trend at the time of calculation. Thus this right-hand plot is the one produced by the NN20 method. The periods when this method is in error are those when the two plots, measured at the same point in time, are not running in the same

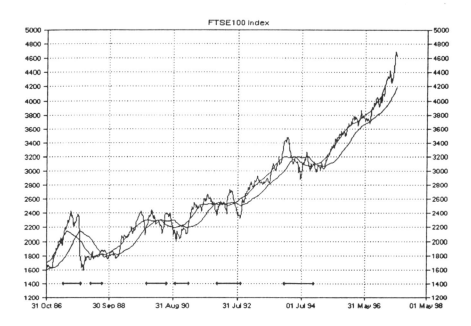

**Figure 7.3** Both the normal and centred 41-week averages plotted for the FTSE100 Index. Periods on the time axis during which both averages are not moving in the same direction are shown by double-headed arrows. During these periods the estimate of a trend provided by the normal average is incorrect

direction. As you might expect, these periods occur between the date at which the actual trend changes direction and the date at which the up-to-date plot makes its change later. A clearer view of the differences between the two averages is given in Figure 7.4 where a section of Figure 7.3 has been expanded.

Thus when such changes are few and far between, as in the period from early 1991 to June 1997, the NN20 method gives good results. On the other hand, in those periods when the trend changes direction frequently, such as from the middle of 1989 to the middle of 1990, or from mid-1991 to mid-1992, the NN20 method is wrong more often than it is right. Thus investors using this method would be extremely pleased by their performance from 1991, but exceedingly disappointed by their performance previous to this.

Rather more information about the success or otherwise of the NN20 method can be obtained by analysing the data numerically rather than graphically. Taking the period from April 1983, the estimate of the current trend direction provided by the NN20 procedure was correct for 184 consecutive weeks up to early 1987 owing to the long, unbroken uptrend. Taking the whole period to 8th May 1992, out of 449 weekly calculations of the average, the estimate was correct on 359 weeks. This corresponds to

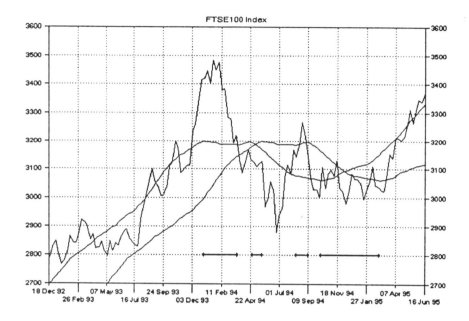

**Figure 7.4** An expanded view of a section of Figure 7.3 gives a clearer view of the times when the normal average is moving in the opposite direction to the centred average

80% of the overall time period, a good performance. On the other hand, if we change the period being analysed to the 240 weeks from October 1987 to May 1992, then the estimate was correct on 152 weeks. Thus the accuracy has fallen from 80% to 63%, a relatively poor performance. An even worse period can be found, that running from April 1990 to April 1991, when the estimate was correct for only 21 weeks out of 52, i.e. just 40% of the time. The reason was of course that the trend changed direction so many times during this period, six times in all.

We can see that the performance of the NN20 method, which relies upon the latest calculation of the average being a true estimate of the latest position of the trend, can range from very good, being correct 80% of the time, to abysmal, being correct only 40% of the time. With such methods, the investor is totally at the mercy of events. He may be lucky in that his investments may coincide with a long uptrend in the market, or he may be unlucky in being subject to a constant switchback such as that in 1990 to 1991.

To make more consistent returns in the market, it is essential to improve on this extremely basic use of long term averages. The aim is to reduce the gap (Figure 7.2) between the signal given by the change in direction of the average and the turning point in the trend itself.

## False Signals

Reduction of the delay in signalling the end of a trend is not the only problem with averages. Figure 7.5 shows an expanded part of the plot. We see that the average is not as smooth as it appears to be on the longer timescale. There are many occasions when it appears that the average has changed direction only for it to resume its previous course within a few weeks. Decisions taken because of such apparent changes in direction, while correct at the time they are taken, will result in losses, which might become quite large if stop-losses are not used. These erroneous signals are known as false signals. We can throw rather more light on them by looking at the lengths of the trends in the 41-week average of the FTSE100 Index from April 1983. These are as follows, the length of the trend in weeks being followed by an indication of the direction, + for rising or – for falling:

| 167+ | 1–  | 42+ | 40– | 18+ | 4–  | 67+           |
|------|-----|-----|-----|-----|-----|---------------|
| 10–  | 1+  | 1–  | 6+  | 24– | 45+ | 2–            |
| 2+   | 2–  | 2+  | 1–  | 3+  | 4–  | 10+           |
| 13–  | 90+ | 8–  | 5+  | 26– | 20+ | (still rising) |

In the last chapter we discussed the properties of an average in terms of the relationship between its span and the wavelengths which it removes. It

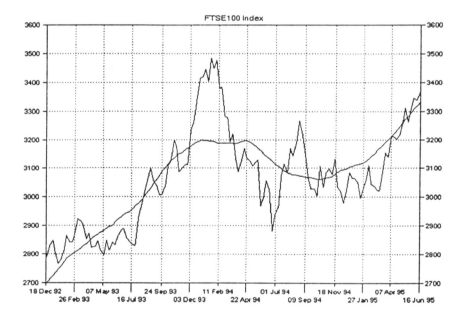

**Figure 7.5**  In this expanded part of the plot it can be seen that the 41-week average is not very smooth, with a number of changes of direction apparent in the middle of the chart

is 100% efficient at removing cycles of the same wavelength as its span, but not as efficient at removing wavelengths shorter than its span. This inefficiency is amply demonstrated by the data above, since we have not removed all trends of less than 20 weeks' duration, i.e. those corresponding to wavelengths of less than 41 weeks. There are 15 such short duration trends apparent in the 41-week average. These short term influences are particularly confusing over the sequence which runs 2–, 2+, 2–, 2+, 1–, 3+, 4– such that no sensible approach can be possible using just a simple 41-week average. The estimated trend direction would be constantly incorrect. Thus any method capable of improving the estimate of the current status of the dominant trend must be capable of alerting the investor to these periods of inconclusive overall direction.

## THE MINI-MARKET

We showed in Chapter 3 that a great deal of information is available to investors if the behaviour of the individual shares is monitored as well as changes in the FTSE100 Index itself. It would be logical to assume that it would be an advantage to monitor the moving averages of a pool of shares such as those used in Chapter 3.

There is of course a great deal of additional work involved in setting up a system to do this, although the data on this pool of shares and the running 41-week totals are available (see Appendix) to ease the burden. A computer system is a great help in such a task, but it is perfectly possible to carry out the monitoring manually. Each week, it is necessary to log the 100 or so share prices, add these in to the running total and subtract the appropriate drop-point. There is no point in dividing by 41 to get the actual average, since it is the direction of the average at the time of calculation which is important. Note also that since we are not going to plot these averages or use them to investigate the position of dominant trends, we do not have to worry about using an additional column to shift the average back in time in order to convert it to a centred one. Thus there are 100 additions and 100 subtractions. As we will show shortly, this work is amply repaid by the early warning achieved and the avoidance of false signalling of changes in the direction of the dominant trend.

The results of such calculations on the pool of 123 shares used previously are shown in Table 7.2, from August 1994 to April 1995. This period was chosen since it covers the last turning point in the 41-week average of the FTSE100 Index. Alongside the data in Table 7.2 is shown the direction of the average compared with the calculation the previous week. Thus a falling average is denoted by a –, while a rising one is denoted by a +. There are no occasions where the average showed no change over its value the previous week. The last column gives the percentage of shares out of the 123 whose 41-week averages are rising at the date

**Table 7.2**    Analysis of the 41-week moving averages of the FTSE100 Index and a pool of 123 shares. A + or – is used to designate a rising or falling average. The third column is the percentage of the 123 shares with a rising average

| Date | 41-week FTSE | % risers | Date | 41-week FTSE | % risers |
|------|------|------|------|------|------|
| 26/08/94 | – | 74 | 23/12/94 | – | 31 |
| 02/09/94 | – | 70 | 30/12/94 | – | 26 |
| 09/09/94 | – | 64 | 06/01/95 | – | 32 |
| 16/09/94 | – | 40 | 13/01/95 | – | 33 |
| 23/09/94 | – | 33 | 20/01/95 | – | 29 |
| 30/09/94 | – | 26 | 27/01/95 | – | 29 |
| 07/10/94 | – | 23 | 03/02/95 | – | 32 |
| 14/10/94 | – | 26 | 10/02/95 | – | 37 |
| 21/10/94 | – | 20 | 17/02/95 | – | 32 |
| 28/10/94 | – | 22 | 24/02/95 | – | 31 |
| 04/11/94 | – | 15 | 03/03/95 | + | 32 |
| 11/11/94 | – | 19 | 10/03/95 | + | 47 |
| 18/11/94 | – | 19 | 17/03/95 | + | 52 |
| 25/11/94 | – | 20 | 24/03/95 | + | 54 |
| 02/12/94 | – | 17 | 31/03/95 | + | 59 |
| 09/12/94 | – | 21 | 07/04/95 | + | 71 |
| 16/12/94 | – | 20 | 14/04/95 | + | 69 |

of calculation. As we might have expected following the discussion in Chapter 3, the individuality of shares means that there are no occasions when all the moving averages are travelling in the same direction. There are always shares which differ from the main group.

The whole purpose of the analysis is to establish whether we are getting advance warning of a change in the direction of the long term trend (represented by the centred 41-week average of the FTSE100 Index) by virtue of a change in the proportion of the shares whose calculated 41-week averages are rising. The answer is an unqualified "yes". We see quite clearly that, from September 1994 onwards, the percentage of shares with rising 41-week averages is falling gradually from its previous value in the 70% plus region until it reaches a low of only 15% on 4th November 1994. It then stays around the 19–21% mark for several weeks until a jump up to 31% in late December. The 41-week average of the FTSE100 Index has been falling all of this time, and continues to do so until 3rd March 1995, when it then begins to rise.

It seems that the rise to a position where 30% of the shares have rising 41-week averages is indicating in advance that the FTSE100 Index average will change direction. At the actual point where the FTSE100 average begins to rise, 32% of the constituents are rising, a figure which rapidly climbs to the 60–70% level over the next few weeks.

The previous edition of this book looked at the reverse case when the average in the FTSE100 Index topped out. Again, this method of using the mini-market of shares was useful in predicting the turn, and a level of 60%

rising shares was deemed the minimum to continue to sustain the market. In order to increase certainty a little, the figures should be rounded to one-third to two-thirds. Thus, when the proportion of risers in a falling market rises to one-third, a change in market conditions is being signalled, and when the proportion falls to two-thirds in a rising market again a change is being signalled.

It is not intended that the investor takes instant action when these proportions are being reached, rather that the investor should be getting ready for the impending change in the market direction, either by watching any shareholdings extremely carefully (if the market is rising), or by making last-minute adjustments to his potential selections for investment as the buying point approaches.

Thus we can be comfortable with a rising 41-week average of the FTSE100 Index as long as at least 60% of the shares have rising 41-week averages. Once the percentage drops below this, the rise in the FTSE100 average is being sustained by fewer shares and is becoming much more suspect. Such an approach would have told us on 2nd February 1990 that the FTSE100 average was running out of steam, giving a clear 11 weeks' warning of the eventual change in the direction of the FTSE100 average. This precious 11 weeks would have enabled us to monitor very closely the performance of any shares that we held, taking action on the first sign of weakness.

This use of the pool of shares to provide advance warning of the end of the dominant trend in the FTSE100 Index is valuable in the sense of helping us to avoid unexpected falls in the share price once we are invested. In this way we help to consolidate the gains which we have made by virtue of a correct investment in the first place. The much more valuable use of the pool of shares is to keep us out of the market at times when the risk is too high by helping us to determine the status of the 41-week average at the time the buying signal is generated by the methods discussed later. It is vital that the dominant trend is moving favourably, both in the share itself and in the FTSE100 Index. Thus it is necessary to look more closely at Table 7.2 for the behaviour of individual shares at the time when the FTSE100 Index had apparently changed from a falling mode to a rising mode, i.e. the investment climate had apparently changed from rain to shine.

## DEDUCING THE CURRENT STATUS BY EXTRAPOLATION

When drawn as a centred average, we have seen that the 41-week average terminates 20 weeks back in time. If the average is sufficiently smooth then it is possible to extrapolate it by eye to the point NOW, as shown in Figure 7.6. Such extrapolations work better for curves which are obviously

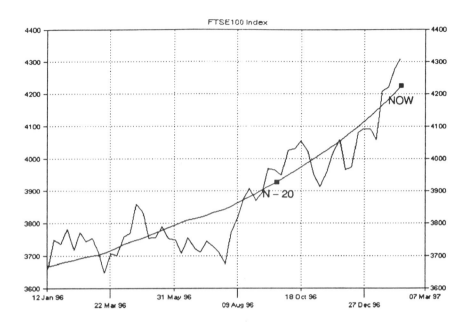

**Figure 7.6** Using graphical extrapolation takes the average curve from its last true point at N – 20 to the present. These two extremes are marked by the two solid squares. The extrapolation takes account of the change in slope of the average prior to N – 20

approaching a smooth maximum or minimum. Where the maximum or minimum occurred sometime in the past, the impression is given that the future curve will continue in the same direction for ever. Since we know that the trend must come to an end sooner or later, then we gain no idea of when this might occur from such curves.

The extrapolation process in this latter case is exactly analogous to the NOW = NOW – 20 method discussed earlier, where it was considered that the average would be moving at the point NOW in exactly the same direction as at its last calculated real value at NOW – 20. In extrapolating a smooth curve which is obviously not approaching a maximum or minimum, we see no reason to interpolate any change in direction between the point NOW – 20 and the point NOW.

When a curve is approaching a maximum or minimum, such as the maximum shown in Figure 7.7, then we have an advantage over the NN20 method. The inference from the NN20 method is simply that the average is still moving in the same direction at NOW as at NOW – 20. No notice is taken of the rate at which the average is changing. In a graphical extrapolation where we are approaching a turning point, we begin to see the rate of ascent or descent slackening off, and we build a similar slowdown into the extrapolation. Because of this, it is possible to end up with an extrapolation that changes direction between NOW – 20 and NOW, i.e. one which

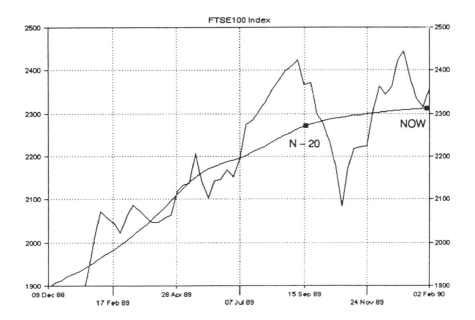

**Figure 7.7** Using the extrapolation method gives a good indication that the dominant trend has run out of steam. The extrapolated portion is marked by the two solid squares

recognises that the trend has changed direction between these two points. The actual course which the 41-week average took over this period of time is shown in Figure 7.7. The data were obtained 20 weeks later, so that the plotted values are real, calculated ones. Figure 7.8 shows a plot of the average obtained 20 weeks after the NOW point in Figure 7.7, i.e. at a point where a true calculated value could be obtained for the average at the point NOW.

It can be seen that the extrapolated average in Figure 7.7 was acceptably close to the real average, thus giving credence to the method.

Just as the NN20 method suffered from the problem of false signals, then so does the extrapolation method. If an average has just changed direction a week or two before its last true point at NOW − 20, then it will always be extrapolated in this new direction, so that another change of direction shortly afterwards will cause a divergence between the two.

## THE PRICE ANALYSIS METHOD

It is also possible to improve on the estimate of the current status of the 41-week average provided by the NN20 method by looking closely at the price movement over the last 41 weeks. Although the result is still subject to the vagaries of chance, it is based upon probability and therefore has a sound basis which will pay off in the long run.

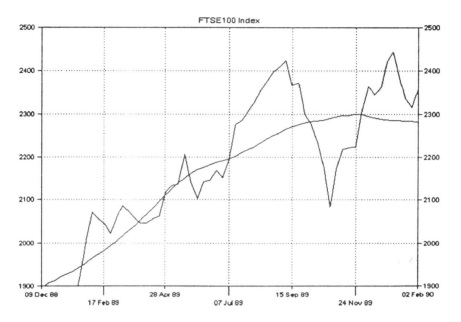

**Figure 7.8**   Once 20 weeks have passed from the time of the extrapolation in Figure 7.7, it is possible to calculate the course that the 41-week average actually took. This shows that the estimate of the trend provided by the extrapolation method was excellent

Taking a portion of the FTSE100 Index movement as an example, the position on 22nd April 1994 is shown in Figure 7.9. There are 41 weekly values across the chart from the left-hand axis to the right-hand axis. The point at the right-hand side, i.e. the latest point, is labelled NOW, and the last calculated value of the 41-week average is plotted half a span back in time at NOW – 20, i.e. in the middle of the time axis of the chart.

The principle by which the plotted average moves from its last known position at NOW – 20 to its current unknown value at NOW depends upon the mathematics of the averaging process. We have already looked at the procedure by which the next point is added in and the drop-point sub-tracted to get the new value of the running total. To take the average forwards from its position at NOW – 20 to the next position at NOW – 19, we have to drop the point at NOW – 40, i.e. the first point in the 41 price values displayed in the chart. This part of the procedure is perfectly straightforward, since we know the exact value at NOW – 40. What is not quite as straightforward is to determine the next value to be added in. This is a future value, the one that we will obtain next week. Obviously we can only estimate this value.

Because of our knowledge of the past history of weekly movements in the FTSE100 Index, we could give a range within which next week's Friday value of the FTSE100 Index will lie. Thus we do not expect the Index to fall by 1000 points or rise by 1000 points by next week, but rises or

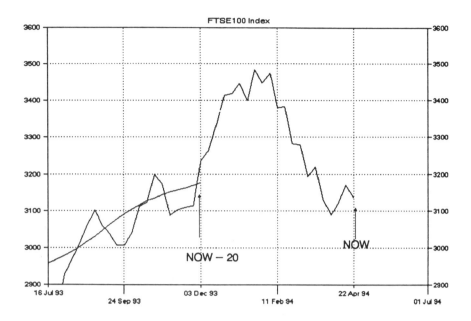

**Figure 7.9** A section of a chart of the FTSE100 Index as it appeared on 22nd April 1994. The 41-week average is also shown, terminating in the middle of the chart

falls of 100 points are perfectly possible. An analysis of all weekly movements in the Index would give the probability of each of the possible rises and falls, but this lies outside the scope of this book. In the absence of such an analysis, a moment's thought should convince the investor that the best option is the middle option, i.e. to guess that the Index will remain the same. If we opt for a rise or a fall, we can be 100% wrong or 100% right. We could thus find ourselves 100% wrong over a long period of such estimations. If we opt for the middle road, then we are not going to be 100% correct all of the time, but neither are we going to be 100% wrong. Thus the middle road is the best option.

By doing this, we are putting a value on the next point, even though it is the same value as the last closing value of the Index. Thus we now have values for both the drop-point and the next point, and we can therefore calculate the running total. If the drop-point is lower than the next point then the running total and hence the average will rise, whereas if the drop-point is higher than the next point then the total and average will fall.

We can proceed in this way for 20 successive drop-points, which will then have allowed us to estimate successive points for the average so as to fill in the gap from NOW –20 to NOW. The numerical procedure is shown in Table 7.3, while these points are plotted in Figure 7.10.

As we move on from the last real calculated value in the middle of the chart, quite naturally our assumption about the future course of the share price remaining at a constant level will be subject to an increasing error.

**Table 7.3**    Calculation of predicted 41-week average from data available on 22nd April 1994. It is assumed that the Index remains at its value on 22nd April

| Date | Index | Subtract | Total | Centred | Average |
|---|---|---|---|---|---|
| 16/07/93 | 2833.0 | x | | | |
| 23/07/93 | 2827.7 | x | | | |
| 30/07/93 | 2926.5 | x | | | |
| 06/08/93 | 2969.8 | x | | | |
| 13/08/93 | 3010.1 | x | | | |
| 20/08/93 | 3057.6 | x | | | |
| 27/08/93 | 3100.6 | x | | | |
| 03/09/93 | 3057.3 | x | | | |
| 10/09/93 | 3037.0 | x | | | |
| 17/09/93 | 3005.5 | x | | | |
| 24/09/93 | 3005.2 | x | | | |
| 01/10/93 | 3039.3 | x | | | |
| 08/10/93 | 3108.6 | x | | | |
| 15/10/93 | 3120.8 | x | | | |
| 22/10/93 | 3199.0 | x | | | |
| 29/10/93 | 3171.0 | x | | | |
| 05/11/93 | 3085.6 | x | | | |
| 12/11/93 | 3099.1 | x | | | |
| 19/11/93 | 3108.1 | x | | | |
| 26/11/93 | 3111.4 | x | | | |
| 03/12/93 | 3234.2 | | | 130159.0 | 3174.61 |
| 10/12/93 | 3261.3 | | | 130459.7 | 3181.94 |
| 17/12/93 | 3337.1 | | | 130765.7 | 3189.41 |
| 24/12/93 | 3412.3 | | | 130972.9 | 3194.46 |
| 31/12/93 | 3418.4 | | | 131136.8 | 3198.46 |
| 07/01/94 | 3446.0 | | | 131260.4 | 3201.47 |
| 14/01/94 | 3400.6 | | | 131336.5 | 3203.33 |
| 21/01/94 | 3484.2 | | | 131369.6 | 3204.14 |
| 28/01/94 | 3447.4 | | | 131446.0 | 3206.00 |
| 04/02/94 | 3475.4 | | | 131542.7 | 3208.36 |
| 11/02/94 | 3378.9 | | | 131670.9 | 3211.49 |
| 18/02/94 | 3382.6 | | | 131799.4 | 3214.62 |
| 25/02/94 | 3281.2 | | | 131893.8 | 3216.92 |
| 04/03/94 | 3278.0 | | | 131918.9 | 3217.53 |
| 11/03/94 | 3191.9 | | | 131931.8 | 3217.85 |
| 18/03/94 | 3218.1 | | | 131866.5 | 3216.26 |
| 25/03/94 | 3129.0 | | | 131829.2 | 3215.35 |
| 01/04/94 | 3086.4 | | | 131877.3 | 3216.52 |
| 08/04/94 | 3120.8 | | | 131911.9 | 3217.36 |
| 15/04/94 | 3168.3 | | | 131937.5 | 3217.99 |
| 22/04/94 | 3133.7 | | 130159.0 | 131959.8 | 3218.53 |
| 29/04/94 | 3133.7 | | 130459.7 | | |
| 06/05/94 | 3133.7 | | 130765.7 | | |
| 13/05/94 | 3133.7 | | 130972.9 | | |
| 20/05/94 | 3133.7 | | 131136.8 | | |
| 27/05/94 | 3133.7 | | 131260.4 | | |
| 03/06/94 | 3133.7 | | 131336.6 | | |
| 10/06/94 | 3133.7 | | 131369.6 | | |
| 17/06/94 | 3133.7 | | 131446.0 | | |
| 24/06/94 | 3133.7 | | 131542.7 | | |

**Table 7.3**  (*continued*)

| Date | Index | Subtract | Total | Centred | Average |
|------|-------|----------|-------|---------|---------|
| 01/07/94 | 3133.7 | | 131670.9 | | |
| 08/07/94 | 3133.7 | | 131799.4 | | |
| 15/07/94 | 3133.7 | | 131893.8 | | |
| 22/07/94 | 3133.7 | | 131918.9 | | |
| 29/07/94 | 3133.7 | | 131931.8 | | |
| 05/08/94 | 3133.7 | | 131866.5 | | |
| 12/08/94 | 3133.7 | | 131829.2 | | |
| 19/08/94 | 3133.7 | | 131877.3 | | |
| 26/08/94 | 3133.7 | | 131911.9 | | |
| 02/09/94 | 3133.7 | | 131937.5 | | |
| 09/09/94 | 3133.7 | | 131959.8 | | |

Our first estimated point, plotted at NOW – 19, will be the least erroneous, while the last, plotted at NOW, will be the most erroneous, since it is based on a prediction of the share price 20 weeks on into the future.

It is only a further 20 weeks on from the NOW position in Figures 7.8 and 7.9 we will have acquired real data points to calculate the real values of the average up to and including the NOW position. It is of interest to see how the estimated and the actual values compare. The actual values calculated some 20 weeks later are plotted in Figure 7.11. We can see the effect of the increasing error to which the estimate is subject as we move

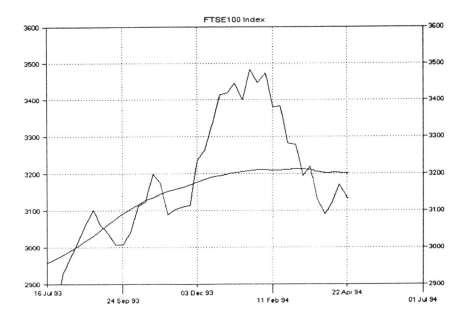

**Figure 7.10**  The predicted values of the average from Table 7.3 are now plotted, taking the estimated average to the latest point of 22nd April

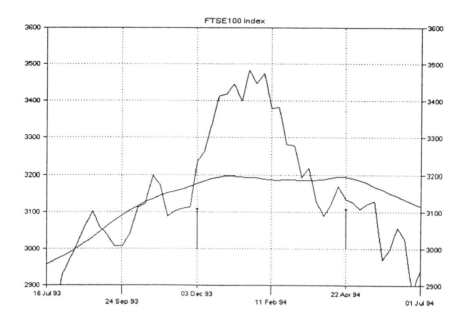

**Figure 7.11**   The actual path of the 41-week average, calculated once an additional 20 points of data were available

on from NOW – 20 in the divergence between the predicted position of the average and the actual position.

It is useful to compare the predicted values with the actual values calculated over the 20 weeks from this date of the estimates. Thus the closing price on 29th April would enable us to calculate the actual average for 3rd December 1993, and prices from the weeks following 29th April would enable us eventually to calculate the actual prices across the gap. This allows us an appreciation of the quality of this type of prediction. These data are shown in Table 7.4. The first estimated value, i.e. at the position NOW – 19, is in error by only 0.006%. The percentage error gradually increases until it reaches 1.0% at the point 14 weeks into the gap, while at the point NOW, i.e. 22nd April 1994, the estimated value is 3218.53 against the true value of 3194.69. This is an error of only 0.74%, an amazingly close prediction.

Also important is the fact that the method correctly predicted the direction of the average, showing a peak, then a trough, the latest estimate being that the average has just started to rise again. This is exactly in line with the actual progress of the average across the gap.

## Improving the Price Analysis Method

As presented so far, the NN20 method and the price analysis method represent two extremes, as shown in Figure 7.12. The price analysis

**Table 7.4**  A comparison of the estimated 41-week average across the gap from NOW – 20 to NOW and the actual average calculated 20 weeks later

| Date | Index | Est. total | Est. average | Actual average | % error |
|------|-------|-----------|--------------|----------------|---------|
| 03/12/93 | 3234.2 | 130159.0 | 3174.61 | 3174.61 | 0.00 |
| 10/12/93 | 3261.3 | 130459.7 | 3181.94 | 3181.74 | 0.006 |
| 17/12/93 | 3337.1 | 130765.7 | 3189.41 | 3188.53 | 0.03 |
| 24/12/93 | 3412.3 | 130972.9 | 3194.46 | 3193.22 | 0.04 |
| 31/12/93 | 3418.4 | 131136.8 | 3198.46 | 3197.07 | 0.04 |
| 07/01/94 | 3446.0 | 131260.4 | 3201.47 | 3196.00 | 0.17 |
| 14/01/94 | 3400.6 | 131336.5 | 3203.33 | 3194.54 | 0.27 |
| 21/01/94 | 3484.2 | 131369.6 | 3204.14 | 3193.45 | 0.33 |
| 28/01/94 | 3447.4 | 131446.0 | 3206.00 | 3192.62 | 0.40 |
| 04/02/94 | 3475.4 | 131542.7 | 3208.36 | 3188.70 | 0.62 |
| 11/02/94 | 3378.9 | 131670.9 | 3211.49 | 3187.12 | 0.76 |
| 18/02/94 | 3382.6 | 131799.4 | 3214.62 | 3185.97 | 0.90 |
| 25/02/94 | 3281.2 | 131893.8 | 3216.92 | 3186.84 | 0.95 |
| 04/03/94 | 3278.0 | 131918.9 | 3217.53 | 3186.99 | 0.96 |
| 11/03/94 | 3191.9 | 131931.8 | 3217.85 | 3186.06 | 1.00 |
| 18/03/94 | 3218.1 | 131866.5 | 3216.26 | 3185.29 | 0.97 |
| 25/03/94 | 3129.0 | 131829.2 | 3215.35 | 3184.59 | 0.97 |
| 01/04/94 | 3086.4 | 131877.3 | 3216.52 | 3187.17 | 0.92 |
| 08/04/94 | 3120.8 | 131911.9 | 3217.36 | 3191.22 | 0.82 |
| 15/04/94 | 3168.3 | 131937.5 | 3217.99 | 3194.01 | 0.75 |
| 22/04/94 | 3133.7 | 131959.8 | 3218.53 | 3194.69 | 0.74 |

method estimates how much the average may have moved up or down from its last calculated position (at NOW – 20) by the time we have reached the present time (NOW). It does this by measuring the gap between the latest price and the first 20 prices in the series and assessing how likely it is that the price can close this gap. The NN20 method simply assumes that there has been no change in the average over the 20-week period from NOW – 20 to NOW.

Since we have a 100% correct value for the average as it was 20 weeks ago, and an estimate for the average as it is now, there are attractions in shifting the estimate from one of the current status to one of the status as it was halfway across the gap, i.e. at NOW – 10. As far as the NN20 method is concerned, we will have to rename it the NN10 method, since it now takes the current calculation of the average as being a perfect estimate of what the average was 10 weeks ago. We saw in Table 7.4 that the error in the price analysis method was least at the beginning of the gap and increased as we moved across the gap. Although in the current example the error decreased again in the last few weeks to the NOW position, this is not normally the case, and the error is usually highest at the end of the gap, i.e. at the point NOW. Thus we would expect the estimation of the average as it was 10 weeks ago to be an improvement over the estimation of the average as it is at NOW. It would be an advantage to calculate, each week, a rolling estimate of the average 10 weeks ago, i.e. at NOW – 10.

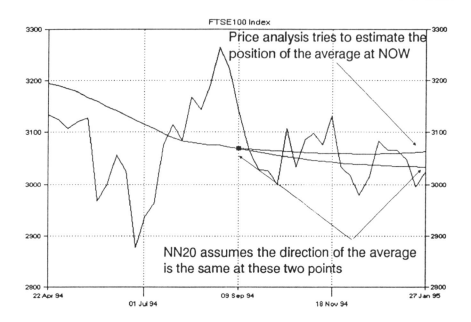

**Figure 7.12** Comparison of the NN20 and price analysis methods. The former simply estimates the current direction of the average, while the latter attempts to estimate the amount by which the average might have risen or fallen by the time it has crossed the gap from NOW – 20 to NOW. NOW – 20 is represented by the solid square

The mechanics of the price analysis method to obtain an estimate of the position of the average 10 weeks ago are quite easy.

As well as the usual 41-week running total, we need the running total of the first 10 points of the 41 points used for the 41-week total. Taking the first value of the 41-week running total of 130159 calculated on 22nd April, we multiply the current price (3133.7) by 10, and subtract the 10-week running total. This gives a value of 131670.9. Dividing this by 41 gives the estimate of the average as 3211.49.

This estimate is for the value of the 41-week average as it was 10 weeks ago. Thus the value of 3211.49 is placed not at the latest date of 22nd April, but 10 weeks back, i.e. at the point corresponding to 11th February. Each subsequently calculated point is similarly shifted back in time by this fixed amount of 10 weeks. These calculations, for the same period as was used in Table 7.3, are shown in Table 7.5.

Since in Chapter 10 we will be looking at investment during the period from the turn in the FTSE100 Index at the end of 1994, it is of interest to see at what point the turn could have been predicted. The turning point was shown previously at the left-hand section of Figure 7.2. The improved price analysis method for some weeks either side of this turning point is shown in Table 7.6. The calculations have been conveniently carried out

**Table 7.5** The on-going calculation of the estimated current value of the 41-week average a constant 10 weeks in the past

| Date | Index | 41-week subtract | 41-week total | 10-week subtract | 10-week total | Estimated total | Estimated average |
|---|---|---|---|---|---|---|---|
| 16/07/93 | 2833.0 | x | | x | | | |
| 23/07/93 | 2827.7 | x | | x | | | |
| 30/07/93 | 2926.5 | x | | x | | | |
| 06/08/93 | 2969.8 | x | | x | | | |
| 13/08/93 | 3010.1 | x | | x | | | |
| 20/08/93 | 3057.6 | x | | x | | | |
| 27/08/93 | 3100.6 | x | | x | | | |
| 03/09/93 | 3057.3 | x | | x | | | |
| 10/09/93 | 3037.0 | x | | x | | | |
| 17/09/93 | 3005.5 | x | | | 29825.1 | | |
| 24/09/93 | 3005.2 | x | | | 29997.3 | | |
| 01/10/93 | 3039.3 | x | | | 30208.9 | | |
| 08/10/93 | 3108.6 | x | | | 30391.0 | | |
| 15/10/93 | 3120.8 | x | | | 30542.0 | | |
| 22/10/93 | 3199.0 | x | | | 30730.9 | | |
| 29/10/93 | 3171.0 | x | | | 30844.3 | | |
| 05/11/93 | 3085.6 | x | | | 30829.3 | | |
| 12/11/93 | 3099.1 | x | | | 30871.1 | | |
| 19/11/93 | 3108.1 | x | | | 30942.2 | | |
| 26/11/93 | 3111.4 | x | | | | | |
| 03/12/93 | 3234.2 | | | | | | |
| 10/12/93 | 3261.3 | | | | | | |
| 17/12/93 | 3337.1 | | | | | | |
| 24/12/93 | 3412.3 | | | | | | |
| 31/12/93 | 3418.4 | | | | | | |
| 07/01/94 | 3446.0 | | | | | | |
| 14/01/94 | 3400.6 | | | | | | |
| 21/01/94 | 3484.2 | | | | | | |
| 28/01/94 | 3447.4 | | | | | | |
| 04/02/94 | 3475.4 | | | | | | |
| 11/02/94 | 3378.9 | | | | | | 3211.49 |
| 18/02/94 | 3382.6 | | | | | | 3212.37 |
| 25/02/94 | 3281.2 | | | | | | 3209.29 |
| 04/02/94 | 3278.0 | | | | | | 3212.76 |
| 11/03/94 | 3191.9 | | | | | | 3214.90 |
| 18/03/94 | 3218.1 | | | | | | 3169.98 |
| 25/03/94 | 3129.0 | | | | | | 3173.42 |
| 01/04/94 | 3086.4 | | | | | | 3186.86 |
| 08/04/94 | 3120.8 | | | | | | 3176.95 |
| 15/04/94 | 3168.3 | | | | | | 3135.62 |
| 22/04/94 | 3133.7 | | 130159.0 | | | 131670.9 | |
| 29/04/94 | 3125.3 | | 130451.3 | | | 131707.0 | |
| 06/05/94 | 3106.0 | | 130729.6 | | | 131580.7 | |
| 13/05/94 | 3119.2 | | 130922.3 | | | 131723.3 | |
| 20/05/94 | 3127.3 | | 131079.8 | | | 131810.8 | |
| 27/05/94 | 2966.4 | | 131036.1 | | | 129969.2 | |
| 03/06/94 | 2997.8 | | 130976.3 | | | 130110.0 | |
| 10/06/94 | 3055.9 | | 130931.6 | | | 130661.3 | |
| 17/06/94 | 3022.9 | | 130897.2 | | | 130255.1 | |
| 24/06/94 | 2876.7 | | 130736.8 | | | 128560.6 | |

**Table 7.6** The estimated 41-week totals a constant 10 weeks in the past using a spreadsheet calculation. The estimated turning point of the total and therefore the average is at the minimum in the last column, i.e. on 23rd December 1994

| Date | Index | 41-week total | 10-week total | Estimated total |
|------|-------|---------------|---------------|-----------------|
| 09/09/94 | 3139.3 | 130982.4 | 31362.8 | 30362.95 |
| 16/09/94 | 3065.1 | 130813.3 | 31465.5 | 30284.68 |
| 23/09/94 | 3028.2 | 130580.2 | 31418.9 | 30201.86 |
| 30/09/94 | 3026.3 | 130269.4 | 31330.5 | 30132.01 |
| 07/10/94 | 2998.7 | 129855.8 | 31246.6 | 30071.40 |
| 14/10/94 | 3106.7 | 129544.1 | 31185.8 | 30046.51 |
| 21/10/94 | 3032.8 | 129130.9 | 31076.3 | 30015.43 |
| 28/10/94 | 3083.8 | 128814.1 | 30968.7 | 30003.02 |
| 04/11/94 | 3097.6 | 128427.5 | 30801.2 | 29994.47 |
| 11/11/94 | 3075.9 | 128056.0 | 30654.4 | 29966.18 |
| 18/11/94 | 3131.0 | 127711.6 | 30646.1 | 29937.66 |
| 25/11/94 | 3033.5 | 127366.2 | 30614.5 | 29924.42 |
| 02/12/94 | 3017.3 | 127000.9 | 30603.6 | 29924.64 |
| 09/12/94 | 2977.3 | 126697.0 | 30554.6 | 29910.32 |
| 16/12/94 | 3013.6 | 126432.6 | 30569.5 | 29890.56 |
| 23/12/94 | 3083.4 | 126324.1 | 30546.2 | 29866.72 |
| 30/12/94 | 3065.5 | 126171.5 | 30578.9 | 29875.16 |
| 06/01/95 | 3065.0 | 126107.5 | 30560.1 | 29893.95 |
| 13/01/95 | 3048.3 | 126069.4 | 30510.8 | 29914.42 |
| 20/01/95 | 2995.0 | 125943.6 | 30429.9 | 29936.57 |
| 27/01/95 | 3022.2 | 125797.5 | 30321.1 | 30009.66 |
| 03/02/95 | 3059.7 | 125723.5 | 30347.3 | 30071.15 |
| 10/02/95 | 3109.9 | 125708.1 | 30439.9 | 30126.57 |

using a computer spreadsheet. There is now no need to store anything other than the columns of totals, since the estimated turning point is the point at which a minimum occurs in the final column. This point is at 23rd December 1994. It is of interest to see how this compares with the actual position as calculated from subsequent data on the FTSE100 Index. This is shown in Figure 7.13. The average can be seen to have turned about six weeks earlier. Besides this good estimation of the turning point, the most important conclusion from this improved version of the price analysis method is that the direction of the average changed during the gap from NOW − 20 to NOW.

The final proof of the value of this approach is obtained by comparing the NN10 method and this variation of the price analysis method. Over the period from 1983 to date, the price analysis method gave a better estimation of the actual value of the average (calculated 10 weeks later) on no fewer than 91% of occasions.

## False Signals

We have already mentioned the so-called "false" signals given by the 41-week average, the cause of these being the fact that an average is an efficient filter of shorter term trends. The mini-market approach overcame

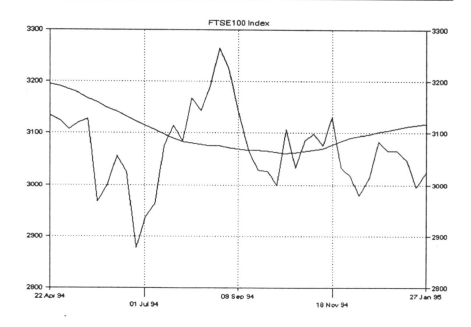

**Figure 7.13** The actual trough in the 41-week average. The estimate in Table 7.6 of the turning point was only a few weeks out

these by drawing attention to the fact that some changes in the direction of the average were not supported by a large enough percentage of shares for the new direction to be maintained.

An alternative way to the mini-market method, and one which requires far less work, is to use a second smoothing process on the 41-week average. Since the averaging process removes much of the shorter term fluctuation in the original FTSE100 data, we would expect a further averaging process to do the same to the 41-week average itself. The most useful average for doing this is one of about half of the span of the original. Since an odd span is advantageous for the eventual plotting as a centred average, the second average which can be applied to the 41-week average is one with a span of 19 weeks.

The calculation of such an average is perfectly straightforward. It is necessary simply to use the results of the 41-week average as the raw material for the application of the second average. This second average requires the evaluation of 19 values of the 41-week average before the first calculation can be made of this 19-week running total. The calculation can proceed in the same way as that for any other average. There is no question of trying to centre the resulting average—the first value of the 41-week average is put alongside the 41st date, and the first value of the 19-week average of this is put alongside the 19th of the average values, i.e. at the 50th data point. If it is necessary to plot this average as a centred one, it should be offset by 29 weeks.

Figure 7.14 shows the original 41-week centred average for the period from the beginning of 1990 to the present. By taking a second 19-week centred average of this first average we can see that there is a great improvement in the shape of the smoothed plot (Figure 7.15), and that the false signals in the middle of 1990 have been removed, as has the uncertainty in the period from late 1991 to the present.

Unfortunately there is a penalty to pay for this removal of the false signals, since the lag in the average is now 29 weeks. This delay can be acceptable in some phases of the market, but unacceptable in others. Thus it kept us out of the market during the false dawn in 1990, but kept us out again in early 1991 for a long period during which the market rose considerably.

## SUMMARY

In this chapter we have presented five methods of dealing with the problem of long term moving averages in order to emphasise how real the problems are and how essential it is to overcome them. The NN20 method was the standard against which other methods have to be judged in terms of their ability to reduce the delay in signalling the change in direction of

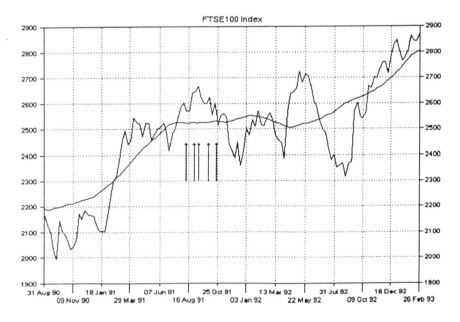

**Figure 7.14**   False signals (arrowed) in the 41-week average during the period June to December 1991. These are the occasions when the average changed direction for only a week or so before resuming its previous course

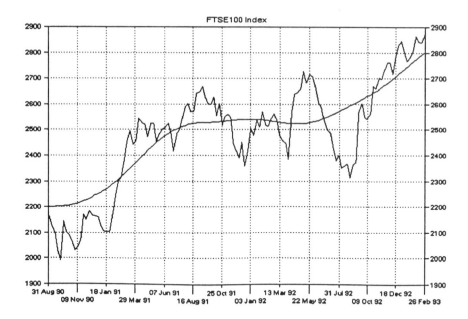

**Figure 7.15** False signals are removed by taking a second, 19-week centred average of the original 41-week average

the long term dominant trend in the FTSE100 Index and their ability to improve the problem of false signalling of the reversal of the dominant trend. The smoothing technique, while giving very impressive curvaceous trends, was actually inferior to the NN20 method in terms of the delay in signalling reversals in the dominant trend, although it did eliminate false signals. The graphical extrapolation method showed some improvement over the NN20 method in certain cases but not in all situations.

The two most useful methods to give early warning that the current status of the dominant trend in the FTSE100 Index had reversed direction were the mini-market and the price analysis method. Although the individual shares of the mini-market are analysed by the NN20 method, and therefore individually are subject to the same drawbacks as when we apply this method to the FTSE100 Index, it is the spread of behaviour, with many shares anticipating a change in direction of the FTSE100 Index, that gives it its power. Because of its advance warning property, and especially because of the excellent way it deals with the question of false signals, it is the method of choice for determining the status of the dominant trend. Having said that, it is useful to have confirmatory evidence from another, different method. Thus, for the sake of the small amount of additional effort, it is well worth while to run the price analysis method to determine the status of the average as it was 10 weeks in the past.

# 8

# Picking Shares

There are so many shares available for investment that the selection of just a handful for further evaluation is a formidable task. Even with a computer system, the time taken to analyse these thousands of shares makes an approach based upon such an analysis totally out of the question. Thus, the only way forward is to use some preliminary filtering system which can, rapidly and efficiently, reduce this large number to much more manageable proportions.

One of the many criteria which can be applied is one of marketability. Since there are so many shares available, it makes no sense to include shares for which there is not a ready market. Even if such shares make a reasonable paper profit, it will be found that the eventual selling price will be profoundly disappointing. The most marketable shares are obviously those in the top 100, i.e. the constituents of the FTSE100 Index. The next group would be those shares that make up the FTSE MID250 Index. Thus we have 350 shares which have already been chosen for us in terms of marketability. While there are occasions when shares outside these two groups offer attractive possibilities, it should be recognised that they will be subject to wider spreads between their buying and selling prices. In this chapter we will present data only from the FTSE100 and MID250 groups.

The potential for profit from a share depends obviously upon its volatility. The more volatile a share is, the larger is the difference between its low value and its high value. Naturally, the larger profit comes from those shares with the largest positive volatility, i.e. the volatility from a low to a high value. Any selection of shares based just on volatility will include shares with negative as well as positive volatilities, but negative volatilities will be weeded out by further analysis.

Since we can only select shares by looking at their historical volatility, then it must be conclusively demonstrated that shares which have been volatile in the most recent past will continue to remain so in the recent future. If this turns out not to be the case, then any selection based upon volatility is a waste of time.

The simplest way of finding the volatility is to run down the column in the newspaper which lists the high and low values for the share over the previous year or part of a year.

Early in the year, the period is split between the current year and the previous year, i.e. "1996/97 High Low", whereas later in the year the period will be restricted to that year, e.g. "1997 High Low". Which of these two forms appear is totally irrelevant, since all we are interested in is the ratio of the high to the low value. We can then write this ratio alongside the name of the share. The next step, which is rather laborious, is to arrange the list in decreasing value of the ratio, i.e. with the most volatile shares first in the listing.

With a computer system in which a database of share prices has been maintained, it is naturally much easier to carry out the complete task. In Table 8.1 we show the FTSE100 constituents with their volatility as computed on 13th June 1996 based on the high and low prices over the previous one-year period. Only those constituents which were still in the Index at the time of writing (June 1997) are included.

Similarly, Table 8.2 shows the constituents of the 100 most volatile shares in the MID250 group with the same criteria applied.

As far as Table 8.1 is concerned, the highest ratio of high to low was 2.24 for Dixons, and the lowest 1.03 for Railtrack. The average volatility was 1.37 for this group. For the MID250 group, the highest ratio of high to low was 4.75 for BTG and the lowest 1.01 for Liberty. The average for this group was 1.52.

Since we have said that, provided the timing of the investment is correct, the more volatile the share the greater the profit, then, comparing the two groups, there is obviously a considerably higher potential for profit with the MID250 group than with the FTSE100 constituents. Thus investors should bias their investment portfolio towards the MID250 group, but not of course to the exclusion of the FTSE100 constituents, since from time to time there may well be better opportunities in the latter group.

Having selected shares on the basis of volatility, the best way to decide if they remain volatile is to compare the volatilities over the following year with those shown in Tables 8.1 and 8.2. Rather than list the new volatilities for the two groups, it is instructive to show just the top 30 in each group based on these new volatilities and then see how many of the previous highly volatile shares appear in these top 30 positions. Thus in Table 8.3 we show the positions held in the previous year's volatility league by each of the top 30 in the June 1996 to June 1997 volatility league for the FTSE100 constituents. Ten shares which were in the top 30 the previous year are still in the top 30. The data for the MID250 shares are shown in Table 8.4. This time 16 shares which were in the top 30 the previous year are still in the top 30. There is therefore a higher representation of previously very volatile shares in the latest lists than would be expected if the appearance or otherwise in the list was purely random, i.e. there is a good

*Winning on the Stock Market*

**Table 8.1**  The volatility of the shares in the FTSE100 Index as at 13th June 1996. The volatility is the ratio of the high price to the low price over the previous year

|                        | High   | Low    | Ratio |
|------------------------|--------|--------|-------|
| Dixons                 | 534    | 237.5  | 2.24  |
| Standard Chartered     | 670    | 335    | 2.00  |
| Burton Group           | 160    | 82.5   | 1.93  |
| British Aerospace      | 976    | 524    | 1.86  |
| Next                   | 578    | 323    | 1.78  |
| BSkyB                  | 480    | 270.5  | 1.77  |
| Ladbroke               | 205.5  | 123    | 1.67  |
| Argos                  | 759    | 457.5  | 1.65  |
| GKN                    | 1007   | 619    | 1.62  |
| Rolls-Royce            | 244    | 150.5  | 1.62  |
| Reuters                | 797    | 510.5  | 1.56  |
| Rentokil Group         | 416    | 267    | 1.55  |
| Bank of Scotland       | 312    | 208    | 1.50  |
| Kingfisher             | 627    | 420    | 1.49  |
| GRE                    | 292    | 196    | 1.48  |
| Siebe                  | 897    | 606    | 1.48  |
| United Newspapers      | 75     | 208    | 1.48  |
| Wolseley               | 486    | 330.5  | 1.47  |
| EMI                    | 1442.3 | 993.3  | 1.45  |
| Royal Bank of Scotland | 608    | 416.5  | 1.45  |
| TI Group               | 552    | 379    | 1.45  |
| Legal & General        | 295.2  | 203.8  | 1.44  |
| Lloyds-TSB             | 358    | 247.6  | 1.44  |
| Asda                   | 120.75 | 84     | 1.43  |
| British Airways        | 570    | 398.5  | 1.43  |
| Enterprise Oil         | 476    | 332.5  | 1.43  |
| Bass                   | 828    | 582    | 1.42  |
| Hays                   | 449    | 314.5  | 1.42  |
| Smiths Industries      | 720    | 506    | 1.42  |
| Abbey National         | 660.5  | 466    | 1.41  |
| Granada                | 843    | 597    | 1.41  |
| National Power         | 453.75 | 320.25 | 1.41  |
| Prudential             | 463    | 327    | 1.41  |
| Rank Group             | 545    | 386    | 1.41  |
| Reed International     | 1210   | 855    | 1.41  |
| HSBC                   | 1124   | 805    | 1.39  |
| Great Universal Stores | 770    | 557    | 1.38  |
| Redland                | 453    | 326    | 1.38  |
| Carlton Communication  | 513    | 373.2  | 1.37  |
| HSBC HK$10             | 1098   | 803    | 1.36  |
| SmithKlineBeecham      | 724.2  | 531.8  | 1.36  |
| BP                     | 599.5  | 443.5  | 1.35  |
| National Grid          | 228    | 168    | 1.35  |
| P & O                  | 618    | 460    | 1.34  |
| Vodafone               | 279.5  | 207.5  | 1.34  |
| Blue Circle            | 374.5  | 281    | 1.33  |
| British Steel          | 200    | 150    | 1.33  |
| Cable and Wireless     | 546    | 408    | 1.33  |
| NatWest Bank           | 711    | 532.5  | 1.33  |

**Table 8.1** (*continued*)

|  | High | Low | Ratio |
|---|---|---|---|
| Sainsbury | 477 | 357 | 1.33 |
| Tomkins | 293 | 220 | 1.33 |
| Zeneca | 1406 | 1052 | 1.33 |
| RTZ | 1074 | 808 | 1.32 |
| Schroders | 1478 | 1114 | 1.32 |
| Glaxo-Wellcome | 969 | 737.5 | 1.31 |
| PowerGen | 608 | 462 | 1.31 |
| Royal & Sun Alliance | 429 | 326 | 1.31 |
| Schroders NV | 1178 | 898 | 1.31 |
| 3I Group | 470 | 360 | 1.30 |
| ICI | 954 | 731.5 | 1.30 |
| Mercury Asset Mgemnt | 992 | 760 | 1.30 |
| Scottish Power | 400.5 | 308 | 1.30 |
| BTR | 344 | 265.5 | 1.29 |
| Lasmo | 194 | 150 | 1.29 |
| Shell | 944 | 727 | 1.29 |
| Boots | 646 | 504 | 1.28 |
| Severn Trent Water | 688 | 536 | 1.28 |
| Tesco | 338 | 263.5 | 1.28 |
| Whitbread | 757 | 589 | 1.28 |
| Scot. & Newcastle Brews. | 699 | 547 | 1.27 |
| Thames Water | 599 | 470 | 1.27 |
| Associated British Foods | 420 | 332 | 1.26 |
| British Telecom | 414 | 326.5 | 1.26 |
| GEC | 378.5 | 299 | 1.26 |
| RMC Group | 1179 | 934 | 1.26 |
| Pearson | 739 | 589 | 1.25 |
| Safeway | 364 | 291 | 1.25 |
| BAT | 585 | 474 | 1.23 |
| Grand Metropolitan | 464 | 376 | 1.23 |
| Barclays Bank | 811 | 664 | 1.22 |
| Cadbury-Schweppes | 561 | 459 | 1.22 |
| General Accident | 694 | 571 | 1.21 |
| United Utilities | 658 | 543 | 1.21 |
| Burmah Castrol | 1090 | 908 | 1.20 |
| Guinness | 532 | 441 | 1.20 |
| Allied Domecq | 559 | 469 | 1.19 |
| British Airports Authority | 554 | 463 | 1.19 |
| BOC Group | 947 | 792 | 1.19 |
| Smith & Nephew | 210.5 | 177 | 1.18 |
| Land Securities | 675 | 573 | 1.17 |
| Marks and Spencer | 474.5 | 403.5 | 1.17 |
| Reckitt & Coleman | 728 | 621 | 1.17 |
| Unilever | 1376 | 1174 | 1.17 |
| Commercial Union | 653 | 561 | 1.16 |
| Tate & Lyle | 497 | 425 | 1.16 |
| Williams | 355 | 304 | 1.16 |
| Orange | 253 | 225.5 | 1.12 |
| Railtrack | 220.5 | 214 | 1.03 |

**Table 8.2**  The 100 most volatile shares in the FTSE MID250 Index as at 13th June 1996. The volatility is the ratio of the high price to the low price over the previous year

|                          | High  | Low   | Ratio |
|--------------------------|-------|-------|-------|
| BTG                      | 385   | 80.96 | 4.75  |
| British Biotechnology    | 331.5 | 74.25 | 4.46  |
| Psion                    | 470   | 127.7 | 3.68  |
| Cairn Energy             | 303   | 83    | 3.65  |
| Biocompatibles           | 517.8 | 150.7 | 3.43  |
| Manchester United        | 485   | 151   | 3.21  |
| Eurotunnel               | 196   | 63    | 3.11  |
| Celltech Group           | 680   | 235.5 | 2.88  |
| ML Laboratories          | 472   | 169   | 2.79  |
| Computer Man. Group      | 678   | 248   | 2.73  |
| Laura Ashley             | 215   | 81    | 2.65  |
| Pizza Express            | 407   | 154   | 2.64  |
| Sage Group               | 500   | 190.8 | 2.62  |
| British Borneo Petroleum | 606   | 238.7 | 2.53  |
| Carpetright              | 640   | 267   | 2.39  |
| Danka Business Systems   | 848   | 378   | 2.24  |
| Misys                    | 848   | 380   | 2.23  |
| Aegis Group              | 56    | 26.5  | 2.11  |
| Stagecoach               | 443.4 | 209.6 | 2.11  |
| Yorkshire-TyneTees TV    | 1130  | 551   | 2.05  |
| DFS Furniture            | 575   | 296   | 1.94  |
| Mayflower Corporation    | 129   | 66.5  | 1.93  |
| Wetherspoon              | 1010  | 531   | 1.90  |
| Arjo Wiggins             | 288   | 154.5 | 1.86  |
| CRT Group                | 164   | 88    | 1.86  |
| Scotia Holdings          | 808   | 435   | 1.85  |
| Mirror Group             | 239   | 133   | 1.79  |
| Sema Group               | 710   | 395   | 1.79  |
| Burford Holdings         | 133.2 | 74.6  | 1.78  |
| Compass Group            | 613.5 | 345   | 1.77  |
| T & N                    | 261.3 | 148   | 1.76  |
| Logica                   | 641   | 367   | 1.74  |
| Taylor Woodrow           | 174   | 100   | 1.74  |
| WPP Group                | 211   | 121   | 1.74  |
| Chelsfield               | 276   | 160   | 1.72  |
| London Electricity       | 855   | 496.8 | 1.72  |
| Perpetual                | 2568  | 1493  | 1.72  |
| Nynex                    | 147   | 85.5  | 1.71  |
| Scottish TV              | 735   | 428   | 1.71  |
| Capital Radio            | 733   | 431   | 1.70  |
| Inchcape                 | 353   | 206.5 | 1.70  |
| Kwik Save                | 731   | 428   | 1.70  |
| Serco Group              | 554   | 325   | 1.70  |
| Cobham                   | 639   | 376   | 1.69  |
| Berkeley Group           | 597   | 355   | 1.68  |
| Clyde Petroleum          | 69    | 41    | 1.68  |
| Cordiant                 | 138   | 83    | 1.66  |
| Southern Electricity     | 903   | 547.1 | 1.65  |
| Tarmac                   | 134   | 81    | 1.65  |
| United Assurance         | 539   | 326   | 1.65  |

**Table 8.2** (*continued*)

| | High | Low | Ratio |
|---|---|---|---|
| Yorkshire Electricity | 898 | 542.8 | 1.65 |
| Hardy Oil and Gas | 260 | 158.5 | 1.64 |
| Telewest Communications | 194 | 118 | 1.64 |
| Bellway | 344 | 210 | 1.63 |
| Dorling Kindersley | 645 | 394 | 1.63 |
| RJB Mining | 625 | 383 | 1.63 |
| MFI Furniture | 185 | 113.5 | 1.62 |
| Beazer Homes | 212 | 131 | 1.61 |
| Travis Perkins | 458 | 284 | 1.61 |
| Peel Holdings | 429 | 267 | 1.60 |
| TBI | 74.5 | 46.5 | 1.60 |
| Barrat Developments | 280 | 176 | 1.59 |
| Kwik-Fit Holdings | 247 | 156 | 1.58 |
| Kalon Group | 159 | 101 | 1.57 |
| Persimmon | 242 | 153.5 | 1.57 |
| Provident Financial | 495 | 314.5 | 1.57 |
| Rexam | 517 | 328 | 1.57 |
| Cattles | 276 | 178 | 1.55 |
| Emap | 713 | 458 | 1.55 |
| Savoy Hotel | 1375 | 883 | 1.55 |
| W.H. Smith | 505 | 324 | 1.55 |
| United Biscuits | 338 | 218 | 1.55 |
| Wimpey | 154 | 99 | 1.55 |
| English China Clay | 413 | 267 | 1.54 |
| Hewden Stuart | 187 | 121 | 1.54 |
| Johnston Press | 222 | 144 | 1.54 |
| Meyer International | 465 | 301 | 1.54 |
| Caradon | 269 | 175 | 1.53 |
| Henlys | 658 | 429 | 1.53 |
| London Clubs Internatl | 277 | 181 | 1.53 |
| Bodycote International | 529.5 | 347 | 1.52 |
| Fairey Group | 688 | 452 | 1.52 |
| N Brown Group | 347 | 229 | 1.51 |
| Eurotherm | 644 | 425 | 1.51 |
| Molins | 1037 | 685 | 1.51 |
| Body Shop | 189 | 126 | 1.50 |
| Powerscreen | 481 | 319 | 1.50 |
| Stakis | 107.5 | 71 | 1.50 |
| Britannic Assurance | 821 | 549 | 1.49 |
| Cowie Group | 395.2 | 265.1 | 1.49 |
| House of Fraser | 190 | 127 | 1.49 |
| Inspec Group | 380 | 255 | 1.49 |
| BBA Group | 348 | 235 | 1.48 |
| National Express | 514 | 345 | 1.48 |
| Powell Duffryn | 600 | 403 | 1.48 |
| Lonrho | 217 | 147.5 | 1.47 |
| Trinity Holdings | 458 | 311 | 1.47 |
| Flextech | 535 | 365 | 1.46 |
| Ocean Group | 455 | 310 | 1.46 |
| Bunzl | 242 | 166 | 1.45 |

chance that a volatile share will remain volatile. Since the thrust of this book is to enable the investor to maximise his performance, then it is obvious that this prior selection of the most volatile shares is an essential part of this process.

**Table 8.3**  The 30 most volatile shares from the FTSE100 constituents during the period 13th June 1996 to 12th June 1997. Their position in the volatility ranking in Table 8.1 is shown in the final column

|                          | High   | Low   | Ratio | 1996 Position |
|--------------------------|--------|-------|-------|---------------|
| Railtrack                | 494    | 208   | 2.37  | 98            |
| Rentokil Group           | 489    | 225.5 | 2.16  | 12            |
| Lloyds-TSB               | 646    | 305   | 2.11  | 23            |
| Reed International        | 1202.5 | 590   | 2.03  | 35            |
| HSBC                     | 1927.5 | 979   | 1.96  | 36            |
| HSBC HK$10               | 1857.5 | 957   | 1.94  | 40            |
| Bank of Scotland         | 426.5  | 229   | 1.86  | 13            |
| Legal & General          | 481.5  | 266   | 1.81  | 22            |
| Barclays                 | 1285   | 760   | 1.69  | 80            |
| Prudential               | 674    | 403   | 1.67  | 33            |
| BSkyB                    | 696.5  | 422   | 1.65  | 6             |
| SmithKlineBeecham        | 1100.5 | 664   | 1.65  | 41            |
| Mercury Asset Mgemnt     | 1463.5 | 894   | 1.63  | 61            |
| Schroders NV             | 1557.5 | 961   | 1.62  | 58            |
| Lasmo                    | 275.5  | 172   | 1.60  | 64            |
| Standard Chartered       | 1018.5 | 633   | 1.60  | 2             |
| General Accident         | 974    | 619   | 1.57  | 82            |
| BTR                      | 284    | 184.5 | 1.53  | 63            |
| Enterprise Oil           | 701    | 460   | 1.52  | 26            |
| Associated British Foods | 574    | 378.5 | 1.51  | 72            |
| British Aerospace        | 1388   | 918   | 1.51  | 4             |
| Glaxo-Wellcome           | 1285.5 | 848   | 1.51  | 55            |
| Land Securities          | 923.5  | 608   | 1.51  | 90            |
| National Power           | 566.5  | 375   | 1.51  | 32            |
| Severn Trent Water       | 795.5  | 524   | 1.51  | 67            |
| British Airways          | 760    | 506.5 | 1.50  | 25            |
| PowerGen                 | 700    | 465.5 | 1.50  | 56            |
| Orange                   | 252    | 169   | 1.49  | 97            |
| Next                     | 750.5  | 508   | 1.47  | 5             |
| Redland                  | 472.5  | 320.5 | 1.47  | 38            |

**Table 8.4** The 30 most volatile shares from the MID250 constituents during the period 13th June 1996 to 12th June 1997. Their position in the volatility ranking in Table 8.2 is shown in the final column

|  | High | Low | Ratio | 1996 Position |
|---|---|---|---|---|
| Fleming Overseas | 380.5 | 65 | 5.85 | 196 |
| Biocompatibles | 1420 | 356.536 | 3.98 | 5 |
| British Borneo Petroleum | 1542 | 520 | 2.96 | 14 |
| Laura Ashley | 129 | 77 | 2.84 | 11 |
| Thorn | 414.38 | 150 | 2.76 | 101 |
| Telewest Communications | 172 | 63 | 2.73 | 53 |
| ML Laboratories | 449 | 168 | 2.67 | 9 |
| Celltech Group | 671.5 | 273.5 | 2.45 | 8 |
| Computer Man. Group | 1322.5 | 555 | 2.38 | 10 |
| Dorling Kindersley | 613 | 267.5 | 2.29 | 55 |
| Cairn Energy | 634.5 | 278 | 2.28 | 4 |
| Yorkshire Water | 752.5 | 331 | 2.27 | 155 |
| BTG | 682.5 | 310 | 2.20 | 1 |
| Pizza Express | 767.5 | 350 | 2.19 | 12 |
| Scotia Holdings | 772 | 362.5 | 2.12 | 26 |
| Southern Electricity | 800.5 | 384.5 | 2.08 | 48 |
| Sema Group | 1425 | 687 | 2.07 | 28 |
| Danka Business Systems | 784 | 385 | 2.03 | 16 |
| BICC | 337 | 166.5 | 2.02 | 102 |
| Clyde Petroleum | 123 | 61.469 | 2.00 | 46 |
| Stagecoach | 799.5 | 405.594 | 1.97 | 19 |
| Molins | 1012 | 527.5 | 1.91 | 85 |
| Misys | 1425 | 753.5 | 1.89 | 12 |
| Pilkington | 207.5 | 110.5 | 1.87 | 172 |
| CRT Group | 276.5 | 148 | 1.86 | 25 |
| De La Rue | 662.5 | 359 | 1.84 | 203 |
| Eurotunnel | 114 | 63 | 1.80 | 7 |
| Low and Bonar | 572 | 318 | 1.79 | 191 |
| Kwik Save Group | 464 | 265 | 1.75 | 42 |
| Firstbus | 246 | 142 | 1.73 | 118 |

# 9

# Dominant Trends

In the last chapter we saw that volatile shares had a higher potential for profit than non-volatile shares, but also had a higher potential for loss. We now have to develop a further selection procedure that keeps us away from the losing shares and points us in the direction of the winning shares. Since no method of selection is going to be perfect, we have to accept the fact that we will end up with some losers, but as long as we are strict about applying the stop-loss method discussed in Chapter 5, we will not suffer the large losses which appeared in the latter half of Table 5.2.

In Chapter 7 we adopted the rule that we should never invest if the dominant trend in the market is running adversely. The best method of determining the status of the dominant trend in the market was to look at the direction of the 41-week average of the shares in the mini-market of alpha shares. As long as 60% or more of these were rising, then it was acceptable to invest in a share that passed all the further criteria for investment. In this chapter we come to one of these further criteria: the dominant trend in the share itself must be rising at the time it is proposed to invest. We saw the importance of a rising dominant trend in a share price when we discussed the potential gain under various conditions. The maximum gain was obtained when both the long term and the short term trends were rising. Since we have to accept that we will make a certain number of losing investments, it is vital that we maximise the gains from those decisions which are correct, otherwise our overall performance may well be disappointing.

## MOVEMENT OF DOMINANT TRENDS OVER A PERIOD

For the FTSE100 constituent shares listed in Table 8.1 in the last chapter, 78% of these made a profit if the buying point was taken to be 14th June 1996 and the selling point one year later. This of course is a reflection of the 80:20 rule during a period when the market was rising strongly. A chart of the FTSE100 Index with a centred 41-week average (Figure 9.1) confirms this point.

These dates are somewhat artificial from the investment point of view, since we are not suggesting that the shares were actually bought and sold on these particular dates. They are selected purely to cover the behaviour of the market during the year prior to the time of writing. It is important to understand that it was the period between these two dates that was favourable for investment due to the rising market. Only if other criteria were satisfied would any share be bought on 14th June 1996 and sold on 13th June 1997.

There are four possible situations for the dominant trend in a particular share on these two dates:

1. The dominant trend is falling on 14th June 1996 but rising by 13th June 1997.
2. The dominant trend is falling on 14th June 1996 and still falling on 13th June 1997.
3. The dominant trend is rising on 14th June 1996 and still rising on 13th June 1997.
4. The dominant trend is rising on 14th June 1996 but falling on 13th June 1997.

Of these four situations, the second will probably give rise to the largest loss and the third probably the largest gain. In situations 1 and 4 we may

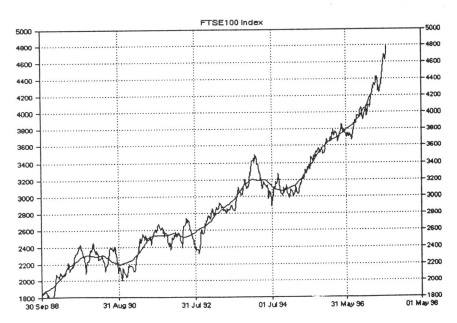

**Figure 9.1** A chart of the FTSE100 Index with a superimposed centred 41-week average shows how strongly the market has been rising over the last few years

achieve a gain or a loss, depending upon where between the two extreme dates the change in direction of the dominant trend occurs.

Thus if, at the point when we think we have been given a signal to buy, the dominant trend in the share price is falling, it is in the lap of the gods as to whether it might change direction sooner rather than later. Although a short term uptrend at the time the investment is made may take the share price up slightly, this initial gain will soon be eroded by the falling dominant trend. Although a stop-loss will have a limiting effect, nonetheless it is inevitable that a loss will be made if the dominant trend continues to fall. Thus it is a pure gamble to invest at such a time just in the hope that the adverse trend will change for the better. The only sensible rule to obey is not to invest unless the dominant trend is rising.

The opposite rule is obviously that we can invest when a buying signal is given provided the dominant trend is rising. There should be a qualification to this rule: if the dominant trend has been rising for a considerable time, say for more than about six months, then the probability is building up that this rise will come to an end. Under such circumstances the investor is better off looking for an alternative investment where the upward dominant trend is still young.

The situations above are best illustrated by examples taken from the list of FTSE100 and MID250 shares. Note that in these examples the 41-week average is plotted as a centred average, i.e. it is a good representation of the dominant trend itself. This will terminate 20 weeks back from 13th June 1997, i.e. on 24th January 1997. Thus we do not know the status of the dominant trend across the whole chart. However, the examples are chosen carefully so that an estimate of the direction of the trend as it would be on 13th June 1997, while it is an estimate, will almost certainly be correct since it represents extremes of share price movement over this particular timescale. Later in the chapter we will see how to estimate more accurately the current status of the dominant trend.

## *Situation 1*

Dominant trend on 14th June 1996 definitely falling; dominant trend on 13th June 1997 almost certainly rising.

Example (a): BAT (Figure 9.2). The reversal of the falling long term trend occurred in September 1996, and the new uptrend swept the price up to higher levels. The price was 507p on 14th June 1996 and 592.5p a year later.

Example (b): ICI (Figure 9.3). The reversal of the falling long term trend occurred later than was the case with BAT, changing in December 1996. The price was 842p on 14th June 1996 and 864p a year later.

## *Situation 2*

Dominant trend on 14th June 1996 definitely falling; dominant trend on 13th June 1997 almost certainly falling.

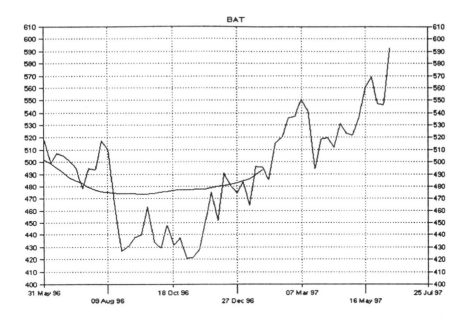

**Figure 9.2** The BAT share price since 14th June 1996 with superimposed 41-week centred average

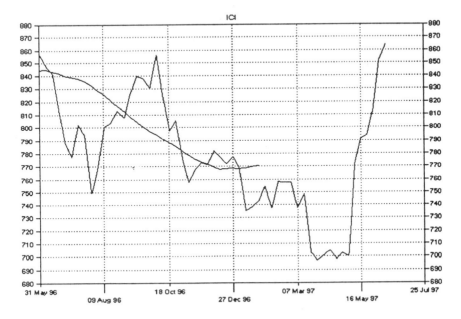

**Figure 9.3** The ICI share price since 14th June 1996 with superimposed 41-week centred average

Example (a): Coats Viyella (Figure 9.4). Here we can see the drastic effect of a continuously falling long term trend. The share price fell from 180.5p to 133.5p over the year.

Example (b): BICC (Figure 9.5). Once again, the effect of a continuously falling trend can be seen in the share price fall from 327p to 178p over the course of the year.

## *Situation 3*

Dominant trend on 14th June 1996 definitely rising; dominant trend on 13th June 1997 almost certainly rising.

Example (a): AB Foods (Figure 9.6). Here we can see exactly the opposite effect to the adverse trend in the previous two examples. The uptrend in AB Foods took the price from 378p to 574p over the year.

Example (b): Barclays Bank (Figure 9.7). Again, the constantly rising trend took the price from 776p to 1249p over the year.

## *Situation 4*

Dominant trend on 14th June 1996 definitely rising; dominant trend on 13th June 1997 almost certainly falling.

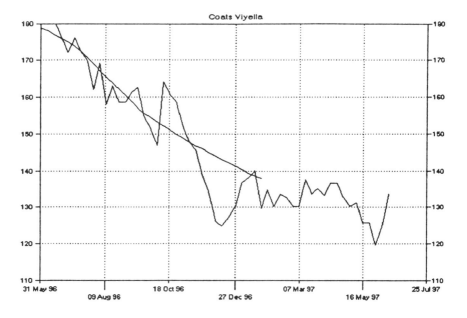

**Figure 9.4**  The Coats Viyella share price since 14th June 1996 with superimposed 41-week centred average

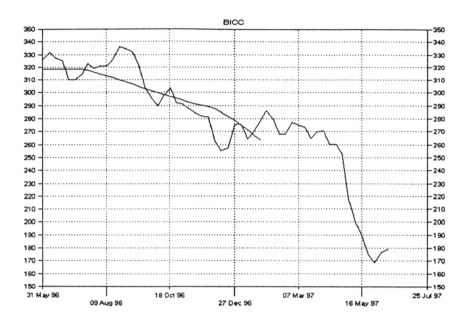

**Figure 9.5** The BICC share price since 14th June 1996 with superimposed 41-week centred average

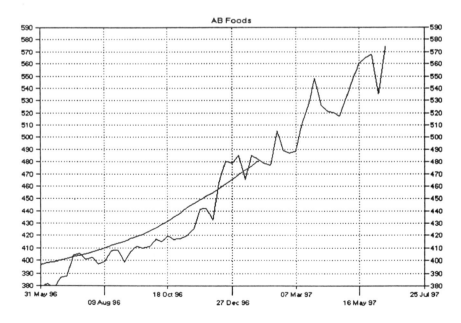

**Figure 9.6** The AB Foods share price since 14th June 1966 with superimposed 41-week centred average

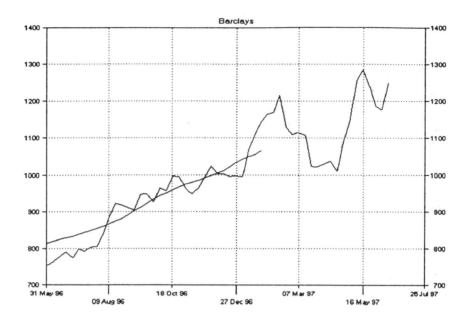

**Figure 9.7**   The Barclays share price since 14th June 1996 with superimposed 41-week centred average

Example (a): Bass (Figure 9.8). The price started at 834p on 14th June 1996, and after rising for a while, fell to a low point of 755p in October 1996. From this point the share price rose and fell in a sawtooth series to end the year at 765.5p.

Example (b): Dixons (Figure 9.9). Here the price started at 548p on 14th June 1996 and ended at 517.5p a year later, having passed through several high points above 570p between the two extremes.

Now we have a clear picture of the directional movement of dominant trends in these examples over the period from June 1996 to June 1997 when the market trend was favourable, and when it is possible to estimate quite easily the current state of the dominant trend in June 1997.

Of course, at intermediate points between the two extremes of the chart it would not be so easy to estimate the status of the dominant trend at these points. It is of interest to see how our estimates of the trends at the time a buying signal was given would affect the final decision to buy or not to buy. The way in which the buying signals were given by short term trends is discussed in the next chapter. The interest in this chapter is in the qualification of the buying signal by estimates of the current status of the long term trend.

When a buying signal is given there are two decisions to be made— either to buy or not to buy. The first thought is that if we decide not to buy, then that is the end of the matter, and our attention should turn to the two

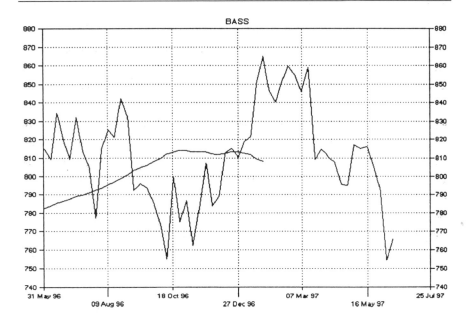

**Figure 9.8** The Bass share price since 14th June 1996 with superimposed 41-week centred average

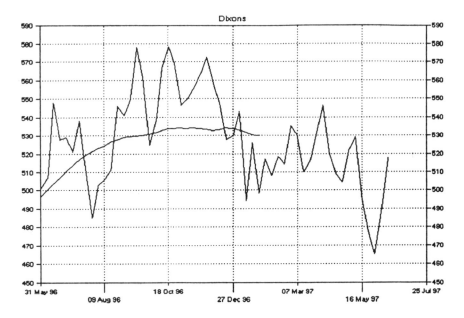

**Figure 9.9** The Dixons share price since 14th June 1966 with superimposed 41-week centred average

outcomes of the decision to buy. These two outcomes are that a profit is enjoyed or a loss endured. We would want any buying method to bring in large profits when the decision is correct, but keep losses low when the decision is incorrect.

However, in evaluating any investment method, the outcomes for a decision not to buy are also important. Again, there are two of these. Either a profit would have been made or a loss would have been made. Thus we would want any buying method to continue to keep us out of the situation where a loss would have been made, but also not to keep us out when a profit would have been made.

**We can now see that there are four outcomes to any buying decision, of which two are positive and two are negative.** The positive ones are to get us in when a profit can be made and keep us out when a loss will be made. The negative ones are to keep us out when a profit can be made and get us in when a loss will be made. An investment method can therefore only be properly tested against an alternative method by comparing each of these four possibilities at the time a signal to buy or not to buy is given.

As we saw in the last chapter, there are several ways in which the current status can be estimated. The NN20 method, in which the calculated value of the 41-week average at a point in time is taken as the estimate of the current status of the trend, was seen to be the least accurate, but had the virtue of simplicity, since only the one calculation is needed. The price analysis method required more effort, but gave a much better picture in most cases of the current direction of the trend, and whether the 41-week average might have changed direction during the intervening 20-week gap. Although these two methods were compared for the FTSE100 Index, it is necessary to compare these two methods in the case of particular shares, looking closely at the four possible outcomes mentioned above, in order to demonstrate conclusively the merits of the price analysis case.

## APPLYING THE NN20 METHOD

The buying points are those which would be indicated by the methods shown in Chapter 10. The direction of the dominant trend is simply taken from a calculation of the 41-week average on the date of the buying point and comparing it with the value of the average as calculated one week previously. The starred items are those where the 41-week average is rising. In all cases, whether or not an investment is made, the gain or loss if the investment is still held on 13th June 1997 is shown.

### *Example 1: BAT*

There were four buying signals given by the short term trends in the BAT share price during the period. Price on 13th June 1997: 592p.

2nd August 1996 (price 517p), 41-week average falling (gain 14.6%)
27th September 1996 (434p), 41-week average falling (gain 36.5%)
23rd November 1996 (451.5p), 41-week average falling (gain 31.2%)
*25th April 1997 (523.5p), 41-week average rising (gain 13.2%)

## Example 2: ICI

There were five buying signals for ICI during the period. Price on 13th June 1997: 864p.

*9th August 1996 (800p), 41-week average rising (gain 8.0%)
6th December 1996 (782p), 41-week average falling (gain 10.5%)
28th February 1997 (757.5p), 41-week average falling (gain 14.1%)
14th March 1997 (748p), 41-week average falling (gain 15.5%)
*9th May 1997 (771.5p), 41-week average rising (gain 12.0%)

## Example 3: Coats Viyella

There were five buying signals for Coats Viyella during the period. Price on 13th June 1997: 133.5p.

13th September 1996 (162.5p), 41-week average falling (loss 17.8%)
11th October 1996 (164p), 41-week average falling (loss 18.6%)
25th October 1996 (158.5p), 41-week average falling (loss 15.8%)
3rd January 1997 (136.5p), 41-week average falling (loss 2.2%)
14th March 1997 (137.5p), 41-week average falling (loss 2.9%)

## Example 4: BICC

There were two buying signals in BICC. Price on 13th June 1997: 178.5p.

*2nd August 1996 (321p), 41-week average rising (loss 44.4%)
17th January 1997 (270p), 41-week average falling (loss 33.9%)

## Example 5: AB Foods

There were four buying signals for AB Foods. Price on 13th June 1997: 574p.

*9th August 1996 (399p), 41-week average rising (gain 44.1%)
*30th August 1996 (398.5p) 41-week average rising (gain 44.0%)
*14th February 1997 (505p), 41-week average rising (gain 13.7%)
*9th May 1997 (547p), 41-week average rising (gain 4.9%)

## Example 6: Barclays Bank

There were three buying signals for Barclays. Price on 13th June 1997: 1249p.

*29th November 1996 (1023.5p), 41-week average rising (gain 22.0%)
*10th January 1997 (1067p), 41-week average rising (gain 17.0%)
*25th April 1997 (1088.5p), 41-week average rising (gain 14.7%)

## Example 7: Bass

There were seven buying signals for Bass. Price on 13th June 1997: 765.5p.

*2nd August 1996 (815p), 41-week average rising (loss 6.1%)
*16th August 1996 (821p), 41-week average rising (loss 6.8%)
*18th October 1996 (799.5p), 41-week average rising (loss 4.3%)
*15th November 1996 (783p), 41-week average rising (loss 2.2%)
*13th December 1996 (812.5p), 41-week average rising (loss 5.8%)
14th March 1997 (859p), 41-week average falling (loss 10.9%)
*2nd May 1997 (817p), 41-week average rising (loss 6.3%)

## Example 8: Dixons

There were six buying signals for Dixons. Price on 13th June 1997: 517.5p.

*23rd August 1996 (546p), 41-week average rising (loss 5.2%)
*11th October 1996 (567p), 41-week average rising (loss 8.7%)
*29th November 1996 (572.5p), 41-week average rising (loss 9.6%)
*14th February 1996 (518.5p), 41-week average rising (loss 0.2%)
*28th February 1997 (535p), 41-week average rising (loss 3.3%)
*28th March 1997 (530.5p), 41-week average rising (loss 2.5%)

## Analysis

In summary, out of the 36 buying signals given for these eight shares, there were 23 occasions when the 41-week averages were moving favourably, i.e. positive buys, and 13 when they were not, i.e. negative buys.

Positive buys:  Number of gains: 10    Highest gain: 44.1%
                Number of losses: 13   Largest loss: 44.4%

Negative buys:  Number of gains: 6     Highest gain: 36.5%
                Number of losses: 7    Largest loss: 33.9%

These results have to be seen as extremely poor, coming at a time when the market as a whole was rising quite strongly. Out of 36 buying signals, the net result is that the investor would have acted on only 10 which would have led to a profit, and would have made a loss on 13 other occasions. The average gain for the 23 transactions would have been only 3.5%. The investor would also have missed six other occasions which would have made a profit. The worst effects of the method were that a large loss of over 44% would have been made out of an investment in BICC, and a large profit of 36.5% in BAT would have been missed.

Notwithstanding the point that in practice we may well have sold the shares before or after 13th June 1997, according to the selling method discussed later, and thus made better profits, it has to be said that the performance of this method is extremely poor, virtually guaranteeing the investor a loss.

## THE PRICE ANALYSIS METHOD

The method is familiar from the discussion in the last chapter. If the method is to be an improvement on the NN20 method, it has to be able to allow us to avoid the run of losses in ICI and Bass and take advantage of the rise of 36.5% in BAT which was missed by the NN20 method. Overall, it should get us into most of the 16 winning situations and out of the 20 losing situations.

This is a rather tall order, requiring us to be almost 100% successful. Rather than go through a detailed discussion of all eight shares, the value of the method can be seen quite clearly if it is applied to the three buying signals in BAT, and to the false signals in Bass and ICI, occasions when the NN20 method was particularly poor.

### *BAT*

Taking first the example of BAT, it can be seen from Figure 9.10 that the centred average, representing the dominant trend, reversed direction from a falling mode to a rising one during the period August to September 1996. Thus all buying signals prior to this point would be best ignored. The question is, at what point after September 1996 would the price analysis method show that the dominant trend had begun to rise. The answer is that it did not for the two buying points of 11th October and 22nd November 1996. However, by the time the buying point on 25th April 1997 came along, the position was that shown in Figure 9.11. The point 40 weeks prior to 25th April (i.e. NOW – 40) is on 19th July 1996, with the price at 494.5p. From that point on, with just two exceptions, all points are lower than the value of 523.5p on 25th April. Thus there is no price rise in this period which would continue to drive the downtrend in the dominant trend 40 weeks later at the time we are looking towards an investment. The conclusion must be, therefore, that the dominant trend is rising, and has been rising for some time when the buying signal is given on 25th April. The gain by 13th June 1997 was 13.1%.

The main reason that the price analysis method did not indicate a rising dominant trend at the time the previous two buying signals were given in October and November 1996 was, of course, that it requires an

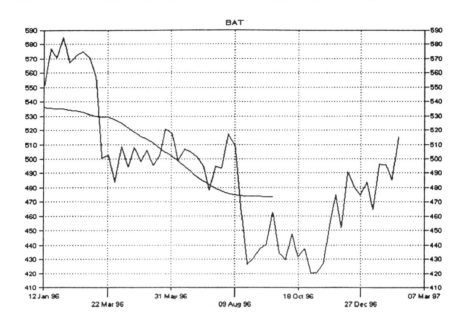

**Figure 9.10**   The position in BAT on 2nd February 1997. It can be seen that the dominant trend, terminating in the middle of the chart, has just begun to turn up

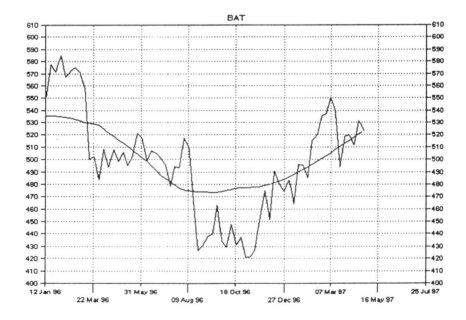

**Figure 9.11**   The position in BAT on 25th April 1997. It can be seen that the dominant trend is rising on the 25th (see text)

anticipation that the price will continue to stay at about the same level as it is at the time the decision is being taken. It does not anticipate, since there is no reason to do so, that there will be a strong rise from that position. In the period October to November the price was in a range of about 420–450p. It was the unpredictable rise to nearly 600p that was responsible for the early turn in the dominant trend.

## ICI

It can be seen from Figure 9.3 that the falling average appeared to change direction around the end of December 1996. It would not be possible to deduce by price analysis this change in direction until quite a few weeks later. Thus the buying points up to and including the one on 14th March 1997 would not be acted upon.

Figure 9.12 shows the position on 16th May 1997, with the price at 790.5p. The point 40 weeks earlier in the chart (9th August 1996) saw a price of 800p. This price level if maintained for a few weeks would see the current status of the dominant trend as falling gently. However, by stepping on just a few weeks from this NOW – 40 point it can be seen that the price rose to 856p, i.e. considerably higher than the latest price of 790.5p. This means that we can expect the dominant trend to be falling more

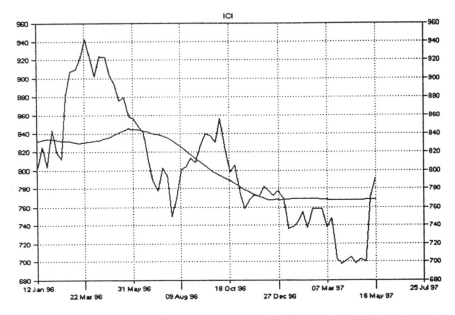

**Figure 9.12** The position in ICI on 16th May 1997. The latest price is 790.5p. It can be deduced by price analysis that the dominant trend is still at an indeterminate stage. It is too soon to invest

rapidly. The price fell consistently from the high of 856p, and therefore we should expect this to be reflected in a reversal of the fall in the dominant trend quite a few weeks in the future. Under such conditions where a positive rise has not yet been established, it is best to avoid any investment. Thus the buying point in May 1997 should be ignored. That it would have yielded a profit of some 12% by 13th June 1997 is due solely to the rapid rise to the 864p level seen in Figure 9.3. Such a rise obviously could not have been predicted on 16th May.

## *Bass*

The position in Bass as at 13th June 1997 was shown in Figure 9.8. It is apparent that the dominant trend passes through a peak. The question is, of course, at what point this could have been determined in the past by the price analysis method.

A chart of the position on 28th March 1997 is shown in Figure 9.13. The price is 814.5p. At the point NOW – 40 (21st June 1996), the price was 819p. Stepping on from the NOW – 40 position we can see that the price stayed above 814.5p for about 10 weeks until 30th August 1996. Thus the prediction is that it should be another 10 weeks, taking us up to 7th June 1997, before an investment could even be considered. Thus the March and May buying points would be ignored.

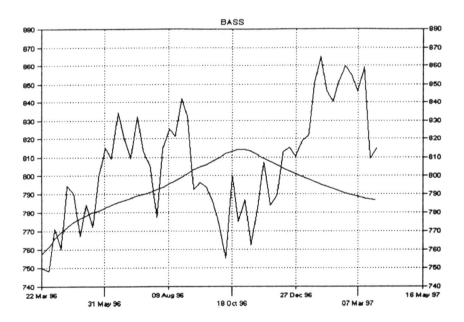

**Figure 9.13** The position in Bass on 28th March 1997. The latest price is 814.5p. It can be deduced by price analysis that the dominant trend is still falling (see text)

## *Dixons*

The position in Dixons as at 13th June 1997 was shown in Figure 9.9. As was the case with Bass, it is clear that the dominant trend passed through a peak and was falling on 13th June.

We see in Figure 9.14 the position on 28th March 1997, with the price on 530.5p. At the point NOW – 40, on 21st June 1996, the price was 527.5p. Stepping on from this point, the price stayed above 530.5p except for a low point of 485p on 26th July 1996. Thus the conclusion is that the dominant trend is headed downwards on 28th March 1997 and an investment should be avoided for some time.

## THE REASON FOR FAILURE OF THE NN20 METHOD

The NN20 method is only satisfactory as an estimator of the current status of the dominant trend at periods when the trend has not changed direction during the gap between the last true plotted point and the last data point. Thus, if a 41-week average is used for highlighting the dominant trend, the dominant trend should not have changed direction during the last 20 weeks. If it has done so, then the NN20 estimate is 100% incorrect. This can be stated in another way: the NN20 method will always give an

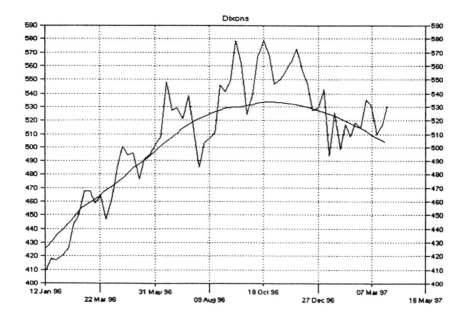

**Figure 9.14**   The position in Dixons on 28th March 1997. The latest price is 530.5p. It can be deduced by price analysis that the dominant trend is still falling (see text)

incorrect estimate of the current status of the dominant trend during the first 20 weeks of the existence of this trend. This shows us that although 200-day and 40-week averages are widely used in investment systems, they have this basic flaw that makes their application certain to lead to losses except for those periods 100 days or 20 weeks after the long term trend has changed direction. Since the most profitable time to enter an uptrend is as close to its beginning as possible, we are faced with two diametrically opposed requirements. In order to be correct about the direction of the dominant trend, we have to hold off an investment until we have just seen a turning point in the 41-week average. Then the new trend will have already been in existence for 20 weeks. The investment will be profitable as long as the dominant trend lasts for say 30 weeks or so. If it does not, and changes direction again before such a time has elapsed, then we will be forced to exit the investment by virtue of the triggering of the stop-loss which we are applying. We saw in the recent behaviour of the FTSE100 Index in Chapter 7 on the Investment Climate that we can have periods in time in which the dominant trend lasts for less than 20 weeks, and even for as little as two to five weeks. Thus any estimation of the current dominant trend using the NN20 method can be hopelessly wrong.

This point can be illustrated clearly by using the short-lived dominant trend in Cookson as an example (Figure 9.15). This was chosen because

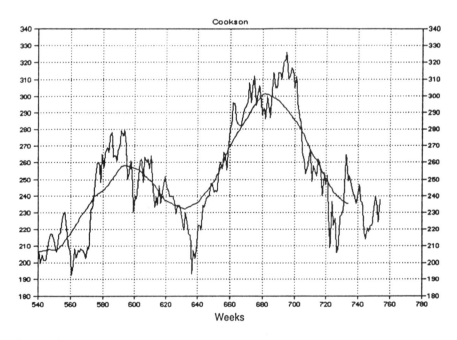

**Figure 9.15**  The dominant trend in Cookson is represented by the centred 41-week average

the dominant trend changed direction twice during the period shown on the chart. The time axis is shown in weeks rather than with dates in order to make it easier to determine timespans.

It is of interest to see at what point after the turns the turning points in the dominant trend (at 632 weeks and 682 weeks) could be deduced using price analysis, so that this can be compared directly with the NN20 method.

Taking first the turn at 632 weeks, we are looking for the first point at which the value NOW is greater than the value at NOW – 40 and is expected to remain so for a number of weeks. A close inspection of the chart suggests that point to be at about week 650. The price (i.e. NOW) is around 240p, while the price 40 weeks previously (NOW – 40) is about 245 and falling rapidly. We thus estimate that the turn could be happening at week 650, with the reservation that the rise from week 612 to 620 may cause a slight hesitation in the turn.

Thus our estimate of a turn at week 650 is suffering a delay of 18 weeks since the turn occurred at week 635.

Taking the second turn, we are now looking for the first point at which the value NOW is less than the value at NOW – 40 and expected to remain so for some weeks. The first point at which this happens is at week 702. Thus now there is a delay of 20 weeks. The reason for this delay is that the turning point is made quite sharp by virtue of the large fall from week 700 to 706. Prior to that, there was nothing to suggest that the trend would top out.

Moving to the NN20 method of determining the turning points, this is illustrated in Figure 9.16. It should be pointed out that the number of weeks covered by the dominant trend is 190. The dominant trend rose for 41 weeks, fell for 39 weeks, rose for 50 weeks and fell for 52 weeks, a total of 182 weeks. The average length of a trend is therefore 182/4 = 45 weeks.

The horizontal arrows show the times during which the dominant trend and the unlagged are moving in the same direction, i.e. the times when the NN20 method gives the correct trend direction. The lengths of these arrows in weeks are approximately 29, 19, 30 and 32. This totals 110 weeks out of a total of 182 weeks. Thus the NN20 estimate of the dominant trend direction is only correct 60% of the time in this particular example.

Taking the particular turning points in which we are interested, the NN20 estimate would give us week 653 as the first turning point, and week 703 as the next. Thus the price analysis method gives us an extra warning of three weeks for the first turn and one week for the second turn.

These extra weeks might seem insignificant, but they have an enormous effect on the profit which will be made.

Let us assume, as one way of illustrating the difference, that the turning points given by the two methods were the points at which an investment was made and then liquidated. The price analysis method would get the investor in at week 650 (16th June 1995) at 242p, and get him out at week

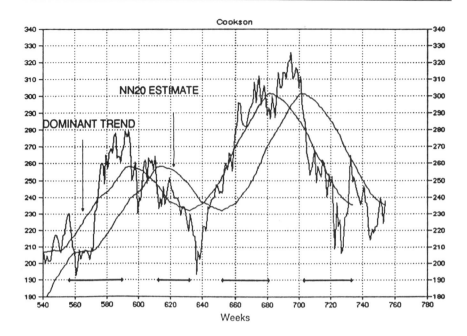

**Figure 9.16** The dominant trend in Cookson is represented by the centred 41-week average, and the estimate provided by the NN20 method is represented by the unlagged 41-week average. Only when these two are moving in the same direction (heavy double-arrowed lines) is the NN20 estimate of the trend direction correct

702 (14th June 1996) at 295p. This gives a nominal profit of 21.9%, very respectable.

On the other hand, the NN20 method gets the investor in at week 653 (7th July 1995) at 256p and out again at week 703 (21st June 1996) at 287p. This represents a profit of 12.1%, almost down to a half of that enjoyed by the price analysis method.

This advantage of a few weeks given by the price analysis method will, in the long run over a good number of transactions, lead to a very substantial increase in profits.

Taking Figure 9.16 as an example once again, it is easy to develop a general formula which will show the number of weeks for which the trends run in the same direction (i.e. coincident weeks), starting from the principle that there is a delay of 20 weeks after the change in direction of the dominant trend before the unlagged average changes direction:

Number of coincident weeks $n$ = length of dominant trend − 20

If we are looking at more than one trend, as in the Cookson example, then we need to take the average length of time of the dominant trend:

Average number of coincident weeks = 45 − 20 = 25

Thus, out of an average length of trend of 45 weeks, the number of coincident weeks is 25, i.e. 56%.

It follows from this relationship that the shorter the average length of trend, the smaller is the percentage of coincident weeks. In the extreme, trends of an average lifetime of 20 weeks would never be coincident.

Because of this factor, it is important, whether the NN20 method or the price analysis method is used, that shares are chosen such that they have a history of long lived dominant trends, rather than short lived ones. Some examples of trends are shown in Table 9.1, arranged in decreasing average lifetime. Once there are more than four trends in the history of a share, the average lifetime rarely gets above 60 weeks. NatWest is a good example of a share with long lifetime trends. Thus the NN20 method would be successful $60 - 20 = 40$ weeks out of 60, i.e. 66.7%. As well as a high average lifetime, it is also necessary to use shares in which the minimum trendlength is also high, preferably over say 10 weeks, since such trends are the ones which will give totally incorrect estimates of the direction of the dominant trend.

At the other extreme in Table 9.1, it can be seen that dominant trends in Vodafone have a mean lifetime of only 19 weeks. Thus most estimates of the dominant trend will be wrong. This excludes the trend which has a lifetime of 33 weeks, since for 13 weeks of this trend the estimate would be correct. Shares at this end of the league table should be avoided at all costs.

The methods of producing buying signals which will be discussed in the next chapter will produce several such signals over the lifetime of a favourable dominant trend if the latter lasts for six months or longer. The first of such signals will almost certainly lie within this 20-week window of error (as far as NN20 is concerned) at the start of the dominant uptrend. Thus we have the option of either ignoring the initial buying signals, or employing the price analysis method to get a better estimate of the current status

**Table 9.1**  The lifetime of dominant trends in some selected shares

| Share | Minimum trendlength | Maximum trendlength | Mean |
|---|---|---|---|
| NatWest | 17 | 161 | 62 |
| GEC | 20 | 108 | 52 |
| Tesco | 12 | 163 | 51 |
| BAT | 19 | 96 | 46 |
| Granada | 14 | 140 | 45 |
| Smith (W.H.) | 19 | 101 | 44 |
| HSBC | 4 | 60 | 32 |
| Hillsdown | 7 | 81 | 31 |
| Thames Water | 9 | 67 | 30 |
| Willis Coroon | 2 | 78 | 27 |
| Unigate | 3 | 63 | 24 |
| Vodafone | 11 | 33 | 19 |

of the dominant trend at this crucial period close to its directional change. If we think about it, there is no contest. If the NN20 estimate is always wrong in this period of time, then any other method must be an improvement!

Occasionally with certain types of price movement, the price analysis method will not be able to predict clearly that the average should turn up before the point is reached at which the true calculated average turns up. More often than not, though, the price analysis method is able to predict the upturn in the 41-week average by up to about five weeks before the actual event. Since the share price will have risen, perhaps by a considerable amount during this period, the five weeks' advance warning of the upturn in the average allows the investor to capture, on average, an extra 4.6% gain. This is an extremely useful additional profit, which will offset the dealing costs involved in the transaction.

The investor should develop this skill at price analysis by constant practice on a few charts of share prices, checking constantly on a weekly basis the estimate he made 20 weeks ago against the current calculation of the 41-week average.

# 10

# Buying and Selling

We have come to the conclusion that a share should be bought at a time when we have estimated that the dominant trend in the market is rising and that the dominant trend in the share itself is rising. We noted towards the end of Chapter 7 that the long upward dominant trend in the FTSE that started towards the end of 1994 was estimated at the time (by the improved price analysis method) to have commenced on 23rd December 1994. Now we have to decide on what is the optimum time to buy during this period in which the dominant trend is headed north.

## INVESTMENT TRENDS

If we look at a section of price history for a share where the dominant trend has reversed direction and is rising, then the shorter term fluctuations in the price provide several opportunities for buying. In Figure 10.1 we show the position for the Boots share price. The dominant trend as highlighted by the centred 41-week average is shown as well as the price movement itself. The dominant trend can be considered to have started with the low price of 464p on 9th December 1994 and has probably ended at the time of writing with a high price of 754p on 13th June 1997 (not shown in the figure), with a gain of over 62%.

During this period there are several obvious buying points. We can use the criterion that a valid buying point is one following which the price does not fall below this level until the next selling point. In other words, the investor is never in a losing situation. Naturally this is only clear from the historical perspective after the event, and in practice we are never going to be able to sustain such a perfect performance. However, identifying such points after the event may lead us to develop methods which have a high probability of avoiding other, more problematical buying points.

Using this criterion, there are six such points from which the investor is guaranteed a profit. Each of these points represents the start of a short term trend which takes the price up for a period of a few weeks at a much

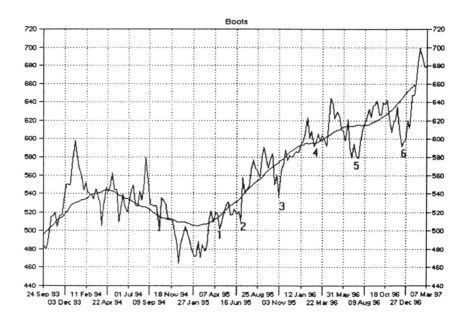

**Figure 10.1**  The Boots share price with a centred 41-week average superimposed. The points labelled 1 to 6 are obvious buying points

higher rate than that of the underlying dominant trend. These are the investment trends, and a method has to be found of identifying them so that the timing of the investment can be fine-tuned during the upward phase of the dominant trend.

Since the investment trends can only be seen to have started on their upward climbs the week after their low points in the case of weekly data such as this, or the day after the low point in the case of daily data, these gaps of one week or one day represent the earliest point at which any signal can get us into the share. This might lead us to think that the most efficient method is the one that generates a buying signal with this minimum delay of one week or one day. However, this is an incorrect perception of the meaning of the word efficiency. The most efficient method is the one that gets us into the share at the next best price after the low points labelled in Figure 10.1. This may or may not be the point one week or one day after the trough—it depends upon the exact nature of the price movement in the weeks or days after the trough.

The distances between the major troughs in the share price are 9, 10, 18, 22, 15, 21 and 24 weeks. As a reasonable approximation they represent cycles with these wavelengths. If we are to use a moving average to isolate short term cycles, we must use a span of less than the shortest cycle, i.e. less than nine weeks. Thus in this particular case the widely used value of a five-week span will still allow through these troughs in the price, so that such an average can be employed to generate a buying signal.

As well as a five-week average, its 25-day equivalent is also used to generate buying signals from daily data, although we shall see that both of these averages can be used in a variety of ways. Whichever span of average we use, and however we analyse the average data, we still need to satisfy two prime requirements:

1. The buying signal should be as close as possible to the best price available after the trough in the share price.
2. The number of false signals, i.e. those where the price fails to rise sufficiently to make a profit, should be minimal.

Criterion 1 will lead us to the maximum profits from correct buying signals, while criterion 2 will reduce the number of incorrect buying signals. It should be realised that because of the partially random nature of share price movement, we can never reduce the number of false signals to zero.

Since the data in Figure 10.1 are weekly data, it is appropriate to apply a five-week moving average. Since we are interested only in whether the five-week average has changed direction or not at its latest calculation, rather than using it as an estimate of the current status of the short term trend, we do not need to plot it as a centred average. Thus in Figure 10.2 we have plotted a centred 41-week average to remind us of the current

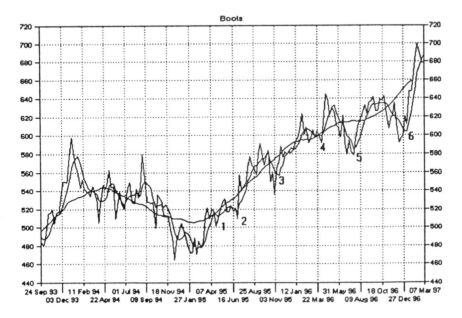

**Figure 10.2** Figure 10.1 with an unlagged five-week average superimposed. The troughs in these signal the start of short term uptrends

status of the dominant trend, and the five-week average with no lag, so as to give us the exact date at which the calculation of the average showed it to have changed direction.

We can see that all of the marked troughs 1 to 6 from Figure 10.1 are reflected by troughs in the five-week average. Trough 5 is a double trough, but yields only one trough in the average.

In order to compare the buying signals generated by the change in direction of the five-week average with the starting points in the trends themselves, it is important to compare like with like.

The start of an uptrend is only confirmed when the price rises on the next occasion from its low point. Thus a 100% perfect trend-calling system would put the investor in not at the trough, but at the next price point. The same argument must be used with turning points in moving averages. Not until the average rises from its low point is the signal generated. In the comparisons made in the following tables, we will call the price point following the price trough the *trend buying point*.

We can see from Table 10.1 that out of the six signals, there was a delay of only one week in two of them, and no disadvantage to the investor, i.e. no profit was missed. Each of the other four signals led to a higher buying price, so that there was a disadvantage to the investor. Overall, the price had risen by 2.7% from the trend buying point by the time the buying signal was given, a very small price to pay for the additional certainty given by using the average. The last point, with a delay of five weeks, as one would expect, was particularly disadvantageous with a loss of 8.5%.

Before moving to a discussion of other ways in which moving averages can be used to generate buying signals, it is instructive to show whether an investor would use the signals in Table 10.1 in the light of the behaviour of the dominant trend. At the time of the first buying signal on 17th February 1995 and the second signal of 24th April 1995, there is no indication by either the NN20 method or the price analysis method that the dominant trend was moving other than downwards. Hence these signals would not

**Table 10.1**  Comparison of dates and prices at the trend buying point with those given by the 5-week average turning point of the Boots share price

| Trend buying point | | Average turning buying point | | | |
|---|---|---|---|---|---|
| Date | Price | Date | Price | Delay (weeks) | % missed |
| 21/04/95 | 510 | 05/05/95 | 518 | 2 | 1.6 |
| 30/06/95 | 557 | 07/07/95 | 557 | 1 | 0 |
| 03/11/95 | 564 | 24/11/95 | 588 | 3 | 4.3 |
| 23/02/96 | 591 | 29/03/96 | 599 | 5 | 1.5 |
| 19/07/96 | 597 | 26/07/96 | 597 | 1 | 0 |
| 13/12/96 | 596.5 | 17/01/97 | 647 | 5 | 8.5 |
| | | Average & missed | | | 2.7 |

be acted upon. This is a general point that can be commented on. Any signals that are given on or just after the time when the dominant trend changes direction (when viewed historically) can never be acted upon, because the estimate of the direction of the dominant trend will be that it is still falling. We have seen that it requires anything from 10 to 20 weeks before an estimate changes to a view that the dominant trend is now rising. Thus any buying signals occurring in this region will have to be ignored. This is the penalty we pay for waiting until the direction of the dominant trend is much more obvious.

By the time the third signal is given on 7th July 1995, the picture is very positive. Historically we can see that at that point we are now some four months past the actual turning point in the dominant trend, and a price analysis carried out at the time, as shown in Figure 10.3, estimates the dominant trend to be rising. This is because for almost all of the price region for 20 weeks from the left-hand side of the chart, the price is below the level of 7th July at the right-hand side of the chart. This should be reflected in a rising 41-week average and hence a rising dominant trend.

The position at the time of the fourth signal on 24th November 1995 is against the background of an extremely positive estimate for the dominant trend (Figure 10.4). Thus the share should be bought at this point. The only slight cautionary note is that the length of time for which the

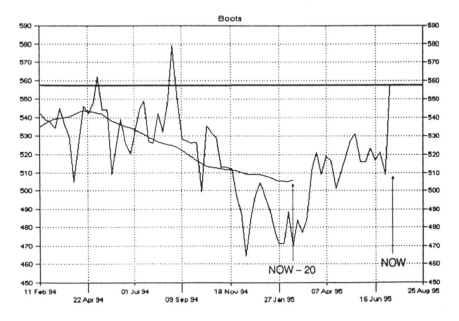

**Figure 10.3** Price history and 41-week average of Boots as at 7th July 1995 (the point NOW). The current estimate of the dominant trend is rising, since the latest price (horizontal line) is above most of the price levels to the left of NOW – 20

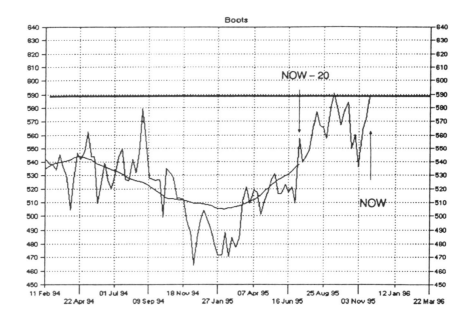

**Figure 10.4** Price history and 41-week average of Boots as at 24th November 1995 (the point NOW). The current estimate of the dominant trend is rising, since the latest price (horizontal line) is well above the price levels to the left of NOW – 20

dominant trend has been rising is some nine months. The reversal in direction of the trend may occur sooner rather than later.

By the time the other two signals are given on 29th March and 26th July 1996, the dominant trend has already been rising for about a year. Thus the probability that it will change direction soon has increased significantly since early 1995. Although price analysis at that time shows that there may still be a few more weeks of a gently rising dominant trend, discretion should cause the investor to look for other opportunities where the dominant trend is much younger.

## PRICE PENETRATION OF THE AVERAGE

The use of a turning point in an average such as the five-week used here is intellectually the most satisfying because the turning point in the average is a reflection of the turning point in the trend, with contributions due to very short term fluctuations almost totally removed. However, another method of using averages has become widely used in investment research. In this alternative method the signal is given by the price rising above the average in the case of buying signals, and falling below it in the case of selling signals. The average is plotted as in the previous figures with no lag.

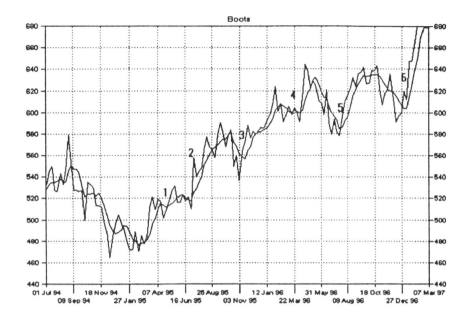

**Figure 10.5** Buying signals (labelled 1 to 6) in the Boots share price generated by the price rising above the five-week average

In Figure 10.5 the places are marked where the price rises above the average so as to generate a buying signal. These signals are compared with those generated by the turning method in Table 10.2.

Three of the signals occurred at the same time as in the turning method, two occurred a week earlier, and one occurred three weeks earlier. Thus on balance there is an advantage in this case to the price penetration method, though across a large group of shares there is virtually no significant difference in performance between the two.

However, there is a difference in the number of signals generated. Between the two extreme dates in Tables 10.1 and 10.2, there are no fewer

**Table 10.2** Comparison of the turning and penetration methods using five-week averages of the Boots share price

| Turning method | | Penetration method | |
|---|---|---|---|
| Date | Price | Date | Price |
| 05/05/95 | 518 | 05/05/95 | 518 |
| 07/07/95 | 557 | 07/07/95 | 557 |
| 24/11/95 | 588 | 16/11/95 | 564 |
| 29/03/96 | 599 | 22/03/96 | 604 |
| 26/07/96 | 597 | 26/07/96 | 597 |
| 17/01/97 | 647 | 03/01/97 | 619.5 |

than nine additional signals generated by the price penetration method. These are shown in Table 10.3 with comments.

The difficulty is that most such signals are false. Thus the price of 580p on 8th September 1995, for example, turned out to be the highest price for two months, putting the investor in a situation where he failed to profit for this length of time. His money could have been more usefully employed elsewhere in a situation which showed an immediate profit from the time of investment. Not only that, but if the investor is operating a stop-loss selling system, then many of these signals would be followed by exit signals leading to losses.

Since a prime aim of any investment strategy is to reduce to a minimum the number of false buying signals, it is of interest to see why the price penetration method gives a signal when there is no turning point in the average.

The basic reason that investors use this method is a misunderstanding of the simple arithmetic involved in the moving average calculation. It might be thought that if the price rises above the average price, which is the situation at the time the penetration signal is given, then the average must subsequently rise at the next calculation. This totally ignores the three components of the average calculation—the running total, the next price point, and the drop-point price. Only if the latter is less than the value of the next point will the average rise. The fact that the current point is above the value of the average does not even guarantee that next week's price is above this week's price, let alone that it is above the drop-point price. Thus there is no relationship whatsoever between what will happen at the next calculation and the fact that the price is currently above the average price. It is this lack of any fundamental relationship between the two that is the cause of so many erroneous signals given by the price crossing method.

## THE 25-DAY AVERAGE

It would seem logical to expect that similar results would be obtained for a 25-day average operating on daily data as for a five-week average

**Table 10.3** Additional signals given by the five-week average price penetration method for Boots

| Date | Price | Comment |
| --- | --- | --- |
| 23/06/95 | 510 | already invested (on 05/05/95) |
| 08/09/95 | 580 | this remains highest price for two months |
| 13/10/95 | 583.5 | this remains highest price for a month |
| 22/12/95 | 583 | already invested (on 24/11/95) |
| 16/02/96 | 608 | poorer price than the next signal |
| 12/04/96 | 615 | very high price |
| 14/06/96 | 621 | very high price |
| 11/10/96 | 639 | top price |
| 29/11/96 | 635 | very high price |

operating on weekly data. This is certainly not the case, and for a very good reason. The sampling of data on a weekly basis from what is fundamentally daily data is in itself a smoothing operation. Thus a five-week average of weekly data would be expected to be smoother than a 25-day average of daily data. That this proves to be the case can be seen from Figure 10.6, where both the daily data and the 25-day average are shown. The figure should be compared with Figure 10.1. It should be obvious that the weekly data are smoother than the daily data, and the weekly average is smoother than the daily one.

The consequence of this is that we will get many more buying and selling signals from the 25-day average than from the five-week average, irrespective of whether we use the turn or price penetration methods. The problem is well illustrated in Figure 10.7, where the chart of the Boots daily price from July 1996 to January 1997 is shown, along with the 25-day average. This was a time period over which we saw just two signals for the five-week turning or price crossing methods. In Figure 10.7 we have marked six signals from the average turning method and seven signals from the price penetration method. Only two of each type can be said to be profitable buying points; the other nine put the investor into a losing position within a few days of buying.

In order to outweigh the highly negative effect of these false signals, the true signals, i.e. those nearest to the four weekly signals produced in the

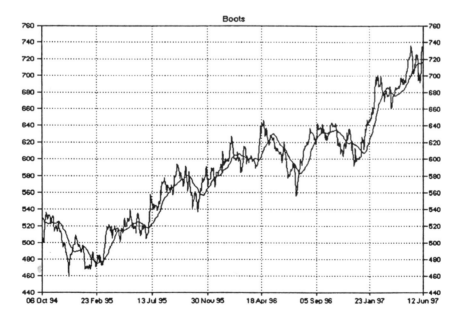

**Figure 10.6**  Daily data and the 25-day average in the Boots share price

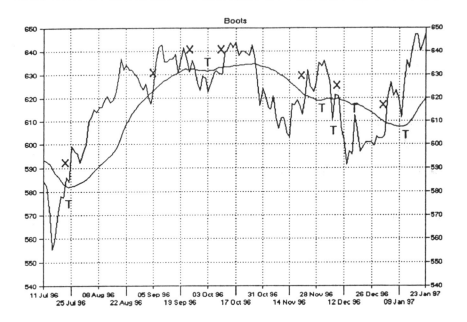

**Figure 10.7** In this expanded chart of the 25-day average, the excessive number of signals generated by daily averages is illustrated by the seven crossing signals (X) and six turning signals (T) shown here. Only two of each type were profitable

weekly data shown previously in Tables 10.1 and 10.2, should produce considerably better buying prices.

Whether this is true or not can be established from the data in Table 10.4, where the results for the signals in the daily data are given.

In the daily data it can be seen that the price penetration method appears to be slightly inferior to the average turning method, getting in at the same price on two occasions and at a better price on one occasion. On three occasions it gave poorer prices. The more interesting comparison is with the weekly data in Table 10.2. The 25-day average penetration method is better than the five-week average penetration method on four

**Table 10.4** Comparison of the turning and penetration methods using 25-day averages of the Boots share price

| Turning method | | Penetration method | |
|---|---|---|---|
| Date | Price | Date | Price |
| 05/05/95 | 528 | 26/04/95 | 517 |
| 05/07/95 | 522 | 05/07/95 | 522 |
| 14/11/95 | 564 | 10/11/95 | 564 |
| 29/03/96 | 599 | 21/03/96 | 602 |
| 24/07/96 | 584 | 23/07/96 | 586 |
| 10/01/97 | 611.5 | 03/01/97 | 619.5 |

occasions, and the same on two occasions. As an average over the six signals, the 25-day average gets the investor in at a price only 1.4% better than the five-week average method.

This small difference may seem surprising to investors brought up on the virtues of daily data. It has to be said that for the extra work entailed in maintaining a daily database by manual methods as opposed to a weekly one by the same method, the additional gain is really not worth the extra effort. When all the additional negative signals are taken into account, the use of daily data may be considered to be an actual disadvantage.

Naturally, as we have maintained throughout this book, it is dangerous to draw conclusions from a limited set of data. When the pool of FTSE100 constituents is examined over a period of time from early 1995 to mid-1997, the conclusion drawn from the study of Boots was fully supported. The number of signals generated by using a 25-day average penetration method is about twice the number generated by the five-week average turning method.

## SELLING SIGNALS

To show the profits (and losses) which can be made from buying on the turn of the five-week average, 10 shares were chosen so as to represent relatively involatile shares, moderately volatile shares and very volatile shares. Only signals which occurred while the dominant trends in both the market (using the FTSE100 Index) and the share itself were estimated to be favourable were taken as genuine buying signals.

### Price Controlled Selling Signals

Although there are many ways in which selling signals can be generated, the stop-loss method we discussed earlier has the virtues of simplicity and the ability to lock in a considerable proportion of the profit from a correct buying decision. Although a 5% stop-loss is a good general purpose value, this percentage can be relaxed somewhat if we have used buying techniques which reduce the overall risk in the investment. The strategy of relying on a favourable dominant trend in the share and the market is such a technique. Since dominant trends are involved, they should maintain the same direction for a reasonable length of time. The advantage of relaxing the stop-loss to say 7.5% means that we should be able to stay in the share for longer periods than if a 5% stop-loss is used, thereby taking advantage of such longer trends. The selling points used in Table 10.5 are generated by triggering of a 7.5% stop-loss.

The buying points listed are those between mid-1995 and June 1997, at the time of writing. Buying points are not listed for occasions when the 41-week average of either the FTSE100 Index or the share was estimated to be falling.

**Table 10.5**   The transactions generated in 10 shares by the five-week average turning method. Signals given when the dominant trend is rising in the market or the share itself are not listed

| Buy date | Price | Sell date | Price | % gain | Weeks invested |
|---|---|---|---|---|---|
| *BSkyB* | | | | | |
| 10/11/95 | 392 | 17/05/96 | 440 | 12.2 | 27 |
| 24/11/95 | 398 | 17/05/96 | 440 | 10.6 | 25 |
| 01/03/96 | 395 | 17/05/96 | 440 | 11.4 | 11 |
| 12/07/96 | 478 | 25/10/96 | 593 | 24.1 | 15 |
| 20/12/96 | 525.5 | 28/02/97 | 597.5 | 13.7 | 10 |
| *Boots* | | | | | |
| 05/05/95 | 518 | 20/10/95 | 549 | 6.0 | 24 |
| 07/07/95 | 557 | 20/10/95 | 549 | −1.4 | 15 |
| 24/11/95 | 588 | 21/06/96 | 589.5 | 0.3 | 30 |
| 29/03/96 | 599 | 21/06/96 | 589.5 | −1.6 | 12 |
| 26/07/96 | 597 | 13/12/96 | 591 | −1.0 | 20 |
| 17/01/97 | 647 | not yet given | | | |
| *Cadbury-Schweppes* | | | | | |
| 28/07/95 | 486.5 | 15/03/96 | 508.5 | 4.5 | 33 |
| 06/10/95 | 497 | 15/03/96 | 508.5 | 2.3 | 23 |
| 02/02/96 | 542 | 15/03/96 | 508.5 | −6.2 | 6 |
| *Dixons* | | | | | |
| 26/05/95 | 247.5 | 20/12/96 | 527.5 | 113.1 | 82 |
| 22/12/95 | 431 | 20/12/96 | 527.5 | 22.4 | 52 |
| 12/04/96 | 485 | 20/12/96 | 527.5 | 8.8 | 36 |
| 31/05/96 | 501 | 20/12/96 | 527.5 | 5.3 | 29 |
| 23/08/96 | 546 | 20/12/96 | 527.5 | −3.4 | 17 |
| 11/10/96 | 567 | 20/12/96 | 527.5 | −7.0 | 10 |
| *Granada* | | | | | |
| 08/09/95 | 654 | 19/07/96 | 796 | 21.7 | 45 |
| 05/01/96 | 647 | 19/07/96 | 796 | 23.0 | 28 |
| 29/03/96 | 750 | 19/07/96 | 796 | 6.1 | 16 |
| 07/06/96 | 815 | 19/07/96 | 796 | −2.3 | 6 |
| 09/08/96 | 838 | 11/04/97 | 881 | 5.1 | 35 |
| 11/10/96 | 871 | 11/04/97 | 881 | 1.1 | 26 |
| 24/01/97 | 867.5 | 11/04/97 | 881 | 1.6 | 11 |
| *Rentokil* | | | | | |
| 28/07/95 | 283 | 08/11/96 | 399.5 | 41.2 | 67 |
| 01/12/95 | 321.5 | 08/11/96 | 399.5 | 24.3 | 49 |
| 23/02/96 | 353 | 08/11/96 | 399.5 | 13.2 | 37 |
| 22/03/96 | 359 | 08/11/96 | 399.5 | 11.3 | 33 |
| 16/08/96 | 417 | 08/11/96 | 399.5 | −4.2 | 11 |
| 29/11/96 | 434 | 14/03/97 | 404.5 | −6.8 | 15 |
| 24/01/97 | 442.5 | 14/03/97 | 404.5 | −8.6 | 7 |
| *RTZ* | | | | | |
| 07/07/95 | 876.5 | 07/06/96 | 971 | 10.8 | 48 |
| 08/09/95 | 927 | 07/06/96 | 971 | 4.7 | 39 |
| 17/11/95 | 909 | 07/06/96 | 971 | 6.8 | 29 |
| 02/02/96 | 951 | 07/06/96 | 971 | 2.1 | 18 |

**Table 10.5** (*continued*)

| Buy date | Price | Sell date | Price | % gain | Weeks invested |
|---|---|---|---|---|---|
| *RTZ (continued)* | | | | | |
| 15/03/96 | 919 | 07/06/96 | 971 | 5.7 | 12 |
| 18/08/96 | 969 | 10/01/97 | 903.5 | −6.8 | 21 |
| 27/09/96 | 977.5 | 10/01/97 | 903.5 | −7.6 | 15 |
| 22/11/96 | 981 | 10/01/97 | 903.5 | −7.9 | 7 |
| 13/12/97 | 933.5 | 10/01.97 | 903.5 | −3.2 | 4 |
| *Tesco* | | | | | |
| 26/05/95 | 287.5 | 20/10/95 | 302 | 5.0 | 21 |
| 08/12/95 | 289 | 09/02/96 | 282.5 | −2.2 | 9 |
| 05/04/96 | 282 | 19/07/96 | 283 | 0.4 | 15 |
| 24/05/96 | 298 | 19/07/96 | 283 | −5.0 | 8 |
| 16/08/96 | 308 | 28/02/97 | 339 | 10.1 | 28 |
| 04/10/96 | 313.5 | 28/02/97 | 339 | 8.1 | 21 |
| 28/03/97 | 349.5 | not yet given | | | |
| *Williams* | | | | | |
| 19/04/96 | 351 | 17/05/96 | 321 | −8.5 | 4 |
| 14/06/96 | 337 | 15/11/96 | 336.5 | −0.1 | 22 |
| 09/08/96 | 340 | 15/11/96 | 336.5 | −1.0 | 14 |
| *Wolseley* | | | | | |
| 27/10/95 | 395 | 29/03/96 | 439 | 11.1 | 22 |
| 19/04/96 | 447 | 26/07/96 | 435 | −8.8 | 14 |
| 07/06/96 | 467 | 26/07/96 | 435 | −6.8 | 7 |
| 10/08/96 | 545 | 01/11/96 | 465.5 | −14.6 | 11 |
| 03/01/97 | 458.5 | 04/04/97 | 480 | 4.7 | 13 |
| 02/05/97 | 497 | 30/05/97 | 465 | −6.4 | 4 |
| Average of 57 signals | | | | 5.9 | 22 |

There are 57 buying and corresponding selling signals for the 10 shares, and the average gain of these is 5.9%. This average of 5.7 transactions per share in just two years is far too high, and ways have to be found of reducing it and possibly increasing the average gain.

## Reducing the Number of False Signals

False signals are those that produce no profit to the investor over a reasonable time span, say six to eight weeks, so that the investor is at best standing still at a time when he could have been more profitably invested. At worst he suffers a considerable loss during this period. Quite obviously, an investor needs a method of reducing these to the very minimum, it being recognised that the random nature of the stock market makes it impossible to eliminate those instances where everything looks perfect for an investment, only to turn sour just a few days or a few weeks later.

There are several sensible and logical rules which we can apply to do this. The first, which will remove a large number of transactions, is to treat as void any buying signal which is given before the selling signal from the previous buying operation has been generated. In other words the investor would be buying into a share which he would still be holding from the previous buying signal. The risk involved in taking two bites at the same short term trend must be considered to be relatively high. Examples would be the transactions from 8th September 1995 to 15th March 1996 in RTZ before the selling signal on 7th June 1996. By adopting this approach we reduce the number of transactions to 25.

The second type of signal which should be ignored is a fall in price from the previous week where the latest calculation of the average shows that it has turned up. **It should be an inviolate rule that an investor never buys on a price fall**. The reason is simple: the start of an uptrend, be it a very short term one or otherwise, is always from a price rise. Thus the investor must wait for a rise to be sure that the uptrend has begun. If the price has fallen from that of the previous week, there is no guarantee that it will not fall the next week. An example of such a rise in the average on a fall in the price is shown for Rentokil in August 1996 (Figure 10.8). The subsequent price action confirms that the buying signal was a false one, and the transaction would have lost the investor 4.3%. Although naturally there are many examples of the reverse behaviour, where although the price has fallen it then recovers and continues upwards, there are many more where

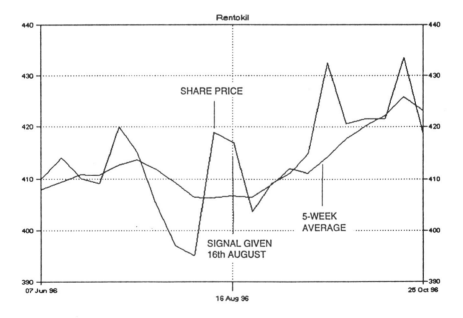

**Figure 10.8**   A false buying signal in the Rentokil share price on 16th August 1996. This should be ignored, since, although the five-week average has risen, this is accompanied by a fall in the share price from the previous week

the buying signal turns out to be false. On balance the risk is too high to take positive action in such circumstances.

The third type of signal is a development of this second type. In this case we ignore a signal when the trend which is even shorter than the one isolated by the five-week average is falling even when the five-week average has turned up. These shorter term trends would be isolated by a three-week average, but for our purposes it is not necessary to calculate such an average. If we think in terms of drop-points, the three-week average turns up when the price at NOW which is added in to the three-week running total is higher than the price at the drop-point at NOW – 3. Thus all we need to do when we get a signal that the five-week average has turned up is to check that the latest price is higher than the price three weeks ago.

On about 90% of the occasions it will be. If it is not, then very short term trends are running adversely, and the signal should be ignored. An example of such a negative signal is shown in Figure 10.9 for the buying signal in Granada in June 1996. The investor who ignored this negative signal would have lost 2.3% from the complete transaction.

These last two methods of eliminating false signals would remove eight signals. These false signals are shown in Table 10.6. Although they do not all lead to losses, their average gain is only 0.5%.

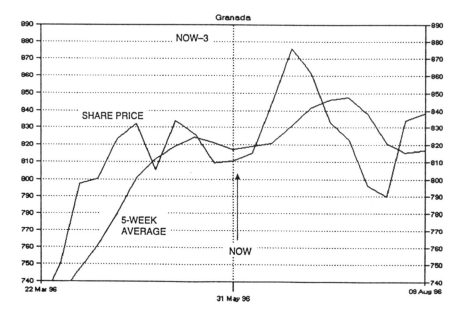

**Figure 10.9** A different type of false buying signal in the Granada share price in June 1996. The very short term trend which would be shown by a three-week average is falling. It is not necessary to calculate this, since a rising three-week average will have the price at NOW higher than the price at NOW – 3. In this example the price at NOW is lower, so the three-week average is falling and the share should not be bought

**Table 10.6** The false signals eliminated (a) because the price has fallen from the previous week even though the five-week average has turned up, or (b) because the price at NOW is lower than the price at NOW − 3 at the time the five-week average turning signal is given

| Buy date | Price | Sell date | Price | % gain | Weeks invested |
|---|---|---|---|---|---|
| *Boots* | | | | | |
| (a) 29/03/96 | 599 | 21/06/96 | 589.5 | −1.6 | 12 |
| *Granada* | | | | | |
| (b) 07/06/96 | 815 | 19/07/96 | 796 | −2.3 | 6 |
| (b) 11/10/96 | 871 | 11/04/97 | 881 | −1.1 | 26 |
| *Rentokil* | | | | | |
| (b) 23/02/96 | 353 | 08/11/96 | 399.5 | 13.2 | 37 |
| (a) 16/08/96 | 417 | 08/11/96 | 399.5 | −4.2 | 11 |
| *RTZ* | | | | | |
| (a) 15/03/96 | 919 | 07/06/96 | 971 | 5.7 | 12 |
| (b) 27/09/96 | 977.5 | 10/01/97 | 903.5 | −7.6 | 15 |
| *Williams* | | | | | |
| (a) 14/06/96 | 337 | 15/11/96 | 336.5 | −0.1 | 14 |

The net result of removing these is to leave us with 24 buying and selling transactions from the 10 shares, i.e. somewhere between two and three per share over the two years. These transactions are shown in Table 10.7. The average gain is now improved to 9.5%, and the average length of time for which the investor would be invested is 26 weeks. This represents a rate of gain of 0.37% per week, before dealing costs are taken into consideration. If we allow 5% for these, then the gain becomes 5% over 27 weeks, or approximately 10% per annum.

Space does not warrant lengthy tables of data, and the 10 shares were chosen deliberately to represent both low, medium and high volatility shares. In practice we would avoid shares of low volatility, since the potential for profit is much less. **In practice, therefore, a correct choice of the more volatile shares should lead to gains of the order of 20–25% per annum.**

## Time Controlled Selling Signals

The results obtained using a stop-loss of say 7.5% were impressive, but it should be pointed out that any method that depends upon the price movement itself to generate a selling signal has a blind spot. It is possible to stay invested for long time periods over which the share price makes no significant advance.

Theoretically the price could see-saw up and down within 2–3% above and below a horizontal long term trend, with the falls from the peaks being too small to trigger the stop-loss. Such a position is shown for BTR in

**Table 10.7** The transactions which remain after elimination of all false signals

| Buy date | Price | Sell date | Price | % gain | Weeks invested |
|----------|-------|-----------|-------|--------|----------------|
| *BSkyB* | | | | | |
| 10/11/95 | 392 | 17/05/96 | 440 | 12.2 | 27 |
| 12/07/96 | 478 | 25/10/96 | 593 | 24.1 | 15 |
| 20/12/96 | 525.5 | 28/02/97 | 597.5 | 13.7 | 10 |
| *Boots* | | | | | |
| 05/05/95 | 518 | 20/10/95 | 549 | 6.0 | 24 |
| 24/11/95 | 588 | 21/06/96 | 589.5 | 0.3 | 30 |
| 26/07/96 | 597 | 13/12/96 | 591 | −1.0 | 20 |
| 17/01/97 | 647 | not yet given | | | |
| *Cadbury-Schweppes* | | | | | |
| 28/07/95 | 486.5 | 15/03/96 | 508.5 | 4.5 | 33 |
| *Dixons* | | | | | |
| 26/05/95 | 247.5 | 20/12/96 | 527.5 | 113.1 | 82 |
| *Granada* | | | | | |
| 08/09/95 | 654 | 19/07/96 | 796 | 21.7 | 45 |
| 09/08/96 | 838 | 11/04/97 | 881 | 5.1 | 35 |
| *Rentokil* | | | | | |
| 28/07/95 | 283 | 08/11/96 | 399.5 | 41.2 | 67 |
| 29/11/96 | 434 | 14/03/97 | 404.5 | −6.8 | 15 |
| *RTZ* | | | | | |
| 07/07/95 | 876.5 | 07/06/96 | 971 | 10.8 | 48 |
| 16/08/96 | 969 | 10/01/97 | 903.5 | −6.8 | 21 |
| *Tesco* | | | | | |
| 26/05/95 | 287.5 | 20/10/95 | 302 | 5.0 | 21 |
| 08/12/95 | 289 | 09/02/96 | 282.5 | −2.2 | 9 |
| 05/04/96 | 282 | 19/07/96 | 283 | 0.4 | 15 |
| 16/08/96 | 308 | 28/02/97 | 339 | 10.1 | 28 |
| 28/03/97 | 349.5 | not yet given | | | |
| *Williams* | | | | | |
| 19/04/96 | 351 | 17/05/96 | 321 | −8.5 | 4 |
| *Wolseley* | | | | | |
| 27/10/95 | 395 | 29/03/96 | 439 | 11.1 | 22 |
| 19/04/96 | 477 | 26/07/96 | 435 | −8.8 | 14 |
| 10/08/96 | 545 | 01/11/96 | 465.5 | −14.6 | 11 |
| 03/01/97 | 458.5 | 04/04/97 | 480 | 4.7 | 13 |
| 02/05/97 | 497 | 30/05/97 | 465 | −6.4 | 4 |
| Average of 24 signals | | | | 9.5 | 26 |

Figure 10.10. The price oscillated in a band between 342p and 316p. The stop-loss 7.5% down from 342p would be just over 316p. It was the final fall to 316p on 29th March 1996 that took the investor out after being in the share for one year. Thus the investor is locked into a situation which is producing no profit. It is of little compensation that he is also apparently

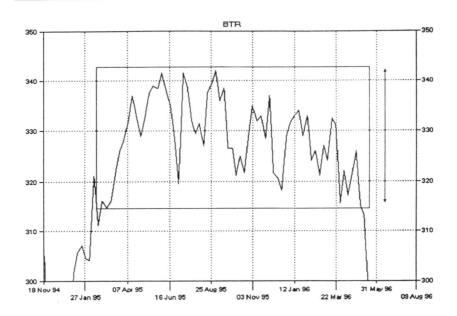

**Figure 10.10**  It is possible to remain invested for a long unprofitable period without a selling signal if the price oscillates within a narrow horizontal band. The falls from peak to trough (double-headed arrow) within the rectangle which represents the period April 1995 to April 1996 are less than 7.5%, hence the stop-loss is not triggered

not losing money while this is happening. Any time spent not making profits must be considered to be wasted time where money could be better employed elsewhere.

Thus we have to have a last-ditch method to prevent such situations building up. Since a price controlled system is the type which fails, we need a back-up system which is independent of price. Since the only two variables in the stock market are price and time, we need to use a back-up system based on time. Thus our selling signal will be given when a certain amount of time has elapsed with no selling signal having been generated by the stop-loss or other selling signal that we are using. The only decision to be made is on the length of time that should be used.

We can get some help with this by looking at the average length of time for which we stayed invested in the 10 shares used as examples in Tables 10.5 and 10.7. This was 26 weeks for the average return of 9.5% (Table 10.7). Rounding this down to 20 weeks, we could adopt a method in which we sell the share after 20 weeks if a selling signal has not been given by the 7.5% stop-loss within that time. In Table 10.7 there were 16 shares that had not given a selling signal within this period of time. It is useful to compare the selling price and gain achieved after 20 weeks with the ultimate selling price and the additional amount of gain achieved during the period after this 20 weeks. This shows us whether the rate of gain was higher during the initial 20 weeks than during the subsequent period. If this turns out to be the case, then there is no point in remaining invested for longer than 20 weeks in the same share; much better returns could be obtained by switching to another share that was just reaching a buying point. The data from this comparison are given in Table 10.8.

The difference between the rates of gain per week during the first 20 weeks of the investment and that made if the investment is held for the full length of time to the stop-loss trigger is large. During the first 20 weeks, the average rate of gain per week was 0.65%, whereas over the longer term it averaged only 0.4% per week. Clearly, therefore, there is a tremendous advantage in terminating the investment at 20 weeks if a stop-loss exit signal has not been given.

By doing this, the gains and number of weeks invested that were shown in Table 10.7 are now changed to those shown in Table 10.9. We have brought down the average length of time for which the investor remains

**Table 10.8** The buying prices, prices at 20 weeks and ultimate selling prices for the longer investment trends. Also given are the rates of gain per week for the first 20 weeks and the period subsequent to this

| Date | Buy price | Price at 20 weeks | Price at signal | Gain per week | |
|------|-----------|-------------------|-----------------|---------------|--------------|
| | | | | At 20 weeks | After 20 weeks |
| *BSkyB* | | | | | |
| 10/11/95 | 392 | 435 | 440 | 0.55 | 0.45 |
| *Boots* | | | | | |
| 05/05/95 | 518 | 580 | 549 | 0.60 | 0.25 |
| 24/11/95 | 588 | 615 | 589.5 | 0.23 | 0.01 |
| *Cadbury-Schweppes* | | | | | |
| 28/07/95 | 486.5 | 546.5 | 508.5 | 0.62 | 0.14 |
| *Dixons* | | | | | |
| 26/05/95 | 247.5 | 386 | 527.5 | 2.80 | 1.38 |
| *Granada* | | | | | |
| 08/09/95 | 654 | 714 | 796 | 0.46 | 0.48 |
| 09/08/96 | 838 | 861 | 881 | 0.14 | 0.15 |
| *Rentokil* | | | | | |
| 28/07/95 | 283 | 335 | 399.5 | 0.92 | 0.61 |
| *RTZ* | | | | | |
| 07/07/95 | 876.5 | 945 | 971 | 0.39 | 0.23 |
| *Tesco* | | | | | |
| 26/05/95 | 287.5 | 268.5 | 302 | −0.33 | 0.23 |
| 16/08/96 | 308 | 352 | 339 | 0.71 | 0.36 |
| *Wolseley* | | | | | |
| 27/10/95 | 395 | 456 | 439 | 0.77 | 0.50 |
| Average | | | | 0.65 | 0.40 |

**Table 10.9**  The transactions which remain after applying the 20-week limit

| Buy date | Price | Sell date | Price | % gain | Weeks invested |
|----------|-------|-----------|-------|--------|----------------|
| *BSkyB* | | | | | |
| 10/11/95 | 392 | 29/03/96 | 435 | 10.9 | 20 |
| 12/07/96 | 478 | 25/10/96 | 593 | 24.1 | 15 |
| 20/12/96 | 525.5 | 28/02/97 | 597.5 | 13.7 | 10 |
| *Boots* | | | | | |
| 05/05/95 | 518 | 22/09/95 | 580 | 12.0 | 20 |
| 24/11/95 | 588 | 12/04/96 | 615 | 4.6 | 20 |
| 26/07/96 | 597 | 13/12/96 | 591 | −1.0 | 20 |
| 17/01/97 | 647 | not yet given | | | |
| *Cadbury-Schweppes* | | | | | |
| 28/07/95 | 486.5 | 15/12/95 | 546.5 | 12.3 | 20 |
| *Dixons* | | | | | |
| 26/05/95 | 247.5 | 13/10/95 | 386 | 56.0 | 20 |
| *Granada* | | | | | |
| 08/09/95 | 654 | 26/01/96 | 714 | 9.2 | 20 |
| 09/08/96 | 838 | 27/12/96 | 861 | 2.7 | 20 |
| *Rentokil* | | | | | |
| 28/07/95 | 283 | 15/12/95 | 335 | 18.4 | 20 |
| 29/11/96 | 434 | 14/03/97 | 404.5 | −6.8 | 15 |
| *RTZ* | | | | | |
| 07/07/95 | 876.5 | 24/11/95 | 945 | 7.8 | 20 |
| 16/08/96 | 969 | 03/01/97 | 932.5 | −3.7 | 20 |
| *Tesco* | | | | | |
| 26/05/95 | 287.5 | 13/10/95 | 318.5 | 10.8 | 20 |
| 08/12/95 | 289 | 09/02/96 | 282.5 | −2.2 | 9 |
| 05/04/96 | 282 | 19/07/96 | 283 | 0.4 | 15 |
| 16/08/96 | 308 | 03/01/97 | 352 | 14.3 | 20 |
| 28/03/97 | 349.5 | not yet given | | | |
| *Williams* | | | | | |
| 19/04/96 | 351 | 17/05/96 | 321 | −8.5 | 4 |
| *Wolseley* | | | | | |
| 27/10/95 | 395 | 25/03/96 | 456 | 15.4 | 20 |
| 19/04/96 | 477 | 26/07/96 | 435 | −8.8 | 14 |
| 10/08/96 | 545 | 01/11/96 | 465.5 | −14.6 | 11 |
| 03/01/97 | 458.5 | 04/04/97 | 480 | 4.7 | 13 |
| 02/05/97 | 497 | 30/05/97 | 465 | −6.4 | 4 |
| Average of 24 signals | | | | 6.9 | 16 |

invested between the buying point and selling point to 16 weeks, while the average gain in this period is 6.9%. Over the year this represents over 22% if dealing costs are ignored. Although dealing costs are considerable, their effect will be partly offset by dividends received. If the average length of time invested is 16 weeks, and an interim or final dividend is paid every six months (26 weeks), then the probability that an investor will receive an interim or final while the share is being held is 16/26, i.e. 62%.

Finally, the purpose behind the discussion in this chapter is to show how a logical approach to filtering out false buying and selling signals can improve the returns dramatically. When this is allied to improved methods of selecting shares in the first place, the investor must make considerable profits over the long run.

# 11

# Channel Analysis

The strategy we have developed so far has simply required us to buy in at the first indication that a rising investment trend has started, against the background of a rising dominant trend in both the share in question and the market itself. The indicator used to determine the start of the investment trend was the turning point in the five-week moving average. No attempt was made to analyse in detail the price movement of the five-week average in the way in which the price movement of the 41-week average was analysed, since good results were obtained simply by eliminating two types of false signal. Implicit in this profitable strategy is that the dominant and investment trends are two unrelated entities. We now show that this simple picture is not true, and that the dominant trend puts limits on the levels to which the short term trends can rise or fall.

Taking a familiar example, Boots, we show in Figure 11.1 a chart of the share price from 1983 upon which we have superimposed the dominant trend as signified by the 41-week average. Looking at the extent to which the shorter term trends oscillate around this average, it becomes obvious that there is a limit to how far vertically above and below the average these short term trends take the price. It is possible to draw a duplicate of the average curve at an equal distance vertically above and below the original position of the average such that the majority of the price movement is contained within these upper and lower levels. This is shown in Figure 11.2. The upper and lower boundaries constitute a channel for the shorter term trends. Such channels can be drawn by computer, as shown here, or by eye, simply by drawing smooth curves through the high and low extremities of the price. It is important that the vertical depth of the channel remains constant, i.e. a fixed number of points in the case of the FTSE100 Index, or a fixed number of pence for a share. Use of percentage envelopes invalidates the channel procedure. The more peaks and troughs that lie on a channel, the more valid is the channel. A small number, say two to four, overshoots of the channel boundaries by the price is permissible, for example the unavoidable overshoots at the time of the 1987 crash, but these should be kept to a minimum.

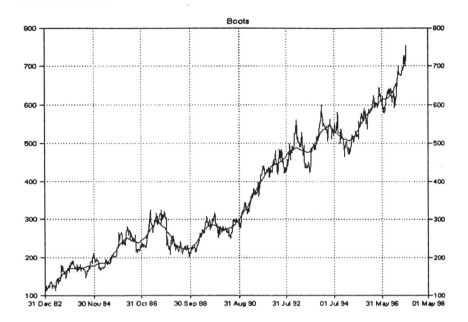

**Figure 11.1** The Boots share price since 1983 with the dominant trend as shown by the centred 41-week average

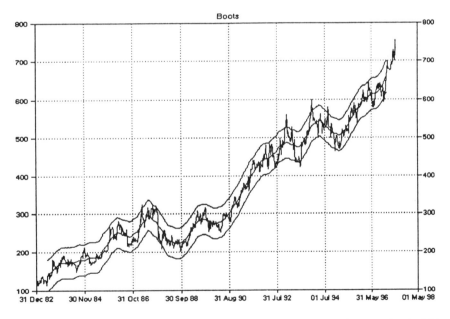

**Figure 11.2** The shorter term trends in the Boots share price can be contained within a channel constructed by duplicating the centred 41-week average above and below the original position

Note that in Figure 11.2 there are at least 24 peaks and troughs that lie almost directly on the channel boundaries. In addition there are a limited number of places where the price overshoots or undershoots the boundaries, such as the section of the chart between 31st July 1992 and 1st July 1994. On these occasions the amount of overshoot is still quite small.

The important implication of these channel boundaries is that there is a limit (in pence or points) to the extent to which the short term trend can normally take the price (or Index) away from the centre of the channel. Having reached this limit the price rebounds back towards the centre. In this example of Boots, we have set the limit at 32p above and below the centre of the channel. Thus the price has a very high probability of bouncing back towards the centre of the channel once this limit is reached. The price is therefore oscillating within a channel which is 64 pence deep throughout its history. On a few occasions during mid-1992 to mid-1994 this limit was exceeded, but only by a few pence.

An idea of the way in which the price moves within a channel can be seen in Figure 11.3. The distance of each price point from the average is plotted in units of 0.5p, and the number of occasions when the price was at each level over the time period spanned by Figure 11.2 is shown on the vertical axis. As we would expect from Figure 11.2, the number of

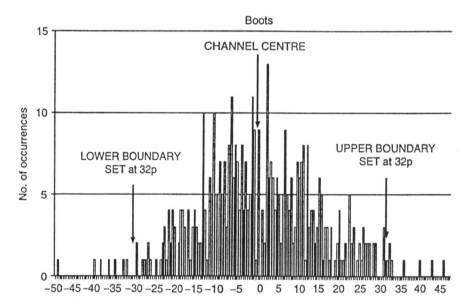

**Figure 11.3** The movement of points within the Boots channel. The horizontal axis shows the distance of the price from the position of the moving average, negative values being below and positive values above the average. The price levels are divided into units of 0.5p and the vertical axis shows the number of points which lie at each position over the period 1983 to the present

occasions when the price is at a large distance, e.g. 30p or more, from the average is quite small. The extremes were 50p above the average and 49p below on just one occasion each. The price spent most of its time within a band 15p either side of the average. The channel boundaries at 32p above and below are also shown, so that the very few occasions on which the price reached or penetrated these boundaries can be seen clearly.

A better view of the underlying theory of channel analysis can be obtained from Figure 11.4. Here the vertical axis expresses a different quantity. The centre point represents the position of the average itself, and to the left of this is the percentage of points that lie further below the average than the particular value on the horizontal axis. For the right-hand side, the percentage refers to those points which are further above the average than the value on the horizontal axis.

Taking particular points on the graph, we can see that 20% of the points below the average lie more than 17p below it, while 20% of the points above the average line lie more than 20p above. The graph is not quite symmetrical because of the effect due to the gradual rise in the Boots share price from 1983 to the present.

The boundary positions of 32p are marked on the chart, and now we can see that a very small percentage (3.5%) of the points lie outside either the lower or upper boundary. In fact, the boundary position was chosen by the

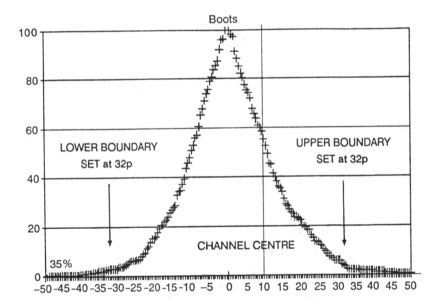

**Figure 11.4** For any point on the horizontal axis, the vertical axis gives the percentage of points that lie further from the position of the average. The left-hand side of the graph represents points lying below, and the right-hand side points lying above the average. At a channel boundary of 32p, only 3.5% of points lie outside the channel

computer program so as to achieve this level of overlap. We can now see that the position of the boundaries is not terribly critical, since moving them in to, say, 25p above and below still leaves only about 5% of the points outside them. This is why it is also quite simple to get good results if the channels are drawn by eye, since the position tolerance is fairly high.

If we think of the vertical axis in terms of probability, we can see why channel analysis works. Once a closing price lies at or very near the boundary, the probability of the next closing price, be it weekly or daily, staying there is only 3.5% in the case of this particular example. The probability is high that it will move in the direction of the centre line of the channel. Having said that, the extent of its movement towards the centre of the channel will depend upon the usual weekly or daily price movement. Thus it would be unrealistic to expect the Boots price to move by 32p to the centre of the channel in one day! A value of 1p to 10p is much more probable. It is the directional probability that we are really concerned with.

It is important to use this picture of channels to reinforce the fundamental significance of centred moving averages and the fundamental insignificance of the unlagged averages so beloved of chartists. By plotting the average as unlagged, the chart shown in Figure 11.5 was obtained. We can see quite clearly that we totally lose the correlation between peaks and

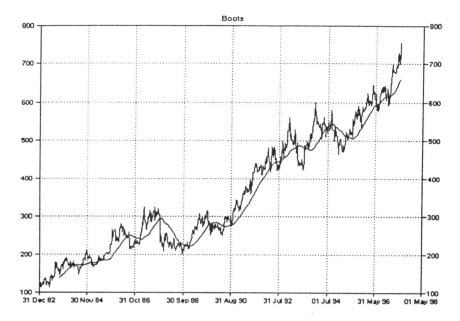

**Figure 11.5** If the 41-week average is plotted as unlagged rather than centred, the coincidence of peaks and troughs in share prices and of the average is lost and channels drawn above and below the unlagged average would be meaningless

troughs in the share price and peaks and troughs in the average. Since channel peaks normally coincide with price peaks and channel troughs normally coincide with price troughs, we can see that any channels drawn around an unlagged average will be meaningless.

To emphasise the validity of the approach, the same channel is shown expanded over the shorter period from August 1990 to the time of writing. There are no fewer than 14 peaks or troughs which lie almost exactly on the channel boundaries. If we extrapolate the 20-week gap to the end of the data, we can see that we expect another two points to lie on the extrapolated channel. Thus, in this seven-year period, we will have encountered 16 occasions on which the price fails to move significantly beyond the boundary. No such result would be obtained if prices moved totally randomly, or if there were no relationship between the dominant trend and the shorter term trends.

It is important to study, as in Figure 11.6, the price movement that occurs once the price retreats from a boundary. The price always appears to retreat to the centre line within a few weeks, but may not continue on to the opposite boundary. In fact, the numbers of half-channel and full-channel movements are about the same.

Since our aim is to be invested only when the dominant trend is rising, it is of interest to analyse the price movements during the upward leg of the

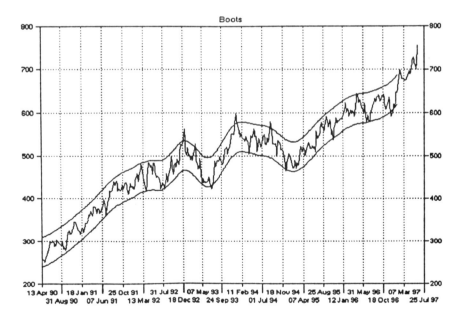

**Figure 11.6** The price retreats towards the centre of the channel once it bounces off a boundary. It may or may not continue to the opposite boundary

channel, i.e. from early 1990 to the end of 1992, and from early 1994 to the present. Although the distance from the channel boundary to the centre, measured vertically, is 32p, the price changes following a bounce from the lower boundary to the centre will be more than this. This is because the channel itself has risen after the bounce, and this rise in the channel must be added to the normal half-channel depth of 32p. Because of this additive effect, useful profits can be made from half-channel rises, although full-channel rises obviously provide the optimum gains. Note that there is no apparent way in which we can predict whether a rise will be a half-channel or full-channel rise at the time the price rebounds from the lower boundary.

Taking some examples of the ultimate gains from such lower boundary bounces in the more recent history of the share, the half-channel bounce from 578p on 19th July 1996 took the price to 632p on 23rd August, a movement of 9% in five weeks. The full-channel bounce from 591p on 13th December 1996 took the price to 699p on 14th February 1997, a movement of 18.3%. Obviously, the earlier in the development of the upward domi-nant trend the bounce occurs, the greater will be the gain expressed as a percentage, since it is starting from a lower base. Since the price rose from the 250p level in April 1990 to the 700p level at the time of writing, a full-channel bounce over the same number of weeks is worth now in 1997 only about a third in percentage terms that it was in early 1990. Although it is not possible to find two half- or full-channel bounces at these two extremes that last exactly the same number of weeks, the point can still be illus-trated by referring to full-channel and half-channel bounces in the period from 1990 to 1991. Thus the half-channel bounce from 276p on 21st Sep-tember 1990 took the price to 323p on 19th October of that year, a gain of 17%. The full-channel bounce on 28th June 1991 took the price from 359p to 439p on 23rd August, a rise of 22.3%.

The price movements above are simply the extent to which the price changes in its rise from the channel boundary. Naturally the limiting prices are not the ones at which the investor could have bought or sold. The investor can only buy when the price has bounced back from the boundary, i.e. has formed a trough. Thus the earliest the investor can buy is at the price immediately after the trough, i.e. one week later in the case of weekly data, or one day later in the case of daily data. The buying and selling signals for the above four price movements would therefore be:

1. Buy on 28th September 1990 at 284p, sell on 26th October 1990 at 313p.
2. Buy on 5th July 1991 at 378p, sell on 30th August 1991 at 429p.
3. Buy on 26th July 1996 at 597p, sell on 30th August 1996 at 623.5p.
4. Buy on 20th December 1996 at 596.5p, sell on 21st February 1997 at 687.5p.

This gives gains of 10.2%, 13.5%, 4.4% and 15.2% respectively.

# NOT QUITE THE HOLY GRAIL

Since we have noted that once the price reaches the lower boundary, it always reacts back to the centre, giving real profits of 10% or more in a short time, we appear to have found a completely foolproof method of profitable investment. This would be true if we knew exactly the position of the channels at the point NOW, i.e. how they have moved, in the case of channels based on a 41-week average, between NOW – 20 and NOW. The problem is exactly the same as that addressed earlier using the price analysis method. Then the approach used was to assume that the price remained constant for 20 weeks into the future and to calculate the resulting average, thus filling in the gap between NOW – 20 and NOW. In the case of channel analysis, we have to use an even better method, since we need an accurate estimate of the current position of the average, and hence the channel boundaries, since the latter are a constant distance below and above the average.

The position of the boundaries up to NOW – 20 has been determined by the more extreme of the peaks and troughs. The boundaries are either drawn by eye so as to pass through these extremes, or calculated by computer so as to allow only a certain small percentage of points, normally about 3.5%, to lie outside the resulting channel. Thus any method to extrapolate the boundaries to NOW should adopt this same procedure. If there are peaks and/or troughs in this 20-week gap that lie close to the estimated position of the boundaries, then the boundaries can be bent upwards or downwards so as to pass through these peaks or troughs. Naturally there must be a limit imposed on the amount of bending towards the centre of the channel which is tolerable. If an unusual bend is required, then the peak or trough in question should be accepted as one which does not lie on the boundary, but some distance inside it. Bending away from the centre of the channel is a different matter. This will be required in those circumstances where the price lies outside the estimated boundary position. Since we allow only a very small proportion of points to lie outside the boundary, and even then not too far outside, we must bend the channel, however extreme this bend may be, in order to keep the peak or trough close to this limit. This will only happen under the very occasional circumstance where the price has moved much more than the typical range of daily or weekly movement.

Before proceeding to such an estimate carried out in this way, it is instructive to see what is a permissible error in the estimate of the boundary position. The effect of error will be different, according to whether we are approaching a lower or upper boundary.

## *Error in Lower Boundary*

If an estimate in the current position of the lower boundary is lower than the correct position, then the price will never reach it. The practical effect to the investor is that the share will never be bought.

If the estimate of the current position is higher than the correct position, then the price will pass down through this incorrect boundary within a few days or weeks. Thus at the time the price is at the estimated boundary, we may take a premature buying decision.

### Error in Upper Boundary

If the estimate in the current position of the upper boundary is lower than the correct position, then the investor may sell prematurely at the apparent boundary, only to see the price re-establish its upward path to the correct higher boundary.

If the estimate in the upper boundary is too high, then an investor relying on the fact of reaching the boundary as the selling signal will never receive such a signal. Thus a loss will inevitably occur if a stop-loss method is not used.

In practice it turns out that the degree of tolerance in boundary position is quite high. Thus in Figure 11.7 we show boundaries that are 20p above and below the centre line rather than the correct value of 32p. If we take the lower boundary in Figure 11.7 to be that which we might have estimated incorrectly, then we can see that the effect of premature buying which this causes is not to give us an eventual loss, but to put us into a position where

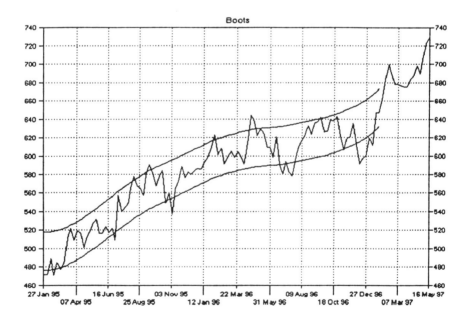

**Figure 11.7** The position if the boundaries are estimated incorrectly. The channel depth is set at 40p, instead of 64p

it is a few weeks before we move into profit. Our annual gain will be reduced by the amount by which our buying price stands above the buying price at which we would enter when the price bounced back from the real channel boundary.

These problems with inaccurate estimates of the channel boundaries can be reduced by two methods. Firstly, we noted that half of the bounces of price from the lower boundary do not take the price to the upper boundary, but only to the approximate midpoint. It is imperative to operate a stop-loss method to ensure against either this incorrect estimate of the boundary, or the premature retreat of the share price because of random influences. Secondly, since peaks and troughs lie on the boundary, where a peak or trough lies close to an estimated position of the boundary the latter can be finely adjusted to touch these peaks or troughs. If we are fortunate, there are a number of such peaks and troughs in the gap between NOW and NOW – 20. Thus we can continually fine-tune the channel boundaries as we proceed to interpolate across the gap from the last true position of the 41-week average, taking care to keep the vertical depth constant.

The thought processes that occur during an estimate of the channel position can best be illustrated by means of three shares.

## Boots (10th November 1995)

This is a straightforward example of channel analysis, but shows the disadvantage that can occur when the price rises quite rapidly from a lower boundary and falls quite rapidly from an upper boundary.

On 10th November 1995 (Figure 11.8) the price has just risen to 564p from its previous value of 536p, this forming a trough at the latter value. In order to put both this trough and the previous trough in late June on the boundary and accommodate the peak in September on the upper boundary, it is necessary to reduce the rate of curvature as shown. By the time the bounce is apparent and it becomes obvious that the trough is on the lower boundary of the channel, the price has already risen by 5% from the trough. The price now appears to be set fair to rise at least to the middle of the channel, if not to the upper boundary. If the latter, we can expect a rise to just above the 600p mark, depending upon how long it takes to rise to the upper boundary. The longer the time taken, the higher will be the price, since the upper boundary is rising all the time.

The price then enjoyed a rise to the middle of the channel by mid-December, and after a few weeks meandering gently along the mid-line saw another large rise to what would be predicted to be the upper boundary of the channel at 623p on 2nd February 1996 (Figure 11.9). Note that the boundaries have to be adjusted again. The only way the trough at 3rd November 1995 and the peak at 2nd February can be accommodated without changing the channel depth is to allow one of them to penetrate

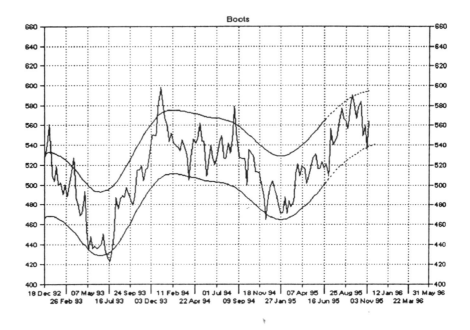

**Figure 11.8**   The extrapolated channels for Boots on 10th November 1995

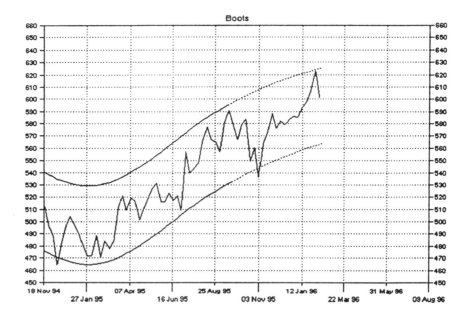

**Figure 11.9**   Within about 10 weeks of the buying position in Figure 11.8, the price has reached the estimated position of the upper boundary and bounced downwards

the boundary, i.e. to contribute to the permissible overlap of 3.5% of points lying outside the boundaries. The rise at that time was about 10%, achieved in about 10 weeks. At this point, the cautious investor would have seen his estimated upper limit of price movement exceeded slightly, and would be happy to take his 10% profit at that point.

By the following week (9th February 1996) the price retreated back to 601p. Thus again, a larger than expected movement took nearly 4% out of the gain leaving the investor with only a 6.5% rise, making it essential to get out with a small profit rather than risk a further fall.

Thus in this example, a boundary to boundary rise of 16.2% was reduced to one of 6.5% by virtue of the movements away from the two boundaries, but these two movements had to take place in order to define accurately the exact positions of the boundaries.

## RTZ (1994 to 1997)

An overall view of the channels which would be drawn for RTZ over the period from April 1994 to mid-1997 is shown in Figure 11.10. The reason for showing this is to show how channel analysis can protect against investing in a share from which it is very difficult to make a profit. In Table 10.4 in the last chapter it was shown that RTZ gave a large number of buying decisions, but that except for the one in July 1995 which gave a 10.8% profit,

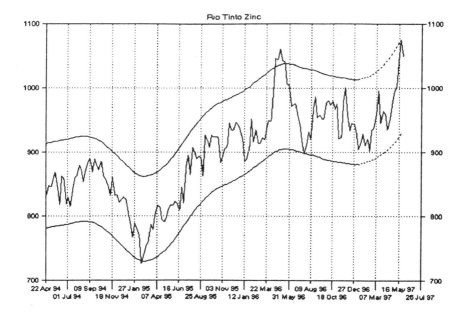

**Figure 11.10**   The channel for RTZ shows that the share price ran along the middle of the channel from April 1994 until March 1996. Thus there would be no buying signals generated by channel analysis and the investor would be kept out of an unprofitable share

they gave rise to either extremely small gains or small losses. Thus the investor would have been tied up in RTZ for a long time with nothing to show for it. The reason can be shown in Figure 11.10. For historical reasons the channel depth has to be around 120p, and with this depth it can be seen that once past the low point of February 1995, the price does not approach a boundary until April 1996. Thus none of the series of buying points indicated by the change in direction of the five-week average would be acted upon by the investor using channel analysis, thus avoiding a disappointing run of narrow share price movement.

## RTZ (7th July 1995)

This point is chosen because it was indicated as a prime buying point when the turn in the five-week average was used. When channels are drawn as shown in Figure 11.11, it can be seen quite clearly that the price is already approaching the upper boundary of the channel. Although it is tempting to curve the channel upwards more sharply than is shown in order to bring the trough on 16th June 1995 onto the lower boundary, the previous share price history would make this an unusually steep rise. Even if this were accepted, it would still be the case that the latest price is at least in mid-channel.

Clearly the potential for further gain in the short term is greatly reduced compared with shares where the price has just left the lower boundary but

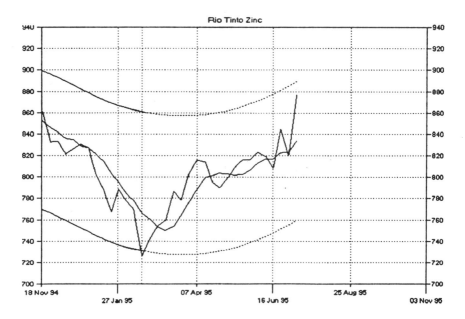

**Figure 11.11**   The position in RTZ on 7th July 1995. In Chapter 10 this was indicated as a buying point. Channel analysis shows that the price is near the top of the channel and therefore the shares would not be bought

is still relatively close to it. The share would definitely not be bought at this point.

## Wolseley (26th January 1996)

The channels drawn on 26th January 1996 are shown in Figure 11.12. It is tempting from this view of the channels to assume that an investor could have got into the share just after the trough on 23rd June 1995 when the price rebounded from the channel boundary at 338p. At the time, however, it could not have been deduced that the channel had reversed direction from its previous fall. It was not until the price had fallen back from its peak of 410p down to 369p on 29th September 1995 and then rose the following week to 373p that the trough formed could be adjudged to be on a rising lower boundary. The price rose again to 380.5p before falling to 377p on 20th October 1995. The investor is now waiting for a rise from that point in order to define the low point of 377p as being a trough and moreover being on a rising boundary. This happens the following week (27th October) by a rise to 395p, at which point the investor could buy.

The rise to the upper boundary took place rapidly, the price reaching 445p by 17th November. The investor would now be waiting for the exact time to sell, based on the relative heights reached by successive peaks. As

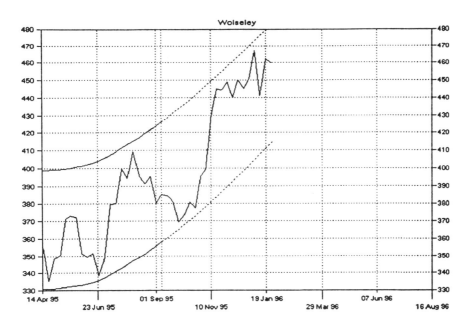

**Figure 11.12** The 41-week channel of the Wolseley share price on 26th January 1996. A very useful rise has been captured by an investment in October 1995 when the price had just rebounded from the lower channel

long as short term peaks reach higher and higher levels, the investor can stay with the share, but as soon as a peak fails to exceed a previous high, it is time to exit the share.

Thus the price fell to 444p the following week, then rose to 449p on 1st December. This was followed by a fall to 440p and a rise to 450p on 15th December, i.e. higher than the previous high of 449p. The next fall was to 445p the following week, and the price then rose to 451p, and rose again the following week to 467p. The investor would now expect to have to sell within a few weeks. Sure enough the price fell to 442p before rising to 462.5p on 19th January 1996. The fall the following week to 460p meant that the peak of 462.5p did not exceed the previous high of 467p, and thus the time has come to sell.

The net result of this investment was a rise from 395p to 460p, a useful gain of 16.5%. The interesting point is the way in which the investor is able to stay in the share past its first peak of 445p, gaining another 15p of profit.

## Dixons (1993 to June 1997)

An overall view of the channel for Dixons is shown in Figure 11.13. This is one of the few shares in which the channel has obviously topped out many months ago and is now falling quite steadily.

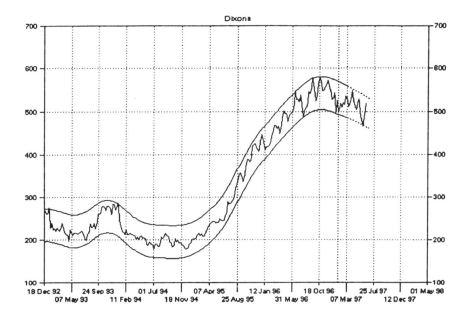

**Figure 11.13**   The 41-week channel of Dixons share price as at 20th June 1997 showed that the channel topped out in October 1996

## Dixons (29th March 1996)

An investment would have been made in Dixons at an early stage in the rise in the dominant trend, on 26th May 1995 at 247.5p. This followed a rise from the value of 238p the previous week, since it was estimated that the trough formed by this rise was on the lower boundary of the channel and that the channel itself was rising.

Figure 11.14 shows the position on 29th March 1996. The price reached a high of 467p on 8th March, fell to 458p and then rose to 464p on the 22nd. A fall to 447p the next week (29th March) established 464p as being a peak, but lower than the previous one at 467p. This is therefore an indication that it is time to leave the share.

Since the investor had entered Dixons at an early stage in the rise of the channel, a large profit was made from this investment, which took the price from 247.5p to 447p, i.e. a gain of 80%. This shows the great advantage of early investment in a rising dominant trend.

## Tesco (10th June 1994)

The position is shown in Figure 11.15. The trough at 205.5p on 22nd April 1994 suggested that the 41-week channel had now reversed direction and had started to rise. From the next peak at 227p on 13th May 1994, the price fell to 209.5p on 3rd June. This proved to be another trough, since the

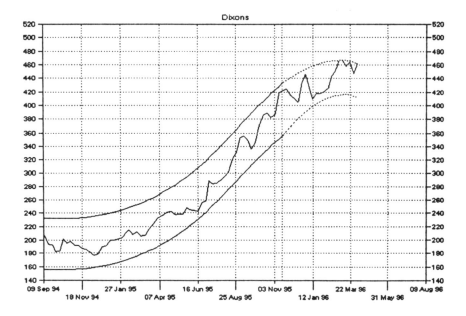

**Figure 11.14** The channel in Dixons as it appeared on 29th March 1996. It is now time to leave the share following a purchase in May

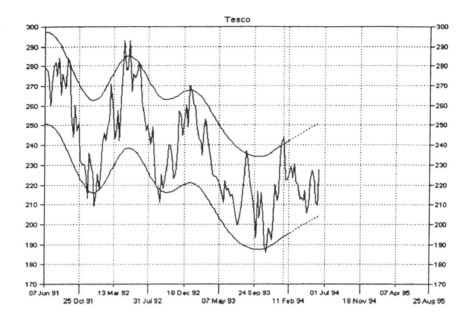

**Figure 11.15**   The 41-week channel in Tesco in June 1994

price rose the following week to 227.5p. The investor would now be comfortable with an investment at 227.5p on 10th June because this second trough is higher than the previous one, and can also be seen to be on the lower boundary as extrapolated from its previous trough. Thus the boundary is now quite clearly rising.

### *Tesco (September 1995)*

The position in Tesco in September 1995 is shown in Figure 11.16. The price shows a double peak at around the 337–338p level. The second peak at 338p on 8th September 1995 was just a penny higher than the previous one. The price then fell to 334p on 15th September. The investor would now be looking for another rise the following week to confirm that the upward trend is still in being. The danger signal is the fact that the price fell again the next week to 318p. This has to be the time to get out from the share. Having invested at a level of 227.5p in June 1994, the investor would be more than satisfied with a gain of 39.8% by 22nd September 1995 in just over 15 months.

### *Rentokil (22nd March 1996)*

The channels in Rentokil as they were on 22nd March 1996 are shown in Figure 11.17. Although the channel has been rising for about a year, there is still an investment opportunity for a short term gain in March 1996. The

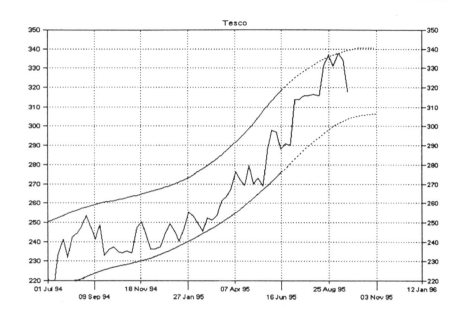

**Figure 11.16** The subsequent movement of the Tesco share price after June 1995

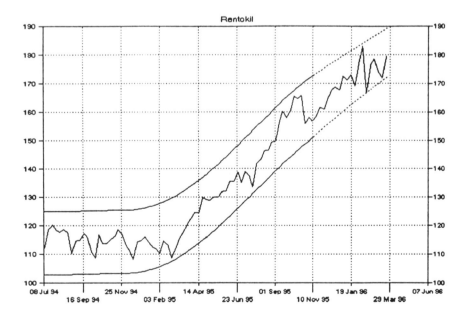

**Figure 11.17** The position in Rentokil on 22nd March 1996

price rose from a trough of 171.75p to 179.5p on 22nd March 1996. The trough before this can be seen to lie on the lower channel boundary which is therefore still rising. Thus an investment could be made at 179.5p, with the proviso that a large profit is not to be expected because of the rise which has already been made in the share price.

### Rentokil (July 1996)

Figure 11.18 shows how the price moved in Rentokil from the investment point in March 1996 to July 1997. The highest point reached was at 210p on 5th July 1996, following a series of peaks at around 205p. The price then fell to 207.5p the following week. The firm impression is given that the upper boundary must now be curving over in order to accommodate this series of peaks as being at the upper boundary. The price fell again the following week to 202.5p. The fact that the price is now below the level of the trough of 204.5 which was formed on 28th June is a firm indication that it is time to sell. The investor would have made a useful short term profit of 12.8%.

## USING DAILY DATA

Whereas the application of moving averages to daily data in order to generate buying signals offers no real advantage over the use of weekly

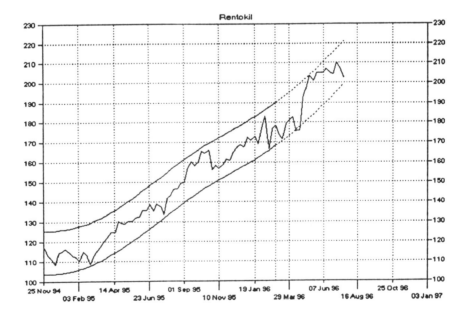

**Figure 11.18**   The position in Rentokil in July 1996

data, the position is rather different with channel analysis. This is because the buying signal is based on a rise from a trough which can be estimated to lie on the lower channel boundary. The trough can be much nearer to the start of the uptrend than is the turning point in the five-week average. In fact, the most powerful aspect of channel analysis is that the trough is more often than not the exact start of the short term uptrend. Thus using daily data the investor can buy into the share at the earliest point that is theoretically possible. Although there will be a few occasions when the price obtained from weekly data is a better one than that from daily data, this only happens when the price falls back slightly from the first point after the trough by the time of the Friday close. On balance, the price at the start of the uptrend will be the best price obtainable.

It is not necessary to keep lengthy daily histories of share prices in order to take advantage of the daily movement at or near the channel boundaries, although such histories are available (see Appendix). The simplest approach is to continue to maintain weekly data, and then when it appears that the price is approaching a lower channel boundary, the price can be monitored daily. Thus it will only be necessary to keep daily data from a point just prior to the approaching buying point to the point at which the share is sold. This reduces the work necessary to an absolute minimum.

To show that there is more often than not an advantage in using daily data in this way, the results obtained can be compared with those obtained using weekly data as shown in the previous examples.

## Boots (November 1995)

The position in Boots on 8th November 1995, with the price at 550p, is shown in Figure 11.19. The price the day before had been at 545p, having fallen from a peak at 550p. Since this trough of 545p is higher than the previous one at 536p, the rise in the channel is confirmed, and the investor can buy at 550p.

## Boots (February 1996)

This is shown in Figure 11.20. The peak price reached was 625p on 1st February 1996. The next day the price fell to 623p, and it fell once again on 5th February to 615p. This value is now lower than the trough at 618p which was formed on 30th January, indicating that the very short term trend is on its way down. It is therefore time to sell.

The net result of the buying and selling operation at 550p and 615p was for a gain of 11.8%. This is a great improvement from the rise of 6.5% made when only weekly data were used to generate the buying and selling signals.

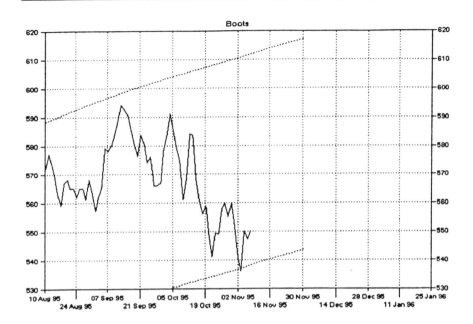

**Figure 11.19**   The position in Boots on 8th November 1995 with daily data

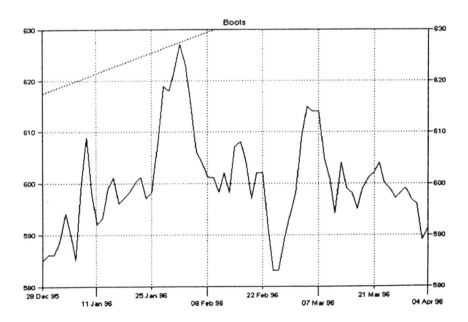

**Figure 11.20**   The position in Boots in February 1996 with daily data

## Wolseley (October 1995)

The lowest point reached in September 1995 was 363p on the 28th (Figure 11.21). The price then rose to 369p and stayed there for two days. This was followed by a small fall before the price rose over the course of the next few days to 374p (6th October). The fall to 367p followed by a rise to 370p on 11th October formed a trough which could be seen to be at the antici-pated position of the lower boundary, confirming also that it is rising. Thus the rise to 370p is a buying signal. This should be compared with the buying signal from weekly data which took the investor in at 395p at the end of October.

## Wolseley (January 1996)

The share price peaked at 474p on 8th January 1996 (Figure 11.22). From that point the price fell to 460p, then 446p. This fall of nearly 6% would of course trigger a 5% stop-loss, taking the investor out at that price for a good 20% profit from the investment. If the stop-loss is higher than 5%, then the investor would rely on the analysis of peaks and troughs in the immediate vicinity. Thus the fact that the price at 446p is below the pre-vious trough (450p on 2nd January) has to be taken as a very negative signal and the investor would sell the share with the same profit as the investor with the 5% stop-loss.

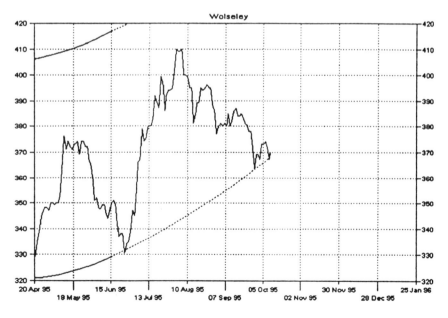

**Figure 11.21** The buying position in Wolseley in October 1995 with daily data

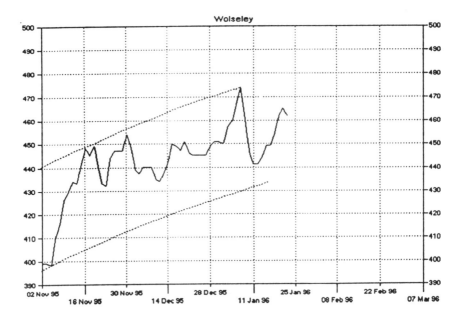

**Figure 11.22**  The selling position in Wolseley in January 1996 with daily data

## Dixons (June 1995)

The position in Dixons in June 1995 is shown in Figure 11.23. After bouncing up from the lower boundary with a rise from 237.5p on 15th June to 243p on 16th June the price continued to rise to 256p. It should be considered that the share has now gained too much in this short time to make this a sensible buying point. However, the price then fell at the end of June (28th) to 247.5p. Once it rose the next day to 251p, the previous price was seen to be a trough on the channel boundary at a higher level than the previous trough. Thus the share could be bought at 251p. Although this is higher than the 247.5p at which the investor using weekly data would have bought, it was a month later, giving the investor a great rate of return from the subsequent rise.

## Dixons (April 1996)

The peak price at the upper boundary was reached on 16th April 1996 at 506p (Figure 11.24). The price fell to 500p, then to 498p, thus establishing 506p as the peak. The price rose to 500p on 19th April and fell back to 492p the next day. Thus 500p was also a peak, but because it is at a lower level than the previous 506p, the indication is that the upper boundary is flattening out, and so the time has come to sell. From this overall investment the profit was 96%, a useful extra 16% compared with the investor using weekly data.

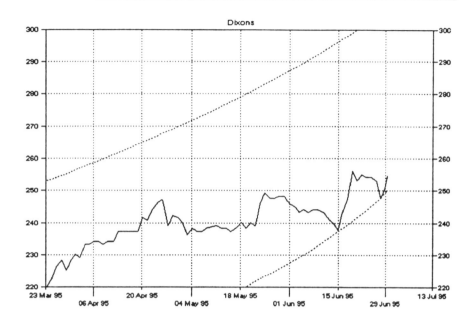

**Figure 11.23**   The buying position in Dixons in June 1995 with daily data

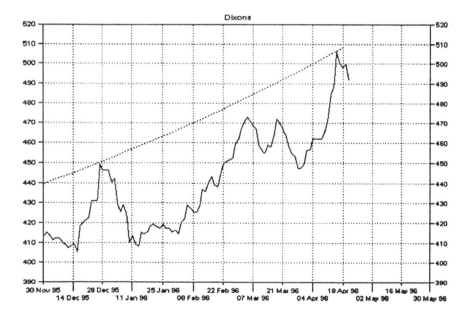

**Figure 11.24**   The selling position in Dixons in April 1996 with daily data

### Tesco (June 1994)

As can be seen from Figure 11.25, there were two troughs in the share price at 209p and 209.5p on 1st and 3rd June 1994. The price rose to 212p on 8th June, thus forming a trough at 210.5p with the previous day's price. Since the latest trough is higher than the previous one, this is a positive signal, so that the share can be bought at 212p. This is a considerable saving compared with the situation with weekly data which would get the investor in at 227.5p a few days later.

### Tesco (September 1995)

This is shown in Figure 11.26. The price reached a peak at 338p on 8th September 1995. The price fell to 329p on 12th September and rose again the next day to 334.5p. The price did not rise from this level, falling back slightly to 334p on 15th September. The failure to surpass the previous peak is a negative signal, and the investor should sell at 334p. The overall profit from the investment in Tesco was 57.5%, considerably higher than the 39.8% enjoyed by the investor using weekly data.

### Rentokil (April 1996)

This is shown in Figure 11.27. There were two troughs in the share price, on 11th April at 175p and on 19th April at 176p. The latter was formed by

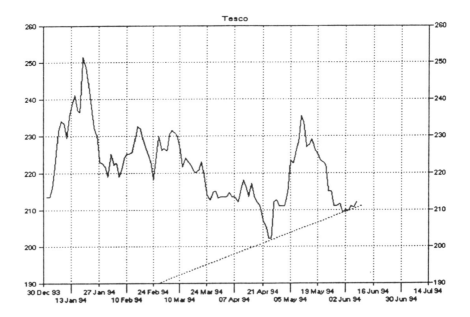

**Figure 11.25**   The buying position in Tesco in June 1994 with daily data

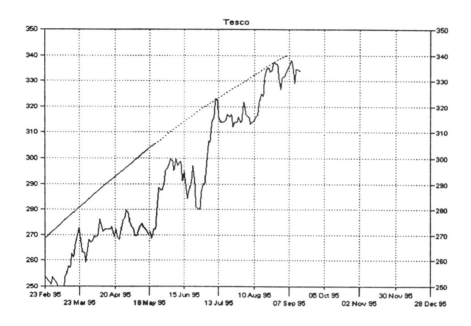

**Figure 11.26** The selling position in Tesco in September 1995 with daily data

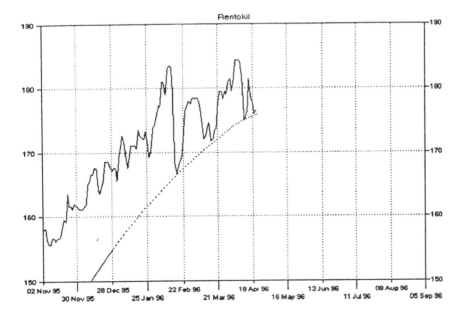

**Figure 11.27** The buying position in Rentokil in April 1996 with daily data

the rise to 176.5p on 22nd April. The fact that this new trough is higher is a positive sign, and the share can be bought at 176.5p.

### Rentokil (June 1996)

In June, only two months later, the position in Figure 11.28 was seen. There was a succession of peaks at 208p. The third one was formed by a fall in price to 207.5p on 20th June 1996. This failure on three recent occasions to pass the 208p level must be taken as a negative signal, and the investor is advised to sell at 207.5p. This gives a profit of 17.6%, compared with the 12.8% made by the investor using weekly data.

It is useful to compare the gains provided by the channel analysis method with those achieved by the methods in Chapter 10. Since it is necessary first of all to compare like with like, transactions carried out using channel analysis on weekly data can be compared with the results obtained using the price analysis and five-week moving average method shown in Table 10.5 in the last chapter. In Chapter 10, false signals were removed by several methods, but the channel analysis method itself will remove such signals. As well as using channel analysis for determination of the buying point, the selling signal was also obtained from an estimation of the position of the upper boundary. As a fall-back position, a stop-loss of 7.5% was also run in parallel.

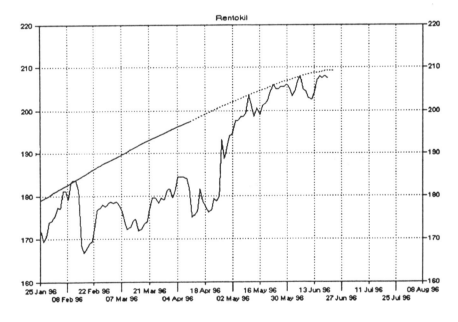

**Figure 11.28**   The selling position in Rentokil in June 1996 with daily data

The results obtained are shown in Table 11.1. There are three reasons why some buying signals have been removed. Firstly, an examination of the price trough showed that it was somewhere in the middle of the channel rather than at the boundary. Secondly, the price may even be near the upper boundary of the channel. The third reason is the requirement for a second trough to be formed in the rise from the boundary. Sometimes such a trough is not formed. This additional level of information is totally missing from any method which relies purely on the turning point in the five-week average or crossing of the average by the price.

The overall result is that the number of transactions is reduced to 14, with an average gain of 16.9%, nearly three times the level of that obtained purely with the five-week average method. There was also only one loser in the list (RTZ) and that lost only 1.3%.

Rather than using Table 10.5, the comparison is perhaps better with the 23 transactions in Table 10.7, where false signals in the five-week average method had been removed. The overall gain in that situation was 10.2%. Thus the gain using channel analysis is over half as much again.

Even at an overall average gain of 16.9%, there is still room for improvement of a few percentage points if daily data are used, since more often than not a slightly better buying and selling price would be obtained. As mentioned earlier, it is not necessary to keep long histories of data, but to use daily data interpolated into the weekly channels as it becomes apparent that the weekly price is approaching a boundary. The results of using this approach can be seen from Table 11.2, where the timing and prices obtained are shown when daily data are used in this way. The overall gain for the 14 transactions has now risen slightly to 21.4%, giving an additional 4.5% return. We can now see the value of the compromise method of using daily data only over the last few weeks of approach of a price to a boundary.

Finally, it is necessary to stress once again that although the channels presented in this chapter were drawn by computer, based upon calculations of the 41-week average, the channels can be drawn on charts of share prices without any calculations being necessary. The investor simply has to follow the rule about minimising the number of occasions when the price penetrates the channel boundaries, positioning the channel carefully so that as many as possible of the peaks and troughs lie on or close to the boundaries. Perhaps the most difficult part of the freehand drawing of such channels is to maintain a constant depth throughout the price history. It might be necessary to have two bites at the cherry, adjusting the first channel by running a ruler held vertically to the price axis along the channel to check its depth. The investor will be surprised at the high quality of the majority of the decisions reached by this method.

**Table 11.1** The gains achieved by channel analysis (CA) of weekly data on the shares analysed previously in Chapter 10. The first column gives the buying date signalled by the five-week average method from Chapter 10, while the second column gives the corresponding transaction using channel analysis for both buying and selling

| Five-week date | CA date | Price | Sell date | Price | % gain |
|---|---|---|---|---|---|
| *BSkyB* | | | | | |
| 10/11/95 | 10/11/95 | 392 | 31/05/96 | 449.5 | 14.7 |
| 24/11/95 | no action | price at middle of channel | | | |
| 01/03/96 | no action | price at middle of channel | | | |
| 12/07/96 | 05/07/96 | 453 | 25/10/96 | 593 | 30.9 |
| 20/12/96 | 27/12/96 | 523.5 | 21/03/97 | 620 | 18.4 |
| *Boots* | | | | | |
| 05/05/95 | no action | price at middle of channel | | | |
| 07/07/95 | no action | price at middle of channel | | | |
| 24/11/95 | 10/11/95 | 564 | 09/02/96 | 601 | 6.6 |
| 29/03/96 | no action | price at middle of channel | | | |
| 26/07/96 | 26/07/96 | 597 | 18/10/96 | 638 | 6.9 |
| 17/01/97 | not yet given | 647 | | | |
| *Cadbury-Schweppes* | | | | | |
| 28/07/95 | no action | price at middle of channel | | | |
| 06/10/95 | 06/10/95 | 497 | 22/12/95 | 532 | 7.0 |
| 02/02/96 | no action | channel topping out | | | |
| *Dixons* | | | | | |
| 26/05/95 | 26/05/95 | 247.5 | 29.03.96 | 447 | 80.6 |
| 22/12/95 | no action | price at middle of channel | | | |
| 12/04/96 | no action | price at middle of channel | | | |
| 31/05/96 | no action | price at middle of channel | | | |
| 23/08/96 | no action | price at middle of channel | | | |
| 11/10/96 | no action | price at top of channel | | | |
| *Granada* | | | | | |
| 08/09/95 | no action | price not forming second trough | | | |
| 05/01/96 | no action | price not forming second trough | | | |
| 29/03/96 | no action | price at middle of channel | | | |
| 07/06/96 | no action | price at middle of channel | | | |
| 09/08/96 | no action | price at middle of channel | | | |
| 11/10/96 | no action | price not forming second trough | | | |
| 24/01/97 | no action | price not forming second trough | | | |
| *Rentokil* | | | | | |
| 28/07/95 | no action | price not forming second trough | | | |
| 01/12/95 | 17/11/95 | 158.5 | 28/06/96 | 202.5 | 27.8 |
| 23/02/96 | no action | price not forming second trough | | | |
| 22/03/96 | no action | price at middle of channel | | | |
| 16/08/96 | 30/08/96 | 204.5 | 25/10/96 | 209.5 | 2.4 |
| 29/11/96 | no action | price at middle of channel | | | |
| 24/01/97 | no action | price at top of channel | | | |

**Table 11.1** (*continued*)

| Five-week date | CA date | Price | Sell date | Price | % gain |
|---|---|---|---|---|---|
| *RTZ* | | | | | |
| 07/07/95 | no action | price at middle of channel | | | |
| 08/09/95 | no action | price not forming second trough | | | |
| 17/11/95 | no action | price not forming second trough | | | |
| 02/02/96 | 16/02/96 | 935 | 24/05/96 | 1007 | 7.7 |
| 15/03/96 | no action | price at middle of channel | | | |
| 16/08/96 | no action | price at middle of channel | | | |
| 27/09/96 | no action | price at middle of channel | | | |
| 22/11/96 | no action | price at top of channel | | | |
| 13/12/96 | 20/12/96 | 945 | 03/01/97 | 932.5 | −1.3 |
| *Tesco* | | | | | |
| 26/05/95 | no action | price at middle of channel | | | |
| 08/12/95 | no action | channel is falling | | | |
| 05/04/96 | no action | channel is falling | | | |
| 24/05/96 | no action | price near top of channel | | | |
| 16/08/96 | no action | price at middle of channel | | | |
| 04/10/96 | 04/10/96 | 313.5 | 10/01/97 | 347 | 10.7 |
| 28/03/97 | not yet given | 349.5 | | | |
| *Williams* | | | | | |
| 19/04/96 | no action | price at middle of channel | | | |
| 14/06/96 | no action | price at middle of channel | | | |
| 09/08/96 | no action | price at middle of channel | | | |
| *Wolseley* | | | | | |
| 27/10/95 | 27/10/95 | 395 | 26/01/96 | 460 | 16.5 |
| 19/04/96 | no action | price at top of channel | | | |
| 07/06/96 | no action | price at top of channel | | | |
| 10/08/96 | 16/08/96 | 454 | 25/10/96 | 490 | 7.9 |
| 03/01/97 | no action | price at middle of channel | | | |
| 02/05/97 | no action | price at middle of channel | | | |
| Average of 14 signals | | | | | 16.9 |

**Table 11.2**  The gains achieved by channel analysis (CA) of weekly data with inter-
polation of daily prices as the weekly prices draw near a boundary. The gains and times
should be compared with those given in Table 11.1 where weekly data alone were used

| Five-week date | CA date | Price | Sell date | Price | % gain |
|---|---|---|---|---|---|
| *BSkyB* | | | | | |
| 10/11/95 | 16/11/95 | 394 | 03/05/96 | 454 | 15.2 |
| 24/11/95 | no action | price at middle of channel | | | |
| 01/03/96 | no action | price at middle of channel | | | |
| 12/07/96 | 26/06/96 | 434 | 23/10/96 | 636 | 46.5 |
| 20/12/96 | 31/12/96 | 522 | 18/02/97 | 633.5 | 21.4 |
| *Boots* | | | | | |
| 05/05/95 | no action | price at middle of channel | | | |
| 07/07/95 | no action | price at middle of channel | | | |
| 24/11/95 | 05/12/95 | 575 | 05/02/96 | 615 | 7.0 |
| 29/03/96 | no action | price at middle of channel | | | |
| 26/07/96 | 01/08/96 | 600 | 21/10/96 | 640 | 6.7 |
| 17/01/97 | not yet given | 647 | | | |
| *Cadbury-Schweppes* | | | | | |
| 28/07/95 | no action | price at middle of channel | | | |
| 06/10/95 | 04/10/95 | 492 | 04/12/95 | 553 | 12.4 |
| 02/02/96 | no action | channel topping out | | | |
| *Dixons* | | | | | |
| 26/05/95 | 22/05/95 | 240 | 20/03/96 | 470 | 95.8 |
| 22/12/95 | no action | price at middle of channel | | | |
| 12/04/96 | no action | price at middle of channel | | | |
| 31/05/96 | no action | price at middle of channel | | | |
| 23/08/96 | no action | price at middle of channel | | | |
| 11/10/96 | no action | price at top of channel | | | |
| *Granada* | | | | | |
| 08/09/95 | no action | price not forming second trough | | | |
| 05/01/96 | no action | price not forming second trough | | | |
| 29/03/96 | no action | price at middle of channel | | | |
| 07/06/96 | no action | price at middle of channel | | | |
| 09/08/96 | no action | price at middle of channel | | | |
| 11/10/96 | no action | price not forming second trough | | | |
| 24/01/97 | no action | price not forming second trough | | | |
| *Rentokil* | | | | | |
| 28/07/95 | no action | price not forming second trough | | | |
| 01/12/95 | 14/11/95 | 156.5 | 16/07/96 | 202.5 | 29.4 |
| 23/02/96 | no action | price not forming second trough | | | |
| 22/03/96 | no action | price at middle of channel | | | |
| 16/08/96 | 02/09/96 | 205.25 | 25/09/96 | 212 | 3.3 |
| 29/11/96 | no action | price at middle of channel | | | |
| 24/01/97 | no action | price at top of channel | | | |

**Table 11.2**   (*continued*)

| Five-week date | CA date | Price | Sell date | Price | % gain |
|---|---|---|---|---|---|
| *RTZ* | | | | | |
| 07/07/95 | no action | price at middle of channel | | | |
| 08/09/95 | no action | price not forming second trough | | | |
| 17/11/95 | no action | price not forming second trough | | | |
| 02/02/96 | 01/03/96 | 913 | 15/05/95 | 1046 | 14.6 |
| 15/03/96 | no action | price at middle of channel | | | |
| 16/08/96 | no action | price at middle of channel | | | |
| 27/09/96 | no action | price at middle of channel | | | |
| 22/11/96 | no action | price at top of channel | | | |
| 13/12/96 | 20/12/96 | 945 | 03/01/97 | 932.5 | −1.3 |
| *Tesco* | | | | | |
| 26/05/95 | no action | price at middle of channel | | | |
| 08/12/95 | no action | channel is falling | | | |
| 05/04/96 | no action | channel is falling | | | |
| 24/05/96 | no action | price near top of channel | | | |
| 16/08/96 | no action | price at middle of channel | | | |
| 04/10/96 | 24/09/96 | 303 | 24/01/97 | 360 | 18.8 |
| 28/03/97 | not yet given | 349.5 | | | |
| *Williams* | | | | | |
| 19/04/96 | no action | price at middle of channel | | | |
| 14/06/96 | no action | price at middle of channel | | | |
| 09/08/96 | no action | price at middle of channel | | | |
| *Wolseley* | | | | | |
| 27/10/95 | 04/10/95 | 373 | 04/12/96 | 439 | 17.7 |
| 19/04/96 | no action | price at top of channel | | | |
| 07/06/96 | no action | price at top of channel | | | |
| 10/08/96 | 12/08/96 | 442 | 22/10/96 | 493 | 11.5 |
| 03/01/97 | no action | price at middle of channel | | | |
| 02/05/97 | no action | price at middle of channel | | | |
| Average of 14 signals | | | | | 21.4 |

# 12

# Summary

The aim of this book has been to develop a method which can minimise the risk and maximise the profit which can be made from investment in shares. There are many examples in existence of what might be called pure mechanical methods for deciding when to buy and when to sell shares. These will give a yes or no response to the question, "Should I buy or sell this share now?", but such methods suffer from many drawbacks. Chief among these is that each method has usually been optimised at a certain point in the market's history, and may not offer the same level of performance during other types of market behaviour.

The methods discussed in this book are not 100% mechanical, and rely on some amount of subjective estimation of probability. This is unavoidable, since we have pointed out that the methods such as moving averages, when used to isolate trends, can only show how a trend was behaving at some point in the recent past, and not what the trend is doing at the exact present. The situation is rather like the view we have of distant galaxies, where the light has taken many millions of years to reach us. The light simply shows us how the galaxies looked these millions of years ago, and we have no firm idea of what has happened to them while their light has been travelling towards us. We do not know how they look now, or even if they are still in existence.

In the case of a trend, a complete reversal of direction could have occurred between the nearest time in the past at which we knew its direction with 100% certainty and the present time.

Chapters 7 and 9 explored the dilemma of this credibility gap and ways in which we could estimate the status of the 41-week moving average at the point NOW, while in Chapter 10 we showed how this dominant trend estimation could be married to a mechanical method of generating buying points by means of turning points in the five-week moving average. Good though this combination method is, once we have removed as many of the false buying signals as possible, it falls well short of the results that can be achieved using channel analysis.

Within the limitations of a book of this kind, channel analysis cannot be made into a purely mechanical process, it relies on an improving skill of the investor to reduce to a minimum the number of occasions on which an incorrect estimate is made of the current status of the dominant trend as represented by the channel.

This skill will be able, unlike the pure mechanical systems, to deal with the many faces that the market shows to the investor: roaring bull markets, growling bear markets, and the difficult periods of indecisive whipsawing.

The decision levels which have to be traversed before an investment can be made are shown in Figure 12.1. Although it looks extensive, the amount of work which has to be done will depend on the investment climate. Thus if there are less than 60% risers in the pool of shares, then no more work will need to be done that week. The investor simply waits another week to see if the percentage of risers has changed.

If it has changed, so that the percentage is now above 60%, then this is the point at which the greatest amount of work has to be carried out. The investor will need to prepare a list of the most volatile shares as was shown in Chapter 8. With a computer and database of say 500 shares, the process will take next to no time. If it is necessary to scan the newspaper share price columns to estimate the ratio of the high to low price, this should take no more than about an hour.

Those shares with very high volatility should be discarded, since they have either fallen so far from their peaks that they must be considered to be bombed out, with no real potential for gain, or they have risen so far from their lows that it is unrealistic to expect any further major advance in price. While there are exceptions to this rule, they are so few that they can be ignored. A useful ceiling on volatility is a ratio of 8 if the FTSE100 Index has been particularly volatile, or 4 if it has been involatile.

The next step is to reduce the group of 100 shares or so down to a much more manageable selection, thus reducing the work that has to be done in preparing charts of each one. Since we should only invest in those shares where the dominant trend is rising, then the procedure for reducing the list is one of quickly deciding whether this trend is rising or not. This can be done by comparing the price of the shares now with the price 40 weeks ago. Retain in the list only those in which the price now is higher.

Now we have a reduced list, we need to prepare a chart of each share covering at least one year of weekly data. We need also to calculate and plot the 41-week averages (centred) of each share and add the channel boundaries above and below the centred average. From this we can deduce whether we are at a buying point in any of the small group of shares. If so, use a portion of the capital sum available to buy this share. If none of the shares is at a buying point, we simply add to the charts each week, adding the new weekly closing value and moving the channels on by one week until such time as one of the shares gives a buying signal.

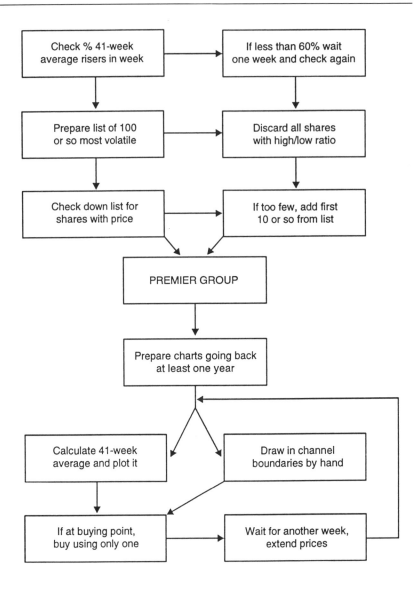

**Figure 12.1**   The decision levels that have to be passed through before an investment is made

## REASONS FOR FAILURE

We have made this low risk and high return method of investment as automatic as possible. Even so, investors may find it difficult to avoid the psychological traps which exist, so a statement of some of the more obvious failings made by all investors from time to time should be particularly useful.

The main reason for failure is, of course, the failure to follow the methods described in this book! These methods have stood the test of time, and since they are probability-based, the investor must come out on the winning side in the long run. The most common failings of the investor are as follows.

## 1. Trying to Pre-empt the Market

This is very common. Having spent some time successfully applying these methods, the investor hopes to steal a march on other investors by getting into a trend earlier. He thus begins to anticipate turning points in the dominant trend. From operating with the odds stacked firmly in his favour, he moves to a position where the odds of correctly predicting the direction of the dominant trend are only 50:50, a sure recipe for disaster.

## 2. Buying on a Price Fall

From some points of view this is similar to the above. The investor does not wait for a price rise to establish a trough and its position relative to the boundary. He anticipates that the price fall will reverse at the next closing, and wishes to buy in at a better price than that which will be obtainable after the rise.

The investor is forgetting a prime rule: a trend will continue until it ends. A downward trend does not end until the price rises.

## 3. Misplaced Patience

The first two failings are a manifestation of investor impatience. Investors are always impatient to buy. On the other hand investors seem to acquire supreme patience once they have bought a share. They patiently watch it fall lower and lower in the belief that it will soon turn around and begin to generate a profit. It is to overcome this misplaced patience that the stop-loss has been devised. Investors must sell once the stop-loss is triggered.

## 4. Holding on for Dividends

It might seem attractive to some investors to buy a share when they become aware that a dividend will be declared shortly. They feel that the dividend received within a few weeks will amply compensate for dealing costs.

This ignores the fact, which investors can check for themselves, that the moment the share price goes ex-dividend, it usually falls by an amount that will offset this dividend. Although strongly rising shares may not do this, or will shrug off the few pence fall within a day or two, most shares take a while to recover this lost price.

The investor must never buy a share because of an impending dividend, but only because the share gives a buying signal when subjected to the procedures discussed in this book.

## 5. *Listening to Advice*

Investors are constantly bombarded with advice from all quarters. The most dangerous is that from certain stockbrokers, since this carries the authority that goes with their position. In this book the investor has been given the tools for the job. If any advice is given to buy or sell a share, the investor should always run the data through these familiar processes. If the share passes the test for investment, all well and good. If it does not, do not buy it.

## 6. *Not Spreading the Risk*

The investor should be invested in no more than about eight to twelve shares at any one time. At the outset, the investor should divide his investment capital into eight equal portions if his capital is small, or up to twelve if it is larger. As the first opportunities arise, he can invest one portion in each share. He must not view the portions so rigidly that he could be forced to buy an odd number of shares. The costs of buying and selling such odd lots are much greater than that for round hundreds or thousands. To reach such a round number of shares, it may be necessary to steal a small amount from the other pots, as long as this is kept to a minimum. Never be tempted to use two portions of capital in one share, even if the buying operations take place at different times. The object is to spread the risk by spreading the number of shares in which the investor has an active interest.

As shares are sold, then an imbalance might occur between the cash in hand and what is about an eighth (or whichever division has been used) of the portfolio. In this case the investor should siphon off some of the excess cash into a reserve. This can be used for those occasions when a good opportunity arises and the investor is fully invested. The reserve can be used for such investments, as long as these occasions are kept to a minimum.

It might seem obvious, but on no account sell a share just because it has been so successful that it has caused an imbalance in the portfolio. A share should be sold only when a selling signal has been generated, either by the stop-loss or by virtue of its position within the channel.

Finally, a reminder of the prime rule of investment: **capital must be preserved**. When the risk in a situation appears to be reaching unacceptable levels, whether it involves a decision to buy or to continue to hold, the investor must go no further. Either do not buy, or sell the existing holding.

# Appendix

## Addresses

For lists of brokers: The Secretary, The International Stock Exchange of the United Kingdom and the Republic of Ireland Ltd, The Stock Exchange, London EC2N 1HP

## Previous Editions by the Author

*Stocks and Shares Simplified* (3rd edn), ISBN 0-471-92131-9, published by John Wiley & Sons Ltd, Chichester.

*Traded Options Simplified* (1st edn), ISBN 1-871857-00-7, published by Qudos Publications, distributed by John Wiley & Sons Ltd, Chichester.

*Channel Analysis* (1st edn), ISBN 1-871857-02-3, published by Qudos Publications, distributed by John Wiley & Sons Ltd, Chichester.

*Winning on the Stock Market* (1st edn), ISBN 0-471-93881-5, published by John Wiley & Sons Ltd, Chichester.

*Profitable Charting Techniques* (1st edn), ISBN 1-871857-03-1, published by Qudos Publications, distributed by John Wiley & Sons Ltd, Chichester.

## Historical Data

Weekly closing prices of shares since 1982 are obtainable in printed form (ISBN 1-871857-01-5) or on floppy disk from:
Qudos Publications, PO Box 27, Bramhall, Stockport, Cheshire SK7 1JH
Tel. 0161 439 3926
Fax 0161 439 2327

## Microcomputer Software

The charts in this book were produced by the Microvest 5.0 and Sigma-p packages published by Qudos Publications Ltd.

# Index